EASY cuisine

meals for a month

300 delicious recipes that save time and money

Linda Larsen

EASY cuisine

meals for
a month

300 delicious recipes that save time and money

I dedicate this book to my dear husband, Doug,
who has always encouraged my every endeavor.

Published by Adams Media, an F+W Publications Company
57 Littlefield Street, Avon, MA 02322 U.S.A.
www.adamsmedia.com

ISBN 10: 1-59869-222-4
ISBN 13: 978-1-59869-222-8

Printed in China.

J   I   H   G   F   E   D   C   B   A

Library of Congress Cataloging-in-Publication Data
available from the publisher.

This publication is designed to provide accurate and authoritative information with regard to the subject matter covered. It is sold with the understanding that the publisher is not engaged in rendering legal, accounting, or other professional advice. If legal advice or other expert assistance is required, the services of a competent professional person should be sought.
—From a *Declaration of Principles* jointly adopted by a Committee of the American Bar Association and a Committee of Publishers and Associations

Easy Cuisine: Meals for a Month is intended as a reference volume only, not as a medical manual. In light of the complex, individual, and specific nature of health problems, this book is not intended to replace professional medical advice. The ideas, procedures, and suggestions in this book are intended to supplement, not replace, the advice of a trained medical professional. Consult your physician before adopting the suggestions in this book, as well as about any condition that may require diagnosis or medical attention. The author and publisher disclaim any liability arising directly or indirectly from the use of this book.

Many of the designations used by manufacturers and sellers to distinguish their products are claimed as trademarks. Where those designations appear in this book and Adams Media was aware of a trademark claim, the designations have been printed with initial capital letters.

Previously published as *The Everything® Meals for a Month Cookbook*.

Contents

Acknowledgments

I'd like to acknowledge the efforts of my agent, Barb Doyen, and my parents, who told me I could be anything I wanted to be and made it possible for me to get the best education. I'd especially like to thank my mother and sisters, who always encouraged my experiments in the kitchen and cleaned up the messes while I was learning to cook.

Introduction

DID YOU KNOW THAT YOU CAN COOK AND BAKE ON ONE DAY and make meals that will feed your family for a month? This increasingly popular form of conveyer-belt cooking isn't as difficult as it sounds, and can actually be a lot of fun. You will learn how to use your freezer, oven, microwave, grill, and slow cooker to cook and store delicious, healthy meals that you can just pull out and reheat for breakfast, lunch, or dinner in minutes. Imagine having the pressure of planning, shopping, cooking, and serving dinner every single day lifted from your shoulders—it's an incredible feeling.

This type of cooking can be adapted to any cuisine. Do you love Mexican food? You can make and freeze a base of meat and vegetables that can be used for enchiladas, tacos, burritos, taco salad, Mexican pizza, fajitas, and Tex-Mex soups and stews. Is your family hooked on Italian cuisine? A base of ground beef can be used for spaghetti, cannelloni, manicotti, and lasagna. The variations are almost endless!

There are a few ways to tackle making meals for a month. You can cook triple batches of your favorite recipes and freeze them in meal-size containers; you can cook ten to thirty individual recipes and freeze them; or you can buy a large quantity of meats and ingredients, cook a big batch of starter foods, and then make lots of different casseroles and entrees from the starter batch.

And did you know you can bake and freeze breads, cookies, bars, cakes, and other desserts? Storing these foods means you will always be prepared when company drops in unexpectedly, and you will be ready for any holiday meal or family celebration.

You'll save money because you can buy what's on special in your supermarket and use every bit. And there's really no better feeling than knowing your freezer is stocked with enough food to feed your family for a month. Once-a-month cooking is one of the best timesavers in the kitchen.

You can also be the best friend and neighbor when you are a devotee of once-a-month cooking. Whenever life becomes difficult for someone you know, you can offer the most wonderful present: a hot, healthy, delicious home-cooked meal at a moment's notice.

Probably the most important bonus of this cooking method is this: preparing fresh, delicious meals for your family helps them live a healthy lifestyle. You won't have to order takeout foods or depend on expensive drive-through restaurants with their sodium-loaded, high-fat foods. Cooking healthy foods for yourself and your family is a way to make everyone feel well fed and cared for.

Chapter 1: How to Make Meals for a Month

On the busiest days of the month, you can come home and have dinner on the table in thirty to forty minutes, with virtually no effort. Think of it: Your freezer will become a grocery store where you can browse for complete meals; you just place a dish in the oven and relax while dinner reheats to perfection. Mealtime can be always this effortless if you learn how to cook once a month and freeze your meals.

What Is Once-a-Month Cooking?

Once-a-month cooking is a marathon cooking session that involves deciding what you want to cook, making lists, shopping, then preparing and freezing enough meals to last for a whole month. With organization, planning skills, and some food-science knowledge, you will never need to order takeout again. You'll pull delicious, healthy meals out of your freezer and reheat them in minutes.

Plan your month by using a blank calendar page. Write down the recipes you want to serve each day, making notes regarding vacation times, times you'll be entertaining, holidays, and days when you're invited out to dinner.

Not only will you find plenty of recipes that are meant to be reheated in the oven or microwave, but this book includes some new variations on once-a-month cooking: meals that go from the freezer to your Slow Cooker, and meals that go from the freezer to your grill. And you can even make your own TV dinners with these recipes. Your family members can choose exactly what they want to eat and reheat their own individual meals.

Foods for breakfast, including waffles, breakfast pizzas, egg sandwiches, and muffins, are also great freezer candidates. You can schedule a special session just for cooking breakfast foods, or add one or two breakfast recipes to a regular cooking session. You'll feed your family a hot, healthy breakfast on even the busiest days.

Frozen Food Basics

If you are new to once-a-month cooking, the process may seem overwhelming. Just take it one step at a time. With each step you complete, your confidence will grow. Before you start, there are some things you need to know about freezing food.

All food is made up of live cells, which are small building blocks. These cells contain enzymes, water, protein, and other chemicals that react with air and water to gradually cause deterioration, known as spoiling, as the food ages. When food is frozen, the functions of cells slow down dramatically; this preserves the food. Freezing cannot improve the quality of food; it simply holds it at the quality it was when frozen. Chemicals in the food will still be active even during the frozen state, although this activity is greatly reduced.

There are several factors in food that affect the freezing process. Here's a brief overview of these facts so you can get the most out of your freezer and this method of cooking.

Bacteria and Molds

Bacteria and molds are present everywhere, even on the food we eat. Freezing does stop the growth of bacteria and mold on foods; however, when the food is thawed, these microorganisms will begin to grow again. That's why it is so important to thaw foods in the refrigerator instead of at room temperature. Bacterial activity is still suppressed in the cold air of the fridge. Cooking destroys bacteria and molds, so it's very important to properly and thoroughly reheat frozen food before eating it.

Freezer Burn

A freezer is a hostile place. Foods that are not properly packaged for the freezer will become damaged very quickly. Freezer burn is the most common problem of the freezing process. It's simply the dehydration of food. When food is improperly wrapped, the dry environment of the freezer draws off moisture as the food freezes. This damages cells in the food and results in dry, hard patches that will not revert to the hydrated state even when thawed. Food that is affected by freezer burn is not unsafe to eat, but it will be tough and lack flavor. If only a small amount of food is affected by freezer burn, you can simply cut off that area and heat and eat the rest. If there is freezer burn over a large area of the food, however, throw it out; the taste and texture will be compromised.

Stews, soups, and other liquid foods that have been affected by freezer burn may be saved. These naturally liquid foods can absorb the damage caused by the dehydration when reheated. Add ¼ cup water to the dish when reheating, and stir gently.

To prevent freezer burn, wrap foods tightly. Also be sure the supplies you purchase to wrap and store your food are specifically developed for the freezer environment.

Enzymes and Oxidation

Enzymes that are naturally present in food cause changes in color, flavor, and texture. Enzymatic processes do not stop when food is frozen, although they do slow down. Some foods, particularly fruits and vegetables, need to be blanched or briefly cooked before freezing to disable these enzymes.

Cells are complete packages with membranes that control water and air exchange. When cells have been damaged (cut, chopped, or torn) by preparing or cooking the food, air combines with enzymes inside the cells. This process is called enzymatic oxidation, and it discolors food and changes flavors. Fats in meat can become rancid. The color of fruits and vegetables can become dull and drab. Freezing minimizes this process, and you can help by removing as much air as possible from the food when packaging it. Also, when you are preparing fruits for the freezer, coat the cut surfaces with an acidic liquid like lemon juice or an ascorbic acid solution to slow down the oxidation process.

Get the Air Out

Air is the enemy when you're freezing foods! Remove as much air as possible when wrapping. When you package food, press down on the container to get rid of excess air. You can use a drinking straw to draw air out before sealing the package. However, liquid items such as soups and stews need a small amount of space, called head space, in the container to allow for expansion during freezing. Leave ½ inch of head space in these containers so the lid doesn't pop off when the food expands as it freezes.

The Freezer(s)

You may want to invest in a stand-alone chest freezer if you are going to make this type of cooking part of your life. The freezer that is part of your refrigerator can also be used as long as it is not overpacked with food.

When adding new packages of food to your freezer, try to place them in the bottom of the freezer or against the sides. These are the coldest parts of the freezer, so the food will freeze more quickly without raising the internal temperature.

Use a freezer thermometer to make sure that your freezer is at a temperature of 0°F or lower before you stock it with food. If possible, turn your freezer to −10°F when you add food. When the food is frozen solid, you can turn the temperature back to 0°F.

If you have an extra stand-alone freezer, store it in the basement or the coolest part of your home. Then, if the power goes off, the ambient air temperature will keep the temperature inside the freezer cooler for a longer period of time. If the power does go off, keep the freezer closed. You may want to wrap it in blankets or towels to help insulate it and keep the temperature down. Most stand-alone freezers will stay at 0°F or less for twenty-four to thirty hours without power.

Many stand-alone freezers need to be defrosted every six to twelve months. Follow manufacturer's instructions for defrosting. While defrosting your freezer, discard packages that are more than a year old and store the remaining frozen items in an insulated ice chest. Place frozen ice packs or bags of ice cubes on top of the food. The food will be safe to refreeze as long as it is still frozen solid.

To Freeze or Not?

Many foods freeze well. Meats, most vegetables, dairy products (including separated egg whites), fruits, sauces, combination dishes, breads, cakes, and casseroles will all hold their quality very well in the freezer and will reheat beautifully. Handling and preparation for storage will be the key factors that determine whether the foods will retain their quality when frozen and reheated.

Foods with a high water content (lettuce, tomatoes, radishes) do not freeze well. All cells contain water, which expands when frozen. Cells of water-rich foods may break down too much as the water within them freezes, resulting in an unacceptable taste or soggy, mushy texture when thawed. Other foods that do not freeze well include:

- Whole hard-cooked eggs
- Raw eggs
- Chopped or cut potatoes
- Celery
- Raw tomatoes
- Mayonnaise
- Custard and cream fillings
- Sour cream
- Fried foods
- Canned refrigerator dough

It's possible to work around some of these problem foods. Purchase already-frozen items, such as frozen potatoes; add them to the recipe after it has cooled; then immediately freeze the dish. When the recipe is thawed and reheated, the potatoes will be tender and perfect. Or you can also simply leave these foods out of the recipe when you're preparing it for the freezer, then add them during the thawing and reheating process.

Creamy dairy products can be frozen if a stabilizer is added to them, like flour or cornstarch. These items may separate when thawed, but a simple stir with a wire whisk will smooth out the sauce.

Buying and Freezing Meat in Bulk

Meat falls into a special category in once-a-month cooking. Since meat will be the most expensive part of your bulk-cooking purchases, always look for sales on meat and add recipes that use that meat to your plan. However, there are very specific rules you need to follow when purchasing and storing large quantities of meat. Most important, pay attention to expiration dates on meat products and never buy or freeze meat that is past those dates.

If you are purchasing large quantities of meat already frozen and plan to defrost the meat before using it in recipes, it must be cooked before being refrozen. Never thaw frozen meat, partially cook it or use it raw in a recipe, and refreeze it. Thaw frozen meat, then cook it completely, and it can be safely refrozen.

Do not freeze meat in its original packaging. Wrap it in freezer wrap, heavy-duty foil, or zipper-lock freezer bags; label; and freeze. Divide the meat into small quantities before you package it for refreezing so it will be easier to thaw and work with. Freeze chicken parts or fish fillets separately, and then combine in a larger bag. Pork chops should be separated by freezer wrap, then combined in a larger bag or wrapped together with freezer wrap. Large quantities of ground beef should be divided into thin portions and packaged divided by parchment or freezer paper.

Make sure you record the meats you are storing in the freezer. When planning each cooking session, refer to this list to use the meat stored in your freezer before you purchase more. Most frozen meat will retain quality for six months to a year. Cured meats like ham and bacon hold their quality in the freezer for only about one month. Because of the curing process, these meats tend to oxidize faster and will become rancid more quickly than uncured meats.

Food Safety

Food safety is the most important part of any food preparation. It doesn't matter if you prepare gourmet foods that everyone loves; if the food makes people sick, all your work is lost. If you have doubts about the purity or safety of the food, throw it out. These rules apply to all cooking and baking, not just once-a-month cooking.

Foods that could cause trouble if mishandled include all fresh and cured meats (cooked and uncooked), eggs, dairy products like milk and cream, seafood, cooked rice and pasta, opened or unsealed home-canned foods, and all foods that contain any of these ingredients.

Whenever you touch raw meats or uncooked eggs (even the shell!), immediately wash your hands with warm, soapy water before touching anything else. Do not open a cupboard, pick up the salt shaker, or touch anything that will be eaten uncooked. Think about keeping a popup container of hand wipes in your kitchen for convenience and to help remind you of this important food-safety factor.

More than 75 million cases of food poisoning occur in the United States every year.

Almost all could be prevented by cooking food to the proper internal temperature.

Follow safe food-handling practices to the letter.

Remember, food poisoning is invisible—it is impossible to tell by taste or smell if food is safe to eat. Most bacteria and the toxins they produce, which cause food-borne illnesses, are not detectable by human senses.

Foods should be left at room temperature for only two hours. At that point, foods must be refrigerated or frozen. Bacteria present in all food grow at temperatures between 40°F and 140°F. Make sure that you keep track of how long potentially hazardous food has been out of refrigeration. For instance, work with all of your ground beef recipes—finish, cool, pack, label, and freeze them—before going on to recipes using chicken. Keep raw meats separate from all other foods. Use a separate cutting board, knife, and fork for preparing raw meats.

Even if the bacteria in food are killed in the cooking process, over time, some bacteria produce toxins that are not destroyed by heat or freezing temperatures. Those toxins will make you sick. That's why you must follow food safety procedures to the letter, heating food quickly, cooling it promptly, and never letting food stand out at room temperature for more than two hours.

If someone in your family falls into a high-risk group (has a compromised immune system or a chronic disease, is elderly, or is under the age of five), you need to be even more careful about food safety. People who fall into these high-risk groups can get so sick form food poisoning they must be hospitalized.

Preparing Food for the Freezer

The food you spend all day preparing also has to be properly packed, wrapped, and frozen to preserve it in the best possible quality. And before the food can be packed and frozen, it must be chilled.

Cool It!

Before placing the food in your freezer, cool it as quickly as you can. Hot foods will raise the temperature of your freezer and could compromise the safety and quality of other foods stored there. When the food has been prepared as the recipe directs, place it in a metal cooking or baking pan, in an ice-water bath, or spread the food in a shallow pan and place it in the refrigerator for thirty to fifty minutes. Then pack the food in the freezer containers or wrap, seal, label, and freeze immediately.

Think about purchasing some large, sturdy, waterproof containers or storage bins to use as ice-water baths. You are going to need all of your mixing bowls and pots for cooking the food, and your sink will be full of sudsy water for cleaning.

Flash Freezing

Flash freezing is simply freezing foods as quickly as possible. Individual appetizers, sandwiches, rolls, cookies, and other small-size foods retain their quality, shape, and form best when flash frozen. Spread a layer of food on a cookie sheet or another flat surface and freeze individually—leave a space of one half to one inch between the individual pieces of food so cold air can circulate freely—then package in one container once frozen solid.

Pack It!

Proper packaging and wrapping will keep your food in excellent condition while it is being frozen and reheated. Make sure that there are no loose wrappings around the food. You can double wrap each recipe after it has frozen solid to make sure that each package is properly sealed. Make sure you use heavy-duty foil or freezer wrap that is heat-resistant. Use freezer tape to seal seams when you use freezer wrap to package food.

Don't store tomato-based foods in foil; the acid in the tomatoes will eat through the foil, exposing the food to air and risking freezer burn. Use heavy-duty heatproof freezer wrap for these foods.

The types of containers you use will determine how much food you'll be able to store in your freezer. Square and flat packages and containers make the best use of space, so you can add more packages to the freezer. Most casseroles can be frozen, removed from their dishes, and then stacked to store. To do this, line casserole and baking dishes with heavy-duty foil or freezer wrap. Assemble the food in the lined dishes, cover tightly with foil or freezer wrap, and freeze. When the food is frozen solid, pop the food out of the dish, wrap again, and store. When you're ready to eat, simply place the frozen food back into the baking dish, thaw, and reheat.

Load It!

Be sure the food is thoroughly cooled before loading your freezer. It's important that food that is already frozen does not thaw or soften because of the addition of unfrozen food. Avoid opening the freezer often during the loading process. Instead, gather up several containers and place them in the freezer at the same time. Every time you open the freezer, the temperature will rise a bit.

Think about dividing your freezer into sections based on the recipes it contains. Place chicken recipes in one area, appetizers in a separate basket or container, and Slow Cooker recipes in another area. You'll be able to find things more easily, and you'll also be able to see which recipe category needs replenishing when you're planning your next once-a-month cooking session.

Permanently attach a notebook or dry erase board to your freezer and update it each time you add or remove food. Make sure that you've used up all the food from your current cycle of once-a-month cooking before you plan another session.

Adding too much to your freezer at once raises the temperature of the freezer and compromises the quality and safety of your stored food. Make sure that you never add the equivalent of more than 40 percent of your freezer space at one time. Be sure to refer to the manufacturer's instruction booklet for specifics for your type and size of freezer.

How to Thaw and Reheat

The second most important technique you need to learn to be a successful cooking and freezing expert is how to thaw and reheat foods. Some foods can be baked directly from the frozen state, while others come out better if thawed first. Each recipe in this book has complete thawing and reheating instructions. Follow these instructions carefully and use an instant-read thermometer to check the temperature of the food before serving.

Add thawing foods to your list of chores you do before bedtime, just as you choose your clothes for the next day and check your children's homework. With a little extra planning, it's very simple to take a casserole from the freezer and store it in the refrigerator to thaw overnight, and then bake it the next evening.

When thawing meat in the refrigerator, place the bagged or wrapped meat in a container so the juices don't drip on any other food. Never thaw frozen meat at room temperature. You can thaw meat in the microwave oven, but only if you are going to cook it right away.

When you reheat thawed food, be sure it is fully cooked before serving it. Casseroles need to reach an internal temperature of 165°F before they are served. Test the casserole in the very center, since that is the last place to reach proper temperature. Meats must also be cooked to certain internal temperatures before they are safe to eat. Here are internal temperatures each meat type should reach when it is done:

Meat Cooking Temperatures	
Type of Meat	Safe Internal Temperature
Chicken parts (light meat)	170°F
Chicken parts (dark meat)	180°F
Whole chickens	180°F
Cuts of beef	145°F
Pork	160°F
Fish	160°F
Ground beef	160°F
Other ground meats	165°F

Be sure to wash the thermometer in hot soapy water in between tests if the meat has not reached the proper temperature the first time you test it.

Organizing and Selecting Recipes

Keep your cookbooks clean and in good condition by keeping them out of the kitchen. Copy recipes from this cookbook and your other favorites onto index cards. It's important to keep the recipes you use for freezing in a separate folder or notebook, along with any notes, lists, and changes to the recipes or lists that you have made. When you want to organize another cook-and-freeze session, all your information will be in one place. Clear vinyl page protectors will hold two 4" × 6" cards on each page in your recipe notebook.

Make photocopies of all of your recipes and tape them in easily accessible areas of your kitchen. You may want to tape recipes to cabinets or to the back of the kitchen door. This way, they stay out of the way, yet are always available when you need to refer to them.

Mix and Match

Think about serving one recipe in different ways. For instance, a beef chili recipe can be served over taco chips and garnished with salsa, cheese, and lettuce as a taco salad. The same recipe can be served over baked potatoes or as a topping for hot dogs. This planning allows you to vary the meals you serve using your tried-and-true recipes, combining similar preparation and cooking steps.

When you are compiling your list of recipes, think not only about the foods your family likes, but also about what's on sale that week at your local supermarket. For instance, if your grocer has a special on ground beef in five-pound packs, pull recipes for meatloaf, spaghetti sauce, and beef manicotti from your collection.

Variety Is Key

Make sure to choose a good variety of recipes for the month. For instance, choose several chicken casseroles, two grilled beef recipes, three slow cooker recipes, one chicken and one ham sandwich recipe, and a pepperoni pizza. Write down the recipes you have chosen on a blank calendar page; it's easier to make sure that you are serving your family a good variety of flavors, textures, colors, and nutrients during the month when you can see the whole month's plan at a glance.

What types of recipes should I choose from my own collection?

Simple recipes freeze best. Avoid recipes with complicated sauces, different cooking times, multiple preparation steps, and those that use exotic ingredients.

Cooking Day Dos and Don'ts

Since you're going to be spending the entire day cooking, the most important "do" of all is enjoy the process. Enjoy the sounds of cooking: the knife blade *chunk*ing into the chopping board, foods *sizzling* in a pan, and even the *clink* of metal on metal as you flip through nested measuring spoons. Think about all the time you're going to save, and how well you are treating yourself and your family. In addition:

- ☑ Do stock up on paper towels and dishrags.
- ☑ Do make sure you have several large plastic garbage bags available, and remove each bag from the kitchen as soon as it is full.
- ☑ Do cook with a helper or two. Split up some of the chores; for instance, one person can cook a few recipes while the other keeps the kitchen clean, and then switch places.
- ☑ Do keep a first-aid kit handy. When you're working with this much food and so many appliances, it pays to be prepared.

☑ Do make sure your knives are sharp and in good condition. A sharp knife slices more easily and is actually safer to use than a dull knife. Dull knives can slip as you work with them, making it all too easy to cut yourself.

☑ Do make an inventory before you start, to make sure you have enough pots, pans, spoons, forks, and knives on hand, and that they are all in good working order.

☑ Do make sure that all your appliances are in good working order and are accurate.

☑ Do schedule more time than you think you'll need.

☑ Do take breaks where you leave the kitchen, sit down, and sip some tea while putting your feet up. Nobody can work for seven or eight hours without a break.

☑ Do think about prepping some of the food on the same day that you shop. You could cut up some vegetables or meats and package them in plastic containers, or start meat cooking in your slow cooker for the next day.

The most important "don't" of all: don't wear yourself out or undertake a day of cooking if you don't feel well. If you're unsure of your strength or stamina, start small by choosing just a few meals to make and freeze. Here are some other important don'ts:

☑ Don't attempt too much, especially on your first experience with this type of cooking. It's much easier to schedule another cooking session if you aren't exhausted by the first attempt.

☑ Don't shop and cook on the same day.

☑ Don't let prepared food sit on the counter while you assemble other recipes. As soon as the recipes are prepared, cool them, then pack, label, and freeze them.

☑ Don't purchase frozen meats and then thaw and refreeze them without cooking. Once a meat has been thawed, it must be cooked before being refrozen.

☑ Don't cook a meal for your family or yourself on C-day. Go out to eat! You deserve some pampering after your marathon cooking session.

Try to make your cooking session fun. If you see it as a positive challenge and do everything you can to make the process enjoyable, you are going to want to schedule another session.

Load up your CD player with lots of songs you love. Upbeat songs with a good tempo will help make the time fly. Make up games as you go along. (Don't play timing games though; racing to see who can chop the most onions in a certain time frame, for instance, can only lead to disaster.)

Cook with a partner—a neighbor, relative, or work colleague. Think about organizing a cooking club and pair off with a different member each month. Your recipe collection will expand exponentially, and you'll pass along this efficient and money-saving cooking method to more people. You will not only expand your collection of freezable recipes, but the time will go by much more quickly when another person is there to share the chores.

Enjoy the aromas as your home fills with delicious smells. Who needs potpourri or air fresheners when bread, cookies, casseroles, and vegetables are baking and simmering? And enjoy the safe, cozy feeling of "putting food by" to feed your family and friends.

Chapter 2: **Bulk Cooking Method**

This chapter contains a complete one-month shopping and cooking plan. This plan will show you how to choose recipes; plan your shopping and "on-hand" lists; plan preparation of ingredients and cooking; prepare ingredients; assemble and cook recipes; and cool, wrap, and freeze the finished dishes.

Recipes for a Month

While you can certainly plan to cook thirty individual recipes for freezing, it's much easier to cook double or triple amounts of ten to fifteen recipes. When you think about it, your family usually requests the same recipe at least twice a month. You'll save lots of time and energy by doubling or tripling a recipe and packaging and freezing that food in meal-size portions. Then rotate the food into your meal plan for the month.

The ten recipes in this cooking model will be tripled, to make a total of thirty entrees that will each serve four to six adults. These recipes are:

- Wild Rice Meatloaf (page 60)

- Easy Lasagna (page 61)

- Cabbage Rolls (page 62)

- Chicken on Cornbread (page 95)

- Chicken Pot Pie (page 111)

- Apricot Pork Chops (page 144)

- Pork Chops and Potatoes Dinner (page 243)

- Slow Cooker Spicy Peanut Chicken (page 209)

- Italian Slow Cooker Chicken (page 210)

When choosing your recipes, you can make adjustments to streamline cooking. For instance, if one recipe calls for ground beef with onions and garlic and another uses just ground beef and onions, add garlic to the second dish or omit garlic from the first one so you can prepare the foods together.

It's important to make sure the recipes you have chosen are cooked with different methods. For instance, you don't want to have thirty baked dishes unless you have three or four ovens. Choose some recipes that are cooked in a skillet or saucepan, some that are baked, some that are frozen without cooking, some that are grilled, and some that are prepared in a Slow Cooker.

Get Ready to Shop

Once you have collected your recipes, pull out a pencil and paper and start making your lists. Lists are your lifeline in this type of cooking. You'll need to create a shopping list and an "on-hand" list that will include every single ingredient listed in each recipe. You'll draw up these lists first, followed by a preparation schedule and a cooking schedule.

Make copies of your recipes to make it easier to work on these lists. Then, using the Equivalents Chart (page 310), convert cups into pounds and ounces, and convert can and bottle sizes. Go through each recipe, writing down each ingredient on your on-hand list if you have it or on the shopping list if you don't, and check off each ingredient as you go. Double-check your lists; your cooking session will be a disaster if you are missing ingredients. You might want to practice making your own shopping and on-hand lists from this session's recipes, then compare them to the lists that follow. (Your own shopping and on-hand lists may be slightly different, depending on what's in your pantry and freezer, and the substitutions you use for the recipes.) Following are the shopping and on-hand lists for the above recipes.

Be sure to double-check your lists and make sure all ingredients, preparation steps, and cooking steps are included.

Make notes as you go through preparation and cooking, to improve your assembly-line process, refine shopping lists and organization of tools and ingredients, and streamline recipe preparation.

Shopping List

- ☑ 2 jalapeno peppers
- ☑ 2 green chilies
- ☑ 23 onions
- ☑ 45 cloves garlic (5–6 heads)
- ☑ 1 (9-ounce) package button mushrooms
- ☑ 3 carrots
- ☑ 3 red bell peppers
- ☑ 3 heads green cabbage

- ☑ 1 pound butter or margarine
- ☑ 1 pint buttermilk
- ☑ 1 quart plus 1 pint whole milk
- ☑ 4 (15-ounce) containers ricotta cheese
- ☑ 11/2 pounds mozzarella cheese
- ☑ 21/2 pounds Parmesan cheese
- ☑ 3 (3-ounce) packages cream cheese
- ☑ 15 eggs
- ☑ 1 pint orange juice

- ☑ 6 pounds boneless, skinless chicken thighs
- ☑ 12 pounds bone-in, skin-on chicken breasts
- ☑ 36 pork chops
- ☑ 6 pounds boneless, skinless chicken breasts
- ☑ 12 pounds lean ground beef
- ☑ 3 pounds ground pork

- ☑ 2 (16-ounce) packages frozen peppers and onions
- ☑ 3 pounds frozen Southern-style hash browns
- ☑ 2 (24-ounce) packages frozen potato wedges
- ☑ 2 (1-pound) packages frozen peas and carrots
- ☑ 5 bags of ice

- ☑ 1 (10-ounce) bottle Worcestershire sauce
- ☑ 1 (10-ounce) bottle soy sauce
- ☑ 1 (16-ounce) bottle Italian salad dressing

- ☑ Mustard
- ☑ Ketchup
- ☑ 3 (15-ounce) cans tomato sauce

- ☑ 6 (26-ounce) jars pasta sauce
- ☑ 1 (18-ounce) jar apricot preserves
- ☑ 3 (8-ounce) cans apricot nectar
- ☑ 1 (28-ounce) jar chunky peanut butter
- ☑ 1 (10-ounce) package dried bread crumbs
- ☑ 3 (10-ounce) cans cream of mushroom soup
- ☑ 3 (10-ounce) cans condensed tomato soup
- ☑ 27 lasagna noodles (two 20-count packages)
- ☑ 2 (1-pound) packages spaghetti
- ☑ 1 (32-ounce) package long-grain rice
- ☑ 1 pound wild rice
- ☑ 3 (10-ounce) packages couscous
- ☑ 3 (10-ounce) cans condensed chicken broth

- ☑ 3 gallon-size zipper-lock bags
- ☑ 18 quart-size zipper-lock bags
- ☑ 6 pint-size zipper-lock bags
- ☑ Waxed paper
- ☑ Heavy-duty freezer wrap
- ☑ Freezer tape
- ☑ Heavy-duty aluminum foil
- ☑ Wax pencil or marker

On-Hand List

- Flour
- Cornmeal
- Baking soda
- Baking powder
- Salt
- Pepper
- Dried marjoram leaves
- Dried thyme leaves
- Dried basil leaves
- Solid shortening
- Olive oil
- Vegetable oil

- 3 8" × 8" baking pans
- At least 3 9" × 9" baking pans
- 3 10" deep-dish pie pans
- At least 3 13" × 9" baking pans

Shortcuts

Depending on your schedule and pocketbook, there are lots of shortcuts available for this cooking plan. If you aren't watching sodium or fat content in your diet, purchasing sauces, gravies, mixes, and other prepared ingredients can save a lot of time. Other shortcuts you might be interested in include the following:

- Purchase canned or bottled chicken gravy for Chicken on Cornbread and Chicken Pot Pie.
- Use a corn muffin mix to make the cornbread.
- Use frozen or refrigerated pie crusts instead of making them from scratch.
- Buy precooked chicken that is sliced or cubed, either from the deli or the frozen foods section of the supermarket.
- Buy precooked, preseasoned ground beef from the meat section of the supermarket.
- Purchase grated and shredded cheese from the deli or dairy section of the supermarket.
- Buy prepared vegetables from a salad bar in your supermarket.
- Purchase cooked rice from a local Chinese restaurant.
- Buy coleslaw mix instead of shredding cabbage; purchase one head of cabbage for the recipe that requires whole leaves.
- Purchase 6 pounds of meatloaf mix instead of 3 each of ground beef and ground pork.

Remember, these shortcuts will cost more than buying items that aren't "value added." Decide whether your budget can handle these added conveniences, and whether the time you will save is worth the extra cost.

Planning and Preparation

There are some tasks that you can do ahead of cooking day. Place all nonperishable foods on your kitchen table in groups as they are needed for the recipes to make sure you have all the ingredients on hand. This can be done two to three days ahead of cooking day. The following preparation steps can be done either the day before or on the morning of cooking day itself.

- Cook the 12 pounds of bone-in chicken breasts in your slow cooker in batches of 4 pounds each for 6 to 7 hours on low, simmer in water for 30 to 45 minutes, or bake in the oven for 50 to 60 minutes. Refrigerate, covered, until needed. (If you cook your chicken by simmering, reserve the broth and use it in place of purchased condensed chicken broth.)
- Peel and chop the onions and garlic, place in zipper-lock bags, and store in the refrigerator.
- Seed and chop the red bell peppers, place in zipper-lock bags, and store in the refrigerator.
- Make pie crust dough, roll out between sheets of waxed paper, wrap again, and refrigerate.
- Cook wild rice until almost tender; drain and refrigerate.

Time for a break! Make yourself a cup of coffee and sit in a comfortable chair while the wild rice is cooking. Put your feet up on an ottoman and listen to some music. Do some simple stretching exercises or massage your feet.

- Seed and chop the jalapenos and green chilies and store in zipper-lock bags in the refrigerator.
- Grate carrots and store in zipper-lock bags in the refrigerator.
- Remove 24 leaves of cabbage from heads; core heads and shred remaining cabbage. Store in zipper-lock bags in the refrigerator.
- Shred the cheeses and store in zipper-lock bags in the refrigerator.
- Group all of the nonperishable and canned foods that you need for each recipe together.
- Divide chicken thighs and boneless chicken breasts into three equal portions each, package in zipper-lock bags, label, and freeze for Slow Cooker Spicy Peanut Chicken and Italian Slow Cooker Chicken.

Time to Get Cooking!

Now that the shopping and preparation phases are complete, it's time to start some serious cooking. As you finish each dish, place it in the refrigerator or in an ice bath to cool quickly, or freeze immediately, depending on the recipe.

When the food is cold, fold wrapping over the food, seal seams, overwrap if necessary, label, and place it in the freezer. Be sure to carefully seal all seams in freezer paper using freezer tape.

Label foods accurately as you go along. Once meals are wrapped and frozen, it will be difficult to identify them. Waterproof markers, grease pencils, and wax markers work well on most freezer wrap and plastic containers. Be sure to record the name of the recipe, the date it was prepared, thawing and reheating instructions, and additional foods needed to finish the recipe.

When casseroles are frozen solid, you can remove them from the baking dishes, then wrap again in freezer wrap or foil and stack to save room. Make sure to rotate food as you add it to your freezer, placing the items frozen for the longest time on top or in the front of the freezer so you'll use them first.

The following steps will see you through the rest of your cooking day:

- If you haven't already cooked the chicken, bake the 12 pounds of bone-in chicken breasts. Sprinkle chicken with salt and pepper and place in several large pans. Cover with foil and bake at 350°F for 30 minutes. Uncover and bake 20 to 30 minutes longer or until meat thermometer registers 170°F. When chicken is done, remove from oven and place in refrigerator until cool enough to handle. Or cook chicken by placing in a stockpot, covering with water, and simmering for 30 to 45 minutes until done. Reserve the broth for your recipes.
- Wash and chop the mushrooms, and prepare any other vegetables you didn't prepare the day before.
- Start cooking the wild rice (if you didn't already) and the white rice and mix the cornbread batter. Bake cornbread until set. When rice is cooked until almost tender, drain if necessary and set aside.
- Combine the recipes for the gravy for Chicken Pot Pie and Chicken on Cornbread in a large stockpot. Let simmer for 5 to 6 minutes. Then chill in the refrigerator.

- Remove meat from cooked and cooled chicken; freeze skin and bones to make broth later if desired. Slice half of chicken and cube half; store in the refrigerator.
- Assemble sauce for Slow Cooker Spicy Peanut Chicken and pour into containers. Attach to bag of chicken thighs, label, and freeze. Set aside couscous in pantry, marked as "reserved."

Time for a break! Do some simple stretches and breathe deeply. Think about changing your shoes to rest your feet. Have a snack of some fresh fruit and cold water or iced tea.

- Add sliced chicken to half of chicken gravy for Chicken on Cornbread. Wrap cornbread, attach bag of chicken in gravy, label, and freeze.
- Combine sauce ingredients for Italian Slow Cooker Chicken and pour into three one-quart zipper-lock bags. Attach three zipper-lock bags of boneless chicken breasts and three more bags with potatoes, label, and freeze.
- Sauté 3 cups chopped onions and 3 cloves minced garlic in olive oil for Wild Rice Meatloaf; refrigerate.
- Sauté, in batches, 9 pounds ground beef, 9 onions, and 27 cloves garlic, minced, for Easy Lasagna, Cabbage Rolls, and Spaghetti. Drain and refrigerate as the meat is cooked; divide mixture into three equal portions. Add pasta sauce and water to one portion for Easy Lasagna and set aside in the fridge.
- Combine all ingredients for Wild Rice Meatloaf and shape into three loaves. Bake as directed until done, then refrigerate until cold.
- Mix lasagna cheese filling; then assemble lasagnas in three lined pans; refrigerate.
- Add thyme, red bell pepper, chicken, and frozen vegetables to chilled chicken gravy for Chicken Pot Pie; form pies, top with pie crusts, wrap, label, and freeze.

Take a break at this point. Update your lists and make notes of the changes you've made to your recipes so far. Make yourself some coffee and sit down in a comfortable chair for fifteen to twenty minutes.

- Brown pork chops for Pork Chops and Potatoes Dinner, add onions, and cook as directed in recipe. Remove pork and vegetables from pan and refrigerate.
- Return one batch of the cooked ground beef/onion/garlic mixture to heavy skillet; add carrots, basil, and pasta sauce and simmer for 25 to 30 minutes for Spaghetti. Cool sauce in the refrigerator.
- Combine remaining batch of cooled ground beef mixture, rice, and remaining ingredients for Cabbage Rolls filling. Stuff and roll cabbage leaves and assemble casseroles; refrigerate.
- Combine all ingredients for Apricot Pork Chops; divide into three portions, wrap, label, and freeze.
- Wrap cooled Wild Rice Meatloaf, label, and freeze.
- Wrap, label, and freeze Cabbage Rolls.
- Wrap, label, and freeze Easy Lasagna.
- Assemble Pork Chops and Potatoes casseroles; wrap, label, and freeze.

And you're done! By now you're tired, but look at what you have accomplished. If possible, have another family member (or two) clean the kitchen. Now, go out to dinner; you've earned it! And enjoy the next thirty days of the simplest dinners ever.

Lessons for Next Time

When you have successfully completed a cooking and freezing plan, be sure to save all your recipes, shopping and on-hand lists, and notes in a loose-leaf notebook. As you become more familiar with this type of cooking, you will find that you are developing your own cooking plans that adapt to your lifestyle and your family's tastes. Before you know it, you'll have five or six cooking plans that can take you through the whole year, and you will have shopping lists, recipes, and preparation plans all figured out..

Olive Tarts

Makes 24

1 onion, chopped
2 cloves garlic, minced
½ cup chopped mushrooms
1 tablespoon olive oil
½ cup sliced black olives
½ cup sliced green olives
½ teaspoon dried thyme
    leaves
2 sheets frozen puff pastry,
    thawed
1 cup shredded Gouda
    cheese

Makes 72

3 onions, chopped
6 cloves garlic, minced
1½ cups chopped
    mushrooms
3 tablespoons olive oil
1½ cups sliced black olives
1½ cups sliced green olives
1½ teaspoons dried thyme
    leaves
6 sheets frozen puff pastry,
    thawed
3 cups shredded Gouda
    cheese

To serve immediately, sprinkle with cheese and bake at
400°F for 10 to 12 minutes or until pastry is golden brown,
filling is set, and cheese is melted and beginning to brown.

1. Preheat oven to 400°F. In heavy skillet, sauté onion, garlic, and mush-rooms in olive oil until tender. Remove from heat and add olives and thyme.

2. Gently roll puff pastry dough with rolling pin until ¼-inch thick. Using a 3-inch cookie cutter, cut 24 circles from pastry. Line muffin cups with dough.

3. Place a spoonful of filling in each pastry-lined cup. Bake at 400°F for 10 to 12 minutes or until crust is golden brown and filling is set.

4. Remove from muffin cups and cool on wire rack. Flash freeze; when frozen solid, pack tarts into zipper-lock bags. Attach zipper-lock bag filled with shredded cheese; label and freeze.

5. *To thaw and reheat:* Thaw tarts in single layer overnight in refrigerator. Top each tart with cheese and bake at 400°F for 5 to 6 minutes or until hot and cheese is melted.

Shrimp Quiches

To serve immediately, bake quiches at 375°F
for 15 to 18 minutes, until filling is set and pastry is browned.
Let cool for 10 minutes before serving.

2 9-inch Pie Crusts (page 299)
½ cup chopped leek, rinsed
1 tablespoon olive oil
2 eggs
½ cup cream
1 (6-ounce) can tiny shrimp, drained
½ teaspoon dried marjoram leaves
½ teaspoon salt
⅛ teaspoon pepper
¾ cup shredded Havarti cheese

1. Using a 2-inch cookie cutter, cut 36 rounds from pie crusts. Place each in a 1¾-inch mini muffin cup, pressing to bottom and sides. Set aside.

2. Sauté leek in olive oil until tender. Beat eggs with cream in medium bowl. Add drained shrimp, cooked leek, marjoram, salt, and pepper, and mix well.

Makes 108

6 9-inch Pie Crusts (page 299)
1½ cups chopped leek, rinsed
3 tablespoons olive oil
6 eggs
1½ cups cream
3 (6-ounce) cans tiny shrimp, drained
1½ teaspoons dried marjoram leaves
1½ teaspoons salt
⅜ teaspoon pepper
2¼ cups shredded Havarti cheese

3. Sprinkle 1 teaspoon cheese into each muffin cup and fill cups with shrimp mixture. Bake at 375°F for 15 to 18 minutes or until pastry is golden and filling is set. Cool in refrigerator until cold, then freeze.

4. Freeze in single layer on baking sheet. When frozen solid, pack in rigid containers, using waxed paper to separate layers. Label and freeze.

5. *To reheat:* Place frozen quiches on baking sheet and bake at 375°F for 8 to 11 minutes or until hot.

Food for Thought

When planning an appetizer reception, plan on four appetizers per person per hour. Also, make sure your menu includes a mix of beef, poultry, seafood, and cheese or a vegetarian offering.

Egg Rolls

Makes 24

½ pound ground pork
½ pound ground shrimp
1 carrot, shredded
2 cloves garlic, minced
1 bunch green onions, finely
  chopped
1 cup shredded Napa
  cabbage
2 tablespoons soy sauce
1 tablespoon oyster sauce
2 tablespoons cornstarch
1 tablespoon water
1 package egg roll wrappers
3 cups peanut oil

Makes 72

1½ pounds ground pork
1½ pounds ground shrimp
3 carrots, shredded
6 cloves garlic, minced
3 bunches green onions,
  finely chopped
3 cups shredded Napa
  cabbage
6 tablespoons soy sauce
3 tablespoons oyster sauce
6 tablespoons cornstarch
3 tablespoons water
3 packages egg roll
  wrappers
3 cups peanut oil

To serve immediately, fry in peanut oil at 375°F for 2 to 3 minutes, until golden brown. To make a dipping sauce, mix 3 tablespoons soy sauce with 1 teaspoon sugar, 1 tablespoon mustard, and 1 tablespoon vinegar.

1. In a large skillet, brown ground pork until almost done. Add ground shrimp, carrot, and garlic; cook and stir for 4 to 6 minutes or until pork is cooked. Remove from heat, drain well, and add green onions, cabbage, soy sauce, and oyster sauce.

2. Combine cornstarch and water in a small bowl and blend well.

3. To form egg rolls, place one wrapper, point-side down, on work surface. Place 1 tablespoon filling 1 inch from corner. Brush all edges of the egg roll wrapper with cornstarch mixture. Fold point over filling, then fold in sides and roll up egg roll, using cornstarch mixture to seal as necessary.

4. At this point, egg rolls may be flash frozen, or you can flash freeze them after frying. Once frozen, pack, label, and freeze in rigid containers.

5. *To reheat unfried egg rolls*: Fry the frozen rolls in peanut oil heated to 375°F for 2 to 3 minutes, turning once, or until deep golden brown.

   To reheat fried egg rolls: Place frozen egg rolls on baking sheet. Bake at 375°F for 8 to 10 minutes or until crisp and hot.

Beefy Mini Pies

Include these pies in an appetizer buffet, or serve them to guests before dinner with a glass of red wine. To serve immediately, bake at 350°F for 7 to 9 minutes; serve hot.

1. Preheat oven to 350°F. Remove rolls from package and divide each roll into 3 rounds. Place each round into a 3-inch muffin cup; press firmly onto bottom and up sides.

2. In a heavy skillet, cook ground beef with onion and garlic until beef is done. Drain well. Place 1 tablespoon beef mixture into each dough-lined muffin cup. Sprinkle cheese over beef mixture. In a small bowl, beat together eggs, half-and-half, and dill weed. Spoon this mixture over beef in muffin cups, making sure not to overfill cups.

3. Bake at 350°F for 10 to 13 minutes or until filling is puffed and set. Flash freeze in single layer on baking sheet. When frozen solid, wrap, label, and freeze.

4. *To thaw and reheat:* Thaw pies in single layer in refrigerator overnight. Bake at 350°F for 7 to 9 minutes or until hot.

Makes 24

1 (10-ounce) package refrigerated flaky dinner rolls
½ pound ground beef
1 small onion, chopped
2 cloves garlic, minced
1 cup shredded Colby cheese
2 eggs
½ cup half-and-half
½ teaspoon dried dill weed

Makes 72

3 (10-ounce) packages refrigerated flaky dinner rolls
1½ pounds ground beef
3 small onions, chopped
6 cloves garlic, minced
3 cups shredded Colby cheese
6 eggs
1½ cups half-and-half
1½ teaspoons dried dill weed

Olive Puffs

Makes 30

_____

5 tablespoons butter,
  softened
1 (3-ounce) package cream
  cheese, softened
1½ cups grated sharp
  Cheddar cheese
1 teaspoon Worcestershire
  sauce
¾ cup flour
 ⅛ teaspoon pepper
30 garlic-stuffed olives

Makes 90

_____

15 tablespoons butter,
  softened
3 (3-ounce) packages cream
  cheese, softened
4½ cups grated sharp
  Cheddar cheese
1 tablespoon Worcestershire
  sauce
2¼ cups flour
 ⅜ teaspoon pepper
90 garlic-stuffed olives

You can make these little puffs with any type of stuffed olive and any type of cheese. To serve immediately, bake at 400°F for 10 to 12 minutes.

1. In medium bowl, combine butter, cream cheese, and Cheddar cheese. Cream well until blended. Add Worcestershire sauce and mix until blended. Add flour and pepper and mix to form dough.

2. Form dough around each olive, covering olive completely. Flash freeze in single layer on baking sheets, then package in zipper-lock bags. Label bag and freeze.

3. *To reheat:* Place frozen puffs on baking sheet. Bake at 400°F for 10 to 12 minutes or until hot, puffed, and golden brown.

What Is a Shallot?

Shallots are a member of the onion family and have a distinct mild flavor. They are used as a flavoring agent in many sauces. Dry shallots are available year-round and should be stored as you would store onions. Fresh shallots are available in the spring and should be stored in the refrigerator.

Nutty Parmesan Sticks

Makes 36

1 package frozen puff
  pastry sheets, thawed
½ cup ground almonds
½ cup grated Parmesan
  cheese
⅛ teaspoon cayenne
  pepper

Makes 72

3 packages frozen puff
  pastry sheets, thawed
1½ cups ground almonds
1½ cups grated Parmesan
  cheese
⅜ teaspoon cayenne
  pepper

To serve immediately, let cool after baking and serve with a soft cheese dip. Store sticks in airtight container at room temperature.

1. Preheat oven to 375°F. In a small bowl, combine almonds, cheese, and pepper; blend well. Sprinkle half of this mixture over work surface and cover with one sheet puff pastry. Using a rolling pin, gently press pastry into cheese mixture. Turn pastry over and press cheese mixture into other side of pastry. Repeat with other half of cheese mixture and second sheet of puff pastry.

2. Using pastry cutter or sharp knife, cut pastry into ½-inch strips. Place on parchment paper– or foil-lined baking sheets, twisting each strip several times. Bake at 375°F for 10 to 15 minutes or until browned and crisp, being careful not to burn sticks. Remove from baking sheet and cool completely on wire racks. Pack carefully into rigid containers, separating layers with waxed paper. Label containers and freeze.

3. *To thaw and reheat:* Thaw sticks at room temperature and serve, or carefully place frozen sticks on baking sheet and bake at 350°F for 4 to 5 minutes or until hot.

Shrimp and Artichoke Puffs

6 slices whole wheat bread
2 shallots, chopped
1 tablespoon olive oil
½ pound cooked shrimp
1 (10-ounce) package
   frozen artichoke hearts,
   thawed
1 (3-ounce) package cream
   cheese, softened
1 cup shredded Gouda
   cheese
½ cup mayonnaise
1 tablespoon lemon juice
1 teaspoon dried basil leaves

Makes about 72

18 slices whole wheat bread
6 shallots, chopped
3 tablespoons olive oil
1½ pounds cooked shrimp
3 (10-ounce) packages
   frozen artichoke hearts,
   thawed
3 (3-ounce) packages cream
   cheese, softened
3 cups shredded Gouda
   cheese
1½ cups mayonnaise
3 tablespoons lemon juice
1 tablespoon dried basil
   leaves

To serve these delicate and delicious puffs immediately, bake at 400°F for 7 to 9 minutes or until hot and bubbling, then offer them to your guests with white wine.

1. Preheat oven to 300°F. Using a 2-inch cookie cutter, cut rounds from bread slices. Place rounds on a baking sheet and bake at 300°F for 7 to 9 minutes, or until crisp, turning once. Remove from oven and cool on wire racks.

2. In a heavy skillet, cook shallots in olive oil over medium heat until tender. Remove from heat. Chop shrimp and add to skillet along with thawed, drained, and chopped artichoke hearts. Add both cheeses, mayonnaise, lemon juice, and basil; stir well to blend.

3. Spoon 1 tablespoon shrimp mixture onto each bread round, covering the top and mounding the filling. Flash freeze on baking sheets. When frozen solid, pack in rigid containers, with waxed paper between layers. Label puffs and freeze.

4. *To reheat:* Place frozen puffs on a baking sheet and bake at 400°F for 10 to 12 minutes or until topping is hot and bubbling.

Stuffed Mushrooms

Lemon juice prevents the mushrooms from darkening
during freezing and adds a fresh flavor. To serve immediately,
bake filled mushrooms at 375°F for 8 to 10 minutes or
until hot and cheese is melted.

1. Preheat oven to 375°F. Remove stems from mushrooms; chop stems and set aside. Combine lemon juice and olive oil in a small bowl and dip mushroom caps into this mixture. Place mushroom caps upside down on baking sheet and bake at 375°F for 6 to 8 minutes, or until slightly softened. Remove from oven and cool.

2. In a heavy skillet, sauté onion and chopped mushroom stems in olive oil until tender. Add chopped apple and walnuts; mix well. Remove from heat and cool for 20 minutes. Stir in cheese, salt, and pepper.

3. Stuff mushrooms with filling mixture, smoothing the top of filling. Flash freeze mushrooms on baking sheets. When frozen, pack mushrooms in rigid containers, with waxed paper separating layers. Label mushrooms and freeze.

4. *To reheat:* Bake frozen mushrooms at 375°F for 15 to 18 minutes or until mushrooms are hot and beginning to brown and cheese is melted.

Makes 30

30 large mushrooms
2 tablespoons lemon juice
2 tablespoons olive oil
1 onion, finely chopped
1 tablespoon olive oil
1 Granny Smith apple,
    peeled and finely
    chopped
½ cup chopped walnuts
1 cup cubed Havarti cheese
½ teaspoon salt
⅛ teaspoon pepper

Makes 90

90 large mushrooms
6 tablespoons lemon juice
6 tablespoons olive oil
3 onions, finely chopped
3 tablespoons olive oil
3 Granny Smith apples,
    peeled and finely
    chopped
1½ cups chopped walnuts
3 cups cubed Havarti cheese
1½ teaspoons salt
⅜ teaspoon pepper

Mini Crab Cakes

Makes about 24

---

1 pound canned lump
   crabmeat
1 cup fresh cilantro leaves
½ cup chopped walnuts
½ cup grated Romano
   cheese
2 tablespoons olive oil
½ cup dried bread crumbs
½ cup mayonnaise
¼ cup minced green onions
3 tablespoons olive oil

Makes about 72

---

3 pounds canned lump
   crabmeat
3 cups fresh cilantro leaves
1½ cups chopped walnuts
1½ cups grated Romano
   cheese
6 tablespoons olive oil
1½ cups dried bread crumbs
1½ cups mayonnaise
¾ cup minced green onions
9 tablespoons olive oil

Serve these crab cakes with mayonnaise blended with cilantro and Romano cheese. To serve immediately, fry until golden and hot, turning once, about 3 to 5 minutes on each side.

---

1. Drain crabmeat well and pick over to remove any cartilage. Set aside in large bowl. In food processor or blender, combine cilantro, walnuts, cheese, and 2 tablespoons olive oil (6 tablespoons for triple batch). Process or blend until mixture forms a paste. Stir into crabmeat.

2. Add bread crumbs, mayonnaise, and green onions to crab mixture. Stir to combine. Form into 2-inch patties about ½-inch thick. Flash freeze on baking sheet. When frozen solid, pack crab cakes in rigid containers, with waxed paper between the layers. Label crab cakes and freeze. Reserve remaining olive oil in pantry.

3. *To thaw and reheat:* Thaw crab cakes in refrigerator overnight. Heat 3 tablespoons olive oil (9 for triple batch) in large, heavy skillet over medium heat. Fry crab cakes until golden and hot, turning once, about 3 to 5 minutes on each side.

Italian Pork Skewers

These skewers are tender and full of flavor. To serve immediately, marinate for 2 to 3 hours, then cook over grill or broil until done.

1. Trim excess fat from tenderloin. Cut pork, on a slant, into ¼-inch-thick slices, each about 4 inches long. In large bowl, combine remaining ingredients and mix well with wire whisk. Add tenderloin slices and mix gently to coat. Cover and refrigerate for 2 to 3 hours. Meanwhile, soak 8-inch wooden skewers in cold water.

2. Remove pork from marinade and thread onto soaked skewers. Flash freeze on baking sheet in single layer. When frozen solid, pack skewers in rigid containers, with layers separated by waxed paper. Label skewers and freeze.

3. *To thaw and reheat:* Thaw overnight in refrigerator. Cook skewers 4 to 6 inches from medium coals on grill, or broil 4 to 6 inches from heat source, for about 4 to 6 minutes or until cooked (160°F on an instant-read thermometer), turning once.

What Is Balsamic Vinegar?

It is an Italian delicacy made from white Trebbiano grape juice. It gets its dark color from aging in barrels of various woods over a period of years. The taste and price of balsamic vinegars vary as much as wines' do. You can improve the flavor of a mid-range quality balsamic by simmering and reducing the volume.

Serves 6–8

2 pounds pork tenderloin
¼ cup balsamic vinegar
¼ cup olive oil
¼ cup finely minced onion
1 teaspoon dried Italian
  seasoning
½ teaspoon salt
⅛ teaspoon pepper

Serves 18–24

6 pounds pork tenderloin
¾ cup balsamic vinegar
¾ cup olive oil
¾ cup finely minced onion
1 tablespoon dried Italian
  seasoning
1½ teaspoons salt
⅜ teaspoon pepper

Cheesy Tomato Gougere Puffs

Makes 48

1 cup milk
¼ cup butter
½ teaspoon salt
Pinch white pepper
1 cup flour
4 eggs
¼ cup oil-packed sun-dried
  tomatoes
1 cup crumbled blue cheese
1 egg yolk
2 teaspoons water
¼ cup grated Parmesan
  cheese

Makes 144

3 cups milk
¾ cup butter
1½ teaspoons salt
 ⅛ teaspoon white pepper
3 cups flour
12 eggs
¾ cup oil-packed sun-dried
  tomatoes
3 cups crumbled blue cheese
3 egg yolks
6 teaspoons water
¾ cup grated Parmesan
  cheese

To serve immediately, bake puffs at 375°F for
15 to 20 minutes or until puffed and browned. Remove from
oven and cut a tiny slit in each puff to let out steam.

1. Preheat oven to 375°F. In heavy saucepan, combine milk, butter, salt, and white pepper and bring to a rolling boil. Add flour all at once, stirring constantly. Cook over medium heat, stirring constantly, until ball of dough forms and cleans sides of pan.

2. Using electric mixer, beat in eggs, one at a time. Remove from heat and let cool for 20 minutes. Drain sun-dried tomatoes well, then mince. Add tomatoes and blue cheese to dough. Stir to combine.

3. Drop teaspoons of dough onto baking sheets lined with parchment paper. Beat egg yolk and water in small bowl and carefully brush over each puff. Sprinkle with Parmesan cheese. Bake at 375°F for 15 to 20 minutes or until puffed, golden brown, and firm. Flash freeze puffs on baking sheet; and then pack, wrap, label, and freeze.

4. *To reheat:* Bake frozen puffs at 375°F for 4 to 6 minutes or until hot.

Seafood Turnovers

To serve immediately, bake at 400°F for 18 to 23 minutes or until pastry is golden brown and filling is hot.

1. In medium bowl, combine shrimp, ricotta, green onions, Havarti, and dill weed and mix well.

2. Gently roll puff pastry into 12-inch by 18-inch rectangle. Cut into 24 3-inch squares. Place 2 teaspoons shrimp mixture in center of each square. Beat egg yolk with water in small bowl. Brush edges of pastry with egg yolk mixture. Fold puff pastry over filling, forming triangles; press edges with fork to seal.

3. Flash freeze turnovers in single layer on baking sheet. Then pack in rigid containers, with waxed paper separating the layers. Label containers and freeze.

4. *To reheat:* Preheat oven to 450°F. Place frozen turnovers on baking sheet. Bake at 450°F for 4 minutes; then turn oven down to 400°F and bake for 12 to 15 minutes longer or until pastry is golden and filling is hot.

Makes 24

1 (6-ounce) can small shrimp, drained
½ cup ricotta cheese
3 green onions, finely chopped
1 cup shredded Havarti cheese
½ teaspoon dried dill weed
1 sheet frozen puff pastry, thawed
1 egg yolk, beaten
1 tablespoon water

Makes 72

3 (6-ounce) cans small shrimp, drained
1½ cups ricotta cheese
9 green onions, finely chopped
3 cups shredded Havarti cheese
1½ teaspoons dried dill weed
3 sheets frozen puff pastry, thawed
3 egg yolks, beaten
3 tablespoons water

Sweet and Sour Meatballs

Serves 8–10

1 pound ground beef
1 egg
½ cup grated Parmesan
   cheese
¼ cup dry bread crumbs
¼ cup apple cider vinegar
1 (10-ounce) can condensed
   tomato soup
⅓ cup sugar
1 (8-ounce) can pineapple
   tidbits, undrained

Serves 24–30

3 pounds ground beef
3 eggs
1½ cups grated Parmesan
   cheese
¾ cup dry bread crumbs
¾ cup apple cider vinegar
3 (10-ounce) cans condensed
   tomato soup
1 cup sugar
3 (8-ounce) cans pineapple
   tidbits, undrained

To serve immediately, combine all sauce ingredients and bring to a boil. Reduce heat, add cooked meatballs, cover, and simmer for 7 to 9 minutes or until meatballs are hot and sauce is slightly thickened.

1. Preheat oven to 350°F. In medium bowl, combine ground beef, egg, cheese, and bread crumbs and mix well to blend. Form into 1-inch meatballs and place on baking sheet. Bake at 350°F for 20 to 25 minutes or until no longer pink in center. Chill meatballs in refrigerator until thoroughly cold.

2. In a medium bowl, combine vinegar, soup, sugar, and pineapple tidbits and juice. Mix well and pour into 1-gallon-size zipper-lock freezer bag. Add meatballs, seal bag, and turn gently to mix. Label bag and freeze.

3. *To thaw and reheat:* Thaw overnight in refrigerator. Pour meatballs and sauce into large skillet and cook over medium heat until sauce comes to a boil. Reduce heat, cover, and simmer meatballs for 8 to 10 minutes or until thoroughly heated, stirring occasionally.

Jalapeno Pops

To serve immediately, heat oil to 375°F.
Fry peppers, a few at a time, until golden brown, about
4 to 6 minutes. Drain on paper towels and serve.

1. Cut slit in side of peppers and gently remove seeds and membranes. Combine Swiss cheese and cream cheese in medium bowl and blend well. Stuff peppers with cheese mixture and press gently to seal.

2. In a small bowl, combine flour, salt, egg, and ginger ale and mix until a thick batter forms. Put cornstarch in another small bowl. Dip each stuffed pepper in cornstarch and shake off excess. Dip each pepper in batter and hold over bowl a few seconds for excess batter to drip off.

3. Flash freeze peppers in single layer on baking sheet. When frozen solid, pack in rigid containers, with waxed paper separating layers. Label peppers and freeze.

4. *To reheat:* Preheat oven to 400°F. Place frozen peppers on baking sheet and bake at 400°F for 20 to 30 minutes or until brown, crisp, and thoroughly heated.

Makes 24

24 small jalapeno peppers
2 cups grated Swiss cheese
1 (8-ounce) package cream cheese, softened
1 cup flour
½ teaspoon salt
1 egg, beaten
⅔ cup ginger ale
3 tablespoons cornstarch

Makes 72

72 small jalapeno peppers
6 cups grated Swiss cheese
3 (8-ounce) packages cream cheese, softened
3 cups flour
1½ teaspoons salt
3 eggs, beaten
2 cups ginger ale
9 tablespoons cornstarch

Cheesy Quesadillas

Makes 5

1 cup oil-packed sun-dried tomatoes

1 cup grated sharp Cheddar cheese

2 cups grated pepper jack cheese

½ cup grated Parmesan cheese

1 teaspoon dried oregano

1 tablespoon olive oil

10 (10-inch) flour tortillas

Makes 15

3 cups oil-packed sun-dried tomatoes

3 cups grated sharp Cheddar cheese

6 cups grated pepper jack cheese

1½ cups grated Parmesan cheese

1 tablespoon dried oregano

3 tablespoons olive oil

30 (10-inch) flour tortillas

To serve immediately, simply cut the stuffed tortillas into wedges after baking. Let quesadillas cool 2 to 3 minutes and serve.

1. Preheat oven to 400°F. Chop sun-dried tomatoes and reserve oil. In medium bowl, combine cheeses, oregano, olive oil, and chopped tomatoes and mix well. Place cheese mixture on 5 tortillas and cover with the other 5. Brush stuffed tortillas on both sides with reserved oil and place on baking sheets. Bake at 400°F for 25 to 35 minutes or until tortillas are golden and cheese is melted.

2. Cool completely in refrigerator, then cut each stuffed tortilla into six wedges. Wrap, label, and freeze.

3. *To reheat:* Place frozen wedges on cookie sheet and bake at 400°F for 7 to 12 minutes, until quesadillas are hot and cheese is melted.

Spicy Snack Mix

Serves 8–10

2 cups salted mixed nuts
2 cups small pretzels
2 cups potato sticks
½ cup butter, melted
3 tablespoons
    Worcestershire sauce
2 teaspoons dried Italian
    seasoning
½ teaspoon crushed red
    pepper flakes
⅛ teaspoon white pepper

To serve immediately, let snack mix cool for 30 to 35 minutes after baking, and serve.

1. Preheat oven to 300°F. Pour nuts, pretzels, and potato sticks onto two cookie sheets with sides. In small saucepan, combine melted butter with remaining ingredients. Drizzle over the nut mixture. Toss to coat. Bake at 300°F for 20 to 25 minutes, or until mixture is glazed and fragrant, stirring once during baking.

2. Cool snack mix and pack into zipper-lock bags. Label bags and freeze.

3. *To thaw and reheat:* Thaw at room temperature for 1 to 3 hours. Spread on baking sheet and reheat in 300°F oven for 5 to 8 minutes, until crisp.

Serves 24–30

6 cups salted mixed nuts
6 cups small pretzels
6 cups potato sticks
1½ cups butter, melted
9 tablespoons
    Worcestershire sauce
6 teaspoons dried Italian
    seasoning
1½ teaspoons crushed red
    pepper flakes
⅜ teaspoon white pepper

Tiny Filled Puffs

Makes about 30

---

1 cup water
½ cup butter
½ teaspoon salt
1 cup flour
3 eggs
½ cup grated Parmesan
    cheese
1 tablespoon dried chives

Makes about 90

---

3 cups water
1½ cups butter
1½ teaspoons salt
3 cups flour
9 eggs
1½ cups grated Parmesan
    cheese
3 tablespoons dried chives

Slice off the top of these tiny puffs and fill them with a mixture of mayonnaise, chopped ham, cubed cheese, and dried basil. Any sandwich filling could be used in these easy little puffs.

---

1. Preheat oven to 375°F. Line baking sheet with parchment paper and set aside. In heavy saucepan, combine water and butter. Bring to a rolling boil that cannot be stirred down. Add salt and flour all at once. Cook and stir over medium heat until dough forms a ball and cleans sides of pan. Remove from heat and beat in eggs, one at a time, until well combined. Stir in cheese and chives.

2. Drop dough by teaspoons onto prepared baking sheet. Bake at 375°F for 18 to 22 minutes or until dough is puffed, golden brown, and firm. Remove from baking sheet and cool on wire rack.

3. Flash freeze puffs in single layer on baking sheet. Then carefully pack into rigid containers. Label puffs and freeze.

4. *To reheat:* Place frozen puffs on baking sheet. Bake in preheated 400°F oven for 5 to 8 minutes, until hot. Let cool slightly, then cut puffs in half and fill with desired filling.

Beefy Enchiladas

Serves 4

1 pound ground beef
1 onion, chopped
1 jalapeno pepper, seeded
    and minced
1 (16-ounce) can refried
    beans
1 (8-ounce) can tomato
    sauce
1 teaspoon cumin
8 flour tortillas
1 (20-ounce) can enchilada
    sauce
1 cup shredded Cheddar
    cheese

Serves 12

3 pounds ground beef
3 onions, chopped
3 jalapeno peppers, seeded
    and minced
3 (16-ounce) cans refried
    beans
3 (8-ounce) cans tomato
    sauce
1 tablespoon cumin
24 flour tortillas
3 (20-ounce) cans enchilada
    sauce
3 cups shredded Cheddar
    cheese

To serve immediately, sprinkle with cheese and bake casserole at 350°F for 20 to 25 minutes until thoroughly heated and bubbling around edges.

1. In heavy skillet, cook ground beef with onions and jalapenos until beef is thoroughly cooked. Drain well. Stir in refried beans, tomato sauce, and cumin. Blend well and simmer, uncovered, for 15 minutes.

2. Stack tortillas and wrap in foil. Place in 350°F oven for 5 minutes to soften.

3. Pour ½ cup enchilada sauce in bottom of a 9" × 9" baking dish. Divide beef filling among tortillas and roll up. Place stuffed tortillas in baking dish. Cover with remaining enchilada sauce.

4. Cool enchiladas in refrigerator, wrap, seal, label, attach zipper-lock bag containing cheese, and freeze.

5. *To thaw and reheat:* Thaw overnight in refrigerator. Sprinkle with cheese and bake at 350°F for 30 to 35 minutes, until casserole is hot in center and bubbling around the edges.

Stuffed Manicotti

Serves 4–6

To serve immediately, sprinkle casserole with cheese and bake at 350°F for 25 to 35 minutes or until bubbly and cheese is melted.

1 pound ground beef
1 onion, chopped
1 cup chopped mushrooms
1 cup bread crumbs
¼ cup milk
1 egg
½ cup grated Parmesan
    cheese
⅛ teaspoon pepper
8 manicotti shells
1 (14-ounce) jar pasta sauce
1 cup grated mozzarella
    cheese
½ cup grated Parmesan
    cheese

1. Brown ground beef with onion in large skillet. Drain well, then add mushrooms. Cook and stir 4 to 5 minutes longer, until mushrooms are tender. Remove from heat and add bread crumbs, milk, egg, first quantity of Parmesan cheese, and pepper. Mix well.

2. Boil manicotti shells as directed on package; drain and rinse with cold water. Place on parchment-lined cookie sheets. Stuff each shell with beef mixture.

3. Spread ½ cup pasta sauce in bottom of 9" × 9" baking dish. Top with stuffed manicotti noodles. Cover with remaining sauce. Chill in refrigerator, then wrap, attach bag of mixed mozzarella and Parmesan, label, and freeze.

4. *To thaw and reheat:* Thaw overnight in refrigerator. Cover and bake at 350°F for 20 to 30 minutes or until hot. Uncover, sprinkle with cheeses, and bake 10 to 15 minutes longer, until casserole bubbles and cheese is melted.

Serves 12–18

3 pounds ground beef
3 onions, chopped
3 cups chopped mushrooms
3 cups bread crumbs
¾ cup milk
3 eggs
1½ cups grated Parmesan
    cheese
⅜ teaspoon pepper
24 manicotti shells
3 (14-ounce) jars pasta sauce
3 cups grated mozzarella
    cheese
1½ cups grated Parmesan
    cheese

Apple Meatloaf

Serves 4

---

1 pound ground beef
¼ cup applesauce
½ cup grated apple
½ cup soft bread crumbs
1 egg
½ cup apple cider
2 tablespoons mustard
1 tablespoon brown sugar

Serves 12

---

3 pounds ground beef
¾ cup applesauce
1½ cups grated apple
1½ cups soft bread crumbs
3 eggs
1½ cups apple cider
6 tablespoons mustard
3 tablespoons brown sugar

Grated apples and applesauce make this meatloaf wonderfully moist and add great flavor. To serve immediately, bake as directed, remove from oven, let stand 10 minutes, and then slice.

1. Preheat oven to 350°F. In large bowl, combine ground beef, applesauce, grated apple, bread crumbs, and egg. Form into loaf shape and place on broiler pan. Bake at 350°F for 30 minutes.

2. Combine apple cider, mustard, and brown sugar in small bowl. Baste meatloaf with half of this mixture and bake 20 minutes longer. Baste with remaining mixture and bake for another 15 to 20 minutes, until meatloaf registers 160°F in center. Cool in refrigerator; wrap, pack, and freeze.

3. *To thaw and reheat:* Thaw overnight in refrigerator. When thawed, slice meatloaf, place in baking dish, and pour ½ cup apple juice over loaf. Bake at 375°F for 20 to 25 minutes, until meat is thoroughly heated.

   To reheat from frozen: Unwrap loaf and place on broiler pan. Bake at 350°F for 1½ hours, until internal temperature registers 155°F, basting occasionally with apple juice.

Goulash

To serve this old-fashioned dish immediately, cook beef mixture and cook pasta until al dente; drain, but don't rinse. Add pasta to beef mixture. Simmer for 10 to 15 minutes, until flavors are blended.

1 pound ground beef
1 onion, chopped
1 (10-ounce) can condensed tomato soup
1 green bell pepper, chopped
1 (8-ounce) can tomato sauce
1 (14-ounce) can diced tomatoes, undrained
2 cups penne pasta

1. In large skillet, cook ground beef with onion until beef is browned and onion is tender. Drain well. Add soup, green pepper, tomato sauce, and undrained tomatoes. Stir well and simmer, uncovered, for 10 minutes to blend flavors.

2. Cook pasta until almost al dente. Drain and rinse with cold water. Stir pasta into mixture in skillet. Cool mixture in refrigerator. Pack, label, and freeze.

3. *To thaw and reheat:* Thaw overnight in refrigerator. Pour into skillet and add ¼ cup water if necessary. Heat mixture until bubbly and serve.

Serves 12

3 pounds ground beef
3 onions, chopped
3 (10-ounce) cans condensed tomato soup
3 green bell peppers, chopped
3 (8-ounce) cans tomato sauce
3 (14-ounce) cans diced tomatoes, undrained
6 cups penne pasta

Spices and Seasonings

The flavor of seasonings can change when frozen. Some spices become stronger; others fade. It's a good idea to use smaller amounts of spices and seasonings when initially preparing food for freezing. You can easily adjust seasoning amounts when you're ready to eat, tasting and correcting the seasoning after the food has heated to a safe temperature.

Mexican Pizza

Serves 8

---

2 cans refrigerated pizza
    dough
2 pounds ground beef
1 onion, chopped
2 cloves garlic, chopped
1 (16-ounce) can refried
    beans
1 (6-ounce) can tomato
    paste
⅓ cup water
1 (12-ounce) jar salsa
1 (4-ounce) can green
    chilies, drained
3 cups shredded mozzarella
    cheese
2 cups shredded Cheddar
    cheese

Serves 24

---

6 cans refrigerated pizza
    dough
6 pounds ground beef
3 onions, chopped
6 cloves garlic, chopped
3 (16-ounce) cans refried
    beans
3 (6-ounce) cans tomato
    paste
1 cup water
3 (12-ounce) jars salsa
3 (4-ounce) cans green
    chilies, drained
9 cups shredded mozzarella
    cheese
6 cups shredded Cheddar
    cheese

To serve immediately, spread each prebaked crust with sauce, top with cheese, and bake at 400°F for 20 to 25 minutes until cheese begins to brown.

---

1. Roll out and prebake each pizza crust at 400°F for 10 minutes or until lightly browned. Set aside.

2. Brown ground beef with onions and garlic in heavy skillet. Drain well and add refried beans, tomato paste, water, salsa, and green chilies. Stir to combine. Simmer, uncovered, for 10 minutes to blend flavors.

3. Divide sauce among pizzas and spread evenly over each crust. Cool in refrigerator; then wrap, attach bags of mozzarella and Cheddar cheese, label, and freeze.

4. *To reheat:* Bake frozen pizzas at 400°F for 12 to 18 minutes until hot. Sprinkle with cheeses and bake 10 to 15 minutes longer, until cheese bubbles and begins to brown.

Beef and Potato Pie

To serve this savory old-fashioned pie immediately, bake as directed and do not refrigerate. Let stand 10 minutes before slicing.

1. Preheat oven to 400°F. Bake unfilled pie crust for 5 to 6 minutes, until set. In large skillet, sauté ground beef with onion and garlic until browned. Drain well. Add drained hash browns, tomato paste, ketchup, water, oregano, and first amount of flour; stir. Simmer for 10 to 15 minutes, until thickened. Pour into prebaked pie crust.

2. In medium bowl, combine cottage cheese, eggs, remaining flour, and Parmesan cheese and beat well with wire whisk. Pour over meat mixture. Bake pie at 350°F for 25 to 30 minutes, until topping is puffed, set, and beginning to brown. Cool pie in refrigerator, and wrap, label, and freeze.

3. *To thaw and reheat:* Let pie thaw in refrigerator overnight. Bake at 350°F for 30 to 35 minutes (cover edges of pie crust with foil if browning too fast), until thoroughly heated.

Serves 6

9-inch Pie Crust (page 299)
1 pound ground beef
1 onion, chopped
2 cloves garlic, chopped
2 cups frozen hash brown potatoes, thawed
2 tablespoons tomato paste
¼ cup ketchup
¼ cup water
½ teaspoon oregano
2 tablespoons flour
1½ cups cottage cheese
3 eggs
2 tablespoons flour
3 tablespoons Parmesan cheese

Serves 18

3 9-inch Pie Crusts (page 299)
3 pounds ground beef
3 onions, chopped
6 cloves garlic, chopped
6 cups frozen hash brown potatoes, thawed
6 tablespoons tomato paste
¾ cup ketchup
¾ cup water
1½ teaspoons oregano
6 tablespoons flour
4½ cups cottage cheese
9 eggs
6 tablespoons flour
9 tablespoons Parmesan cheese

Italian Meatballs

Serves 4

---

2 tablespoons olive oil
1 onion, finely chopped
1 pound ground beef
½ cup chopped prosciutto
    ham
½ cup dried Italian bread
    crumbs
1 egg
1 teaspoon dried Italian
    seasoning
¼ cup milk

Serves 12

---

6 tablespoons olive oil
3 onions, finely chopped
3 pounds ground beef
1½ cups chopped prosciutto
    ham
1½ cups dried Italian bread
    crumbs
3 eggs
1 tablespoon dried Italian
    seasoning
¾ cup milk

You can use these delicious meatballs immediately by mixing with gravy and serving over noodles, or adding some pasta sauce and making a sandwich. The possibilities are endless!

1. In medium skillet, heat olive oil over medium heat. Sauté onion until crisp-tender.

2. In large bowl, combine cooked onion with all other ingredients and mix well to combine. Form into 24 to 30 meatballs. Place meatballs on baking sheet. Bake at 350°F for 20 to 30 minutes, until fully cooked.

3. Place meatballs on another baking sheet and flash freeze. When meatballs are frozen, package them in a zipper-lock bag. Label bag and freeze.

4. *To reheat:* Bake frozen meatballs at 350°F for 10 to 12 minutes until hot, or add to Slow Cooker recipes and cook 7 to 8 hours on low.

Cincinnati Chili

To serve immediately, break spaghetti in half and add to cooked chili; simmer for 8 to 10 minutes or until pasta is al dente. Garnish with grated cheese and chopped onions.

1. In large stockpot, cook ground beef, onion, and garlic until beef is browned. Drain off fat. Add remaining ingredients except spaghetti. Bring to a boil, reduce heat, and simmer for 20 to 30 minutes. Cool chili in refrigerator or ice-water bath.

2. Pour chili into rigid containers, wrap, label, and freeze. Reserve pasta in pantry.

3. *To thaw and reheat:* Thaw chili overnight in refrigerator. Place in saucepan and bring to a boil. Reduce heat and simmer for 10 to 15 minutes or until thoroughly heated. Break spaghetti in half and add to pot, making sure pasta is covered with liquid. Simmer for 8 to 12 minutes or until pasta is tender.

Serves 6

1½ pounds ground beef
1 onion, chopped
3 cloves garlic, minced
1 (14-ounce) can diced tomatoes, undrained
1 (6-ounce) can tomato paste
1 (10-ounce) can condensed beef broth
3 cups water
1 tablespoon apple cider vinegar
2 (16-ounce) cans kidney beans, drained
2 tablespoons chili powder
½ teaspoon cumin
½ teaspoon allspice
1 (6-ounce) package spaghetti pasta

Serves 18

4½ pounds ground beef
3 onions, chopped
9 cloves garlic, minced
3 (14-ounce) cans diced tomatoes, undrained
3 (6-ounce) cans tomato paste
3 (10-ounce) cans condensed beef broth
9 cups water
3 tablespoons apple cider vinegar
6 (16-ounce) cans kidney beans, drained
6 tablespoons chili powder
1½ teaspoons cumin
1½ teaspoons allspice
3 (6-ounce) packages spaghetti pasta

Chunky Spaghetti Sauce

Serves 4

1 pound ground beef
2 onions, chopped
4 cloves garlic, chopped
2 (14-ounce) cans diced
  tomatoes, undrained
1 (6-ounce) can tomato
  paste
1 (10-ounce) can condensed
  beef broth
1 (4-ounce) jar sliced
  mushrooms, undrained
⅛ teaspoon red pepper
  flakes
2 teaspoons sugar

Serves 12

3 pounds ground beef
6 onions, chopped
12 cloves garlic, chopped
6 (14-ounce) cans diced
  tomatoes, undrained
3 (6-ounce) cans tomato
  paste
3 (10-ounce) cans condensed
  beef broth
3 (4-ounce) jars sliced
  mushrooms, undrained
⅜ teaspoon red pepper
  flakes
2 tablespoons sugar

You can serve this sauce immediately after letting it simmer for about 30 minutes to blend flavors. Cook spaghetti or linguine pasta until al dente, drain, and pour sauce over pasta.

1. Brown ground beef, onions, and garlic in large skillet. Drain well, then add remaining ingredients. Bring to a boil, then partially cover pan and simmer over low heat for 25 to 30 minutes to blend flavors, stirring frequently.

2. Cool sauce in refrigerator or ice-water bath, then portion into rigid containers, wrap, label, and freeze.

3. *To thaw and reheat:* Thaw sauce in refrigerator overnight. Reheat in saucepan until bubbly, stirring frequently. Serve over hot cooked pasta and top with grated Parmesan cheese.

Meatball Veggie Casserole

Serves 4

1 pound lean ground beef
¼ cup dry bread crumbs
3 tablespoons milk
1 egg
½ teaspoon salt
⅛ teaspoon pepper
2 tablespoons olive oil
1 onion, chopped
1 cup cut green beans
1 cup chopped carrots
1 cup chopped broccoli
1 (14-ounce) can diced
   tomatoes, undrained
2 tablespoons flour
2 cups mashed potatoes

To serve immediately, after returning meatballs to skillet with vegetables, simmer another 5 to 10 minutes. Assemble and bake as directed until casserole bubbles and potatoes begin to brown.

1. In large bowl, combine beef, bread crumbs, milk, egg, salt, and pepper and mix gently. Form into 24 meatballs. In large skillet, heat olive oil and sauté meatballs on all sides until brown. Remove meatballs from pan as they cook and refrigerate.

2. In drippings remaining in skillet, sauté onions, beans, carrots, and broccoli until crisp-tender. Drain liquid from diced tomatoes and mix liquid with flour until smooth. Add tomatoes and flour mixture to pan. Simmer for 10 minutes. Add meatballs to skillet, stir, and remove from heat.

3. Chill mixture in refrigerator or ice-water bath. Place in 9" × 9" square baking dish and top with mashed potatoes. Wrap, label, and freeze.

4. *To thaw and reheat:* Thaw casserole overnight in refrigerator. Bake at 350°F for 20 to 30 minutes, until casserole is thoroughly heated and potatoes begin to brown.

Serves 12

3 pounds lean ground beef
¾ cup dry bread crumbs
9 tablespoons milk
3 eggs
1½ teaspoons salt
⅜ teaspoon pepper
6 tablespoons olive oil
3 onions, chopped
3 cups cut green beans
3 cups chopped carrots
3 cups chopped broccoli
3 (14-ounce) cans diced
   tomatoes, undrained
6 tablespoons flour
6 cups mashed potatoes

Meatball Pot Pie

Serves 6

---

1 pound lean ground beef
¼ cup dry bread crumbs
3 tablespoons milk
1 egg
½ teaspoon salt
⅛ teaspoon pepper
2 tablespoons olive oil
1 (10-ounce) can cream of
    celery soup
½ cup evaporated milk
2 cups frozen mixed
    vegetables
1 9-inch Pie Crust (page 299)

Serves 18

---

3 pounds lean ground beef
¾ cup dry bread crumbs
9 tablespoons milk
3 eggs
1½ teaspoons salt
⅜ teaspoon pepper
6 tablespoons olive oil
3 (10-ounce) cans cream of
    celery soup
1½ cups evaporated milk
6 cups frozen mixed
    vegetables
3 9-inch Pie Crusts (page
    299)

To serve immediately, combine soup, milk, vegetables, and cooked meatballs in skillet. Cook over medium heat, stirring frequently, for 10 minutes. Place in pie plate, cover with pastry, and bake at 375°F for 30 to 40 minutes, until done.

---

1. In large bowl, combine ground beef, bread crumbs, milk, egg, salt, and pepper and mix gently. Form into 24 meatballs. Heat olive oil in heavy skillet and brown meatballs, turning occasionally, until browned and fully cooked. Drain on paper towels. Cool meatballs in refrigerator.

2. In 9-inch deep-dish pie plate, combine soup, milk, and vegetables. Add cold meatballs and mix gently. Place pastry on top of mixture, seal edges, and flute. Cut slits in a decorative pattern in the top crust. Wrap, label, and freeze.

3. *To thaw and reheat:* Thaw pie overnight in refrigerator. Bake at 375°F for 35 to 45 minutes, until pie is thoroughly heated and bubbling and crust is brown.

Creamy Swiss Meatballs

To serve immediately, pour meatball and sauce mixture
into 9" square baking dish. Bake at 375°F for 20 to 30 minutes,
until bubbly and thoroughly heated.

1 pound lean ground beef
¼ cup dry bread crumbs
3 tablespoons milk
1 egg
½ teaspoon celery salt
⅛ teaspoon pepper
½ cup grated Swiss cheese
2 tablespoons olive oil
1 cup brown rice
1 leek, chopped
2 cloves garlic, chopped
1 (10-ounce) jar Alfredo
    sauce
½ cup evaporated milk
½ cup grated Parmesan
    cheese
1 cup grated Swiss cheese

1. In large bowl, combine beef, bread crumbs, milk, egg, celery salt, pepper, and first quantity of Swiss cheese and mix gently. Form into 20 meatballs. Heat olive oil in large skillet and brown meatballs on all sides, turning occasionally.

2. Meanwhile, cook rice as directed on package, undercooking slightly. When meatballs are done, remove from skillet. Sauté leek and garlic in pan drippings until crisp-tender. Add Alfredo sauce, milk, remaining cheeses, browned meatballs, and cooked rice and mix gently.

3. Pour mixture into 9" × 9" baking dish; wrap, label, and freeze.

4. *To thaw and reheat:* Thaw casserole overnight in refrigerator. Bake at 375°F for 25 to 35 minutes, until casserole bubbles and meatballs are hot in center.

Serves 12

3 pounds lean ground beef
¾ cup dry bread crumbs
9 tablespoons milk
3 eggs
1½ teaspoons celery salt
⅜ teaspoon pepper
1½ cups grated Swiss cheese
6 tablespoons olive oil
3 cups brown rice
3 leeks, chopped
6 cloves garlic, chopped
3 (10-ounce) jars Alfredo
    sauce
1½ cups evaporated milk
1½ cups grated Parmesan
    cheese
3 cups grated Swiss cheese

Mom's Favorite Meatloaf

Serves 4–6

2 pounds ground beef
½ pound ground pork
1 onion, minced
½ cup minced mushrooms
1 egg
½ cup quick oatmeal
½ cup tomato sauce
1 teaspoon seasoned salt
⅛ teaspoon pepper
½ cup Beef Broth (page 302)
½ cup tomato sauce
1 tablespoon mustard

Serves 12–18

6 pounds ground beef
1½ pounds ground pork
3 onions, minced
1½ cups minced mushrooms
3 eggs
1½ cups quick oatmeal
1½ cups tomato sauce
1 tablespoon seasoned salt
⅜ teaspoon pepper
1½ cups Beef Broth (page 302)
1½ cups tomato sauce
3 tablespoons mustard

The mushrooms and oatmeal in this meatloaf recipe add moistness and flavor. To serve immediately, bake meatloaf as directed. Cover with foil and let stand 10 minutes before slicing.

1. In large bowl, combine all ingredients except final tomato sauce and mustard and mix gently but thoroughly. Form into large meatloaf and place on broiling rack. Combine remaining tomato sauce and mustard in small bowl and pour over meatloaf. Bake at 350°F for 55 to 65 minutes, until internal temperature registers 160°F, basting occasionally with pan drippings.

2. Cool meatloaf completely in refrigerator, then wrap, label, and freeze.

3. *To thaw:* Thaw overnight in refrigerator. Since meatloaf is fully cooked, it can be served cold.

   To reheat: Slice meatloaf, place in baking dish, and pour ½ cup of beef broth or beef gravy over loaf. Cover dish and bake at 375°F for 20 to 25 minutes until meat is thoroughly heated.

   To reheat from frozen: Unwrap loaf and place on broiler pan. Bake at 350°F for 1½ hours, until internal temperature registers 155°F, basting occasionally with ½ cup beef broth.

Beefy Bean Burritos

These easy and delicious burritos can be made hot or mild, depending on the salsa and peppers. To serve immediately, spread hot filling on warmed flour tortillas, sprinkle with cheese, and roll up.

1. In large skillet, brown ground beef with onions and garlic until beef is browned. Drain well. Add remaining ingredients except for cheese and tortillas. Stir to combine. Simmer for 10 to 15 minutes to blend flavors.

2. Cool mixture in refrigerator or ice-water bath. Pack into zipper-lock bags, label, attach bag with cheese and bag with tortillas, and freeze. To assemble burritos before freezing, spread chilled filling on tortillas and top with cheese; roll to enclose filling. Flash freeze on a baking sheet, then wrap individually, package, and place in freezer.

3. *To thaw and reheat unassembled burritos:* Thaw overnight in refrigerator. Place meat mixture in skillet and cook over medium heat, stirring frequently, until hot. Wrap tortillas in foil and place in 350°F oven for 10 to 12 minutes, until hot. Assemble burritos and serve.

   To reheat assembled burritos: Wrap each frozen burrito in a microwave-safe paper towel. Microwave, one at a time, on medium for 2 minutes, then rotate and microwave on high for 1 to 2 minutes longer, until hot. Or unwrap and bake frozen burritos at 400°F for 15 to 25 minutes, until hot and crisp.

Serves 4

1 pound ground beef
1 onion, chopped
4 cloves garlic, minced
1 (16-ounce) can refried beans
1 (14-ounce) jar chunky salsa
1 tablespoon chili powder
1 teaspoon cumin
1 (4-ounce) can chopped jalapeno peppers
2 cups shredded Cheddar cheese
12 flour tortillas

Serves 12

3 pounds ground beef
3 onions, chopped
12 cloves garlic, minced
3 (16 ounce) cans refried beans
3 (14 ounce) jars chunky salsa
3 tablespoons chili powder
1 tablespoon cumin
3 (4 ounce) cans chopped jalapeno peppers
6 cups shredded Cheddar cheese
36 flour tortillas

Wild Rice Meatloaf

Serves 6

½ cup wild rice
1 onion, finely chopped
1 clove garlic, minced
1 tablespoon olive oil
¼ cup dried bread crumbs
2 eggs, beaten
½ cup milk
1 tablespoon mustard
1 teaspoon salt
¼ teaspoon pepper
¼ cup grated Parmesan
    cheese
1 teaspoon dried thyme
    leaves
1 teaspoon dried basil leaves
1 pound lean ground beef
1 pound lean ground pork
½ cup Beef Broth (page 302)
    or gravy

Serves 18

1½ cups wild rice
3 onions, finely chopped
3 cloves garlic, minced
3 tablespoons olive oil
¾ cup dried bread crumbs
6 eggs, beaten
1½ cups milk
3 tablespoons mustard
2 teaspoons salt
¾ teaspoon pepper
¾ cup grated Parmesan
    cheese
1 tablespoon dried thyme
    leaves
1 tablespoon dried basil
    leaves
3 pounds lean ground beef
3 pounds lean ground pork
1½ cups Beef Broth (page
    302) or gravy

To serve immediately, bake at 350°F for 60 to 75 minutes, until internal temperature registers 160°F. Let meatloaf stand, covered, 10 minutes before serving.

1. Cook wild rice according to package directions until tender but still firm; drain. In large skillet, sauté onion and garlic in olive oil until almost crisp-tender.

2. In large bowl, combine cooked wild rice, sautéed onion and garlic, bread crumbs, eggs, milk, mustard, salt, pepper, Parmesan cheese, thyme, and basil; mix well. Add meat and mix gently but thoroughly with hands.

3. Form into oblong shape on broiler pan. Cover and bake at 350°F for 60 minutes. Remove cover and bake for 15 to 25 minutes longer until internal temperature registers 165°F. Cool in refrigerator; then wrap, label, and freeze. Reserve beef broth or gravy in freezer.

4. *To thaw:* Thaw overnight in refrigerator. Since meatloaf is fully cooked, it can be served cold.

   To reheat: Slice meatloaf, place in baking dish, and pour ½ cup of beef broth or beef gravy over loaf. Cover dish and bake at 375°F for 20 to 25 minutes, until meat is thoroughly heated.

   To reheat from frozen: Unwrap loaf and place on broiler pan. Bake at 350°F for 1½ hours until internal temperature registers 155°F, basting occasionally with ½ cup beef broth.

Easy Lasagna

To serve without freezing, cover tightly with foil and bake at 350°F for 1 hour. Uncover, sprinkle with cheese, and bake another 10 to 15 minutes, until casserole is bubbling and cheese browns.

1. In large skillet, brown ground beef with onion and garlic; drain. Add pasta sauce and water; mix well.

2. In large bowl, combine ricotta, cream cheese, egg, salt, and pepper and mix well. Stir in mozzarella cheese.

3. In 13" × 9" baking dish lined with freezer wrap, place 1 cup ground beef mixture. Lay 3 uncooked lasagna noodles on top. Spread one third of ricotta filling over noodles and top with one third of the remaining ground beef mixture. Repeat layers twice, ending with ground beef mixture. Chill in refrigerator, then wrap and freeze until firm. Pop lasagna out of pan, wrap again, attach bag with 1 cup grated Parmesan cheese, label, and freeze.

4. *To thaw and reheat:* Unwrap lasagna and place in 13" × 9" pan; thaw overnight in refrigerator. Bake casserole, covered, at 350°F for 60 to 75 minutes, until hot in center. Uncover, sprinkle with reserved Parmesan cheese, and bake 10 to 15 minutes longer, until pasta is tender and casserole is bubbly. Let stand 15 minutes before serving.

Serves 6

1 pound ground beef
1 onion, chopped
3 cloves garlic, minced
1 (26-ounce) jar pasta sauce
1 cup water
2 cups ricotta cheese
1 (3-ounce) package cream cheese
1 egg
1 teaspoon salt
¼ teaspoon pepper
2 cups shredded mozzarella cheese
9 uncooked lasagna noodles
1 cup grated Parmesan cheese

Serves 18

3 pounds ground beef
3 onions, chopped
9 cloves garlic, minced
3 (26-ounce) jars pasta sauce
3 cups water
6 cups ricotta cheese
3 (3-ounce) packages cream cheese
3 eggs
2 teaspoons salt
¾ teaspoon pepper
6 cups shredded mozzarella cheese
27 uncooked lasagna noodles
3 cups grated Parmesan cheese

Cabbage Rolls

Serves 4

---

1 head green cabbage
1 pound ground beef
1 onion, chopped
3 cloves garlic, minced
1 cup cooked long-grain rice
1 tablespoon mustard
2 tablespoons ketchup
1 egg, beaten
¼ teaspoon pepper
1 (15-ounce) can tomato
   sauce
1 (10-ounce) can condensed
   tomato soup

Serves 12

---

3 heads green cabbage
3 pounds ground beef
3 onions, chopped
9 cloves garlic, minced
3 cups cooked long-grain
   rice
3 tablespoons mustard
6 tablespoons ketchup
3 eggs, beaten
¾ teaspoon pepper
3 (15-ounce) cans tomato
   sauce
3 (10-ounce) cans condensed
   tomato soup

To serve immediately, bake at 375°F for 30 to 40 minutes, until sauce bubbles and rolls are thoroughly heated. Any leftover shredded cabbage can be made into coleslaw (see page 162).

1. Core cabbage and carefully remove 8 whole cabbage leaves from head. Soak leaves in hot water while preparing filling. Shred remaining cabbage; set aside 3 cups to use in filling.

2. Cook ground beef, onion, and garlic in heavy skillet until beef is browned and onion and garlic are tender; drain well. Remove from heat and add rice, mustard, and ketchup and mix well. Stir in egg, pepper, and shredded cabbage. Fill each cabbage leaf with filling and roll up.

3. Line a 13" × 9" baking pan with freezer wrap. Pour 1 cup tomato sauce into lined pan. Arrange cabbage rolls, seam-side down, in pan. Place any remaining filling around filled rolls. Mix together remaining tomato sauce and condensed tomato soup and pour over filled rolls. Cool in fridge until cold; then freeze until solid. When frozen solid, pop out of pan, wrap, label, and freeze.

4. *To thaw and reheat:* Unwrap casserole and place in 13" × 9" baking pan; thaw overnight in refrigerator. Cover casserole and bake at 375°F for 50 to 60 minutes or until hot. Remove cover and bake an additional 10 to 15 minutes, until bubbly.

Beef Stew

Serves 4

---

1 pound beef round steak
2 tablespoons flour
½ teaspoon salt
⅛ teaspoon pepper
1 tablespoon olive oil
1 onion, chopped
3 cloves garlic, chopped
1 (9-ounce) bag baby
  carrots
1 (14-ounce) can diced
  tomatoes, undrained
1 (10-ounce) can condensed
  beef broth
1 (8-ounce) can apple juice
2 cups water
1 (16-ounce) bag frozen
  potato wedges
1 cup frozen green beans

Serves 12

---

3 pounds beef round steak
6 tablespoons flour
1½ teaspoons salt
⅜ teaspoon pepper
3 tablespoons olive oil
3 onions, chopped
9 cloves garlic, chopped
3 (9-ounce) bags baby
  carrots
3 (14-ounce) cans diced
  tomatoes, undrained
3 (10-ounce) cans condensed
  beef broth
3 (8-ounce) cans apple juice
6 cups water
3 (16-ounce) bags frozen
  potato wedges
3 cups frozen green beans

To serve this stew immediately, prepare as directed, but don't cool it. Add frozen potato wedges and green beans to stew and simmer for 20 to 30 minutes longer, until vegetables are tender.

---

1. Cut steak into 1-inch pieces and toss with flour, salt, and pepper. In large skillet over medium-high heat, cook beef in olive oil until brown, about 2 to 3 minutes, stirring frequently. Add onion and garlic; cook and stir for 4 to 5 minutes until crisp-tender. Add baby carrots, undrained tomatoes, beef broth, apple juice, and water; stir. Bring to a boil, then cover pan and simmer for 1 to 2 hours, until beef is thoroughly cooked.

2. Cool stew in ice-water bath or in refrigerator, pour into 1-gallon zipper-lock bag, and seal bag. Attach bag containing frozen potatoes and frozen green beans. Label and freeze.

3. *To thaw and reheat:* Thaw stew in refrigerator overnight. Keep potatoes and green beans frozen. Pour stew mixture into large saucepan and bring to a boil. Add potatoes and green beans and bring back to a boil; then reduce heat, cover, and simmer for 20 to 30 minutes, until vegetables are tender and stew is thoroughly heated.

Beef Carbonnade

Beer adds great depth of flavor to this rich beef stew. To serve without freezing, keep simmering stew while you cook the frozen noodles. Drain noodles and serve with the stew.

1. Cut steak into 2-inch pieces. Toss with flour, salt, and pepper. Heat olive oil in large saucepan and cook steak, in batches, until browned, about 5 to 6 minutes per batch. When all the beef is browned, remove from pan and set aside. Cook onions, garlic, and mushrooms in the drippings remaining in saucepan. Cook and stir until onions are crisp-tender.

2. Return beef to saucepan along with beer, thyme, carrots, and broth. Bring to a boil; reduce heat, cover pot, and let simmer for 2 to 3 hours, until beef is cooked and vegetables are tender. Cool in ice-water bath or in refrigerator. Pour into 2-gallon-size zipper-lock bags; attach frozen noodles, label, and freeze.

3. *To thaw and reheat:* Thaw stew overnight in refrigerator. Keep noodles frozen. Place stew in saucepan and add ½ cup water if necessary. Cook over medium-low heat, stirring frequently, until thoroughly heated. Cook noodles according to package directions and serve with stew.

Serves 8

2 pounds beef chuck steak
3 tablespoons flour
½ teaspoon salt
⅛ teaspoon pepper
2 tablespoons olive oil
2 onions, chopped
4 cloves garlic, chopped
1 (8-ounce) package
    mushrooms, chopped
1 (12-ounce) can beer
1 teaspoon dried thyme
3 carrots, sliced
3 cups Beef Broth (page 302)
1 (16-ounce) package frozen
    spaetzle noodles

Serves 24

6 pounds beef chuck steak
9 tablespoons flour
1½ teaspoons salt
⅜ teaspoon pepper
6 tablespoons olive oil
6 onions, chopped
12 cloves garlic, chopped
3 (8-ounce) packages
    mushrooms, chopped
3 (12-ounce) cans beer
1 tablespoon dried thyme
9 carrots, sliced
9 cups Beef Broth (page 302)
3 (16-ounce) packages
    frozen spaetzle noodles

Beef Stroganoff

Serves 4

---

1 pound beef sirloin steak
½ teaspoon salt
⅛ teaspoon pepper
1 tablespoon olive oil
1 tablespoon butter
1 onion, chopped
3 cloves garlic, chopped
1 (8-ounce) package
   mushrooms, chopped
1 (10-ounce) can condensed
   beef broth
1 cup water
1 tablespoon Worcestershire
   sauce
1 teaspoon dried marjoram
1 cup sour cream
2 tablespoons flour
3 cups uncooked egg
   noodles

Serves 12

---

3 pounds beef sirloin steak
1½ teaspoons salt
⅜ teaspoon pepper
3 tablespoons olive oil
3 tablespoons butter
3 onions, chopped
9 cloves garlic, chopped
3 (8-ounce) packages
   mushrooms, chopped
3 (10-ounce) cans condensed
   beef broth
3 cups water
3 tablespoons
   Worcestershire sauce
1 tablespoon dried
   marjoram
3 cups sour cream
6 tablespoons flour
9 cups uncooked egg
   noodles

To serve immediately, mix sour cream with flour and liquid and add to stroganoff. Simmer until thickened and serve with hot egg noodles.

---

1. Cut steak into 1-inch cubes and sprinkle with salt and pepper. Heat olive oil and butter in large saucepan and brown beef cubes in batches, about 4 to 5 minutes per batch. Add onions, garlic, and mushrooms to drippings in saucepan and cook until crisp-tender, stirring frequently.

2. Return beef to saucepan and add broth, water, Worcestershire sauce, and marjoram; stir. Bring to a boil, then reduce heat, cover saucepan, and simmer for 1½ hours until beef is tender. Cool in ice-water bath or in refrigerator.

3. Pour into 1-gallon-size zipper-lock bag; label and freeze. Reserve sour cream in fridge, and flour and egg noodles in pantry.

4. *To thaw and reheat:* Thaw overnight in refrigerator. Pour stroganoff into saucepan and bring to a boil. In medium bowl, combine sour cream, flour, and ⅓ cup of the stroganoff liquid and beat well with wire whisk. Stir into stroganoff and cook until thickened. Cook egg noodles as directed on package and serve with stroganoff.

Pot Roast

To serve this classic savory pot roast immediately, when beef is tender, remove from oven and let stand, covered, for 10 minutes. Slice beef and serve with vegetables and sauce.

---

1. Sprinkle roast on all sides with salt, pepper, and paprika. Heat olive oil in large skillet and brown roast on all sides, about 10 minutes total. Remove roast from skillet and place in large ovenproof casserole or Dutch oven.

2. Add onions, carrots, and garlic to drippings in skillet and cook and stir until crisp-tender. Pour beef broth, marjoram, and tomato paste into skillet. Cook and stir to loosen pan drippings for 4 to 5 minutes. Pour vegetables and sauce over roast in casserole. Cover and bake at 325°F for 3 to 4 hours, until meat is very tender.

3. Cool beef, vegetables, and sauce in ice-water bath or refrigerator. When cold, slice beef. Place beef slices, vegetables, and sauce in 2-gallon-size zipper-lock bags. Seal bags, label, and freeze.

4. *To thaw and reheat:* Thaw overnight in refrigerator. Place contents of bags in heavy skillet. Cook over medium heat, stirring occasionally, until sauce bubbles and meat and vegetables are thoroughly heated, about 10 to 15 minutes.

Serves 10–12

1 (5-pound) chuck roast
1 teaspoon salt
¼ teaspoon pepper
2 teaspoons paprika
¼ cup olive oil
2 onions, chopped
4 carrots, chopped
4 cloves garlic, chopped
1½ cups Beef Broth (page 302)
1 teaspoon dried marjoram leaves
1 (6-ounce) can tomato paste

Serves 30–36

3 (5-pound) chuck roasts
1 tablespoon salt
¾ teaspoon pepper
6 teaspoons paprika
¾ cup olive oil
6 onions, chopped
12 carrots, chopped
12 cloves garlic, chopped
4½ cups Beef Broth (page 302)
1 tablespoon dried marjoram leaves
3 (6-ounce) cans tomato paste

Mini Beef Pizzas

Serves 4–6

---

1 pound round steak
2 tablespoons
   Worcestershire sauce
⅛ teaspoon pepper
1 tablespoon olive oil
12 thin slices Colby cheese
6 English muffins, split
2 cups pizza sauce
1 cup frozen peppers and
   onions
2 cups shredded mozzarella
   cheese

Serves 12–18

---

3 pounds round steak
6 tablespoons
   Worcestershire sauce
⅜ teaspoon pepper
3 tablespoons olive oil
36 thin slices Colby cheese
18 English muffins, split
6 cups pizza sauce
3 cups frozen peppers and
   onions
6 cups shredded mozzarella
   cheese

To serve these pizzas immediately, bake at 375°F for 15 to 20 minutes until pizza is hot, English muffin is toasted and crisp, and cheese is melted and bubbly.

1. Sprinkle steak with Worcestershire sauce, pepper, and olive oil on both sides and let marinate in refrigerator for 1 to 2 hours. Remove from refrigerator and place on broiler pan. Broil 4 to 6 inches from heat for 4 to 5 minutes on each side until beef is slightly pink in center. Let steak stand at room temperature for 10 minutes. Cut steak into ½-inch cubes.

2. Place Colby cheese slices on cut sides of English muffins. Top each with 1 tablespoon of pizza sauce, then divide steak cubes among pizzas. Top with remaining pizza sauce, then peppers and onions. Sprinkle with mozzarella cheese. Wrap pizzas individually, label, and freeze.

3. *To reheat:* Place frozen mini-pizzas on baking sheet and bake in preheated 375°F oven for 20 to 25 minutes, until hot and bubbly.

Italian Beef and Beans

To serve this simple dinner immediately, let steaks marinate in refrigerator for 1 to 2 hours. Then cook steaks over grill or under broiler, heating sauce in saucepan at the same time.

1. In heavy skillet, cook onion and garlic in olive oil over medium heat until crisp-tender. Remove from heat and add beans, undrained tomatoes, and seasoning. Pour into a zipper-lock bag. Rub steaks with red wine vinegar and place in separate zipper-lock bag. Place both bags in larger zipper-lock bag; then label, seal, and freeze.

2. *To thaw and reheat:* Thaw overnight in refrigerator. Broil or grill steaks 4 to 6 inches from heat source for 4 to 5 minutes per side until medium doneness. While steak is cooking, place sauce in heavy saucepan and cook over medium heat, stirring frequently, until sauce boils; boil for 3 to 4 minutes. Serve sauce over steak.

Grading Beef

Prime cuts are usually the most expensive, tender, and flavorful meat with the highest amount of marbling, which is the streaks of white fat throughout the meat that indicate tenderness and flavor. Choice cuts are slightly below prime in cost and marbling. Select cuts are the leanest meats and therefore the least tender and usually require slower cooking methods to make them tender.

Serves 4

1 onion, chopped
3 cloves garlic, chopped
1 tablespoon olive oil
1 (16-ounce) can cannellini beans, drained
1 (14-ounce) can diced tomatoes, undrained
1 teaspoon dried Italian seasoning
4 sirloin steaks
3 tablespoons red wine vinegar

Serves 12

3 onions, chopped
9 cloves garlic, chopped
3 tablespoons olive oil
3 (16-ounce) cans cannellini beans, drained
3 (14-ounce) cans diced tomatoes, undrained
1 tablespoon dried Italian seasoning
12 sirloin steaks
9 tablespoons red wine vinegar

Sauerbraten

Serves 6

2-pound chuck roast
3 tablespoons olive oil
1 teaspoon salt
¼ teaspoon pepper
2 onions, chopped
½ cup red wine vinegar
½ cup red wine
1 cup Beef Broth (page 302)
½ teaspoon ground cloves
⅛ teaspoon allspice
¼ cup brown sugar
2 stalks celery, minced
12 gingersnap cookies
3 cups egg noodles

Serves 18

6-pound chuck roast
9 tablespoons olive oil
1 tablespoon salt
¾ teaspoon pepper
6 onions, chopped
1½ cups red wine vinegar
1½ cups red wine
3 cups Beef Broth (page 302)
1½ teaspoons ground cloves
¼ teaspoon allspice
¾ cup brown sugar
6 stalks celery, minced
36 gingersnap cookies
9 cups egg noodles

To serve immediately, add crushed gingersnap cookies to gravy and simmer 10 to 15 minutes until thickened. Serve over hot cooked egg noodles.

---

1. Trim excess fat off roast and cut into 1½-inch cubes. Heat olive oil in Dutch oven or large ovenproof casserole. Sprinkle meat with salt and pepper and brown on all sides over medium heat.

2. Add onions; cook and stir for 3 to 4 minutes longer to partially cook onions. Add all remaining ingredients except gingersnaps and egg noodles. Cover casserole and bring sauce to a boil. Then reduce heat to low and simmer for 2½ to 3 hours until beef is very tender.

3. Cool casserole in ice-water bath or refrigerator. Slice beef into ½-inch-thick slices. Place beef and sauce in gallon-size zipper-lock bags. Attach small bag with gingersnap cookies. Label bags and freeze. Reserve egg noodles in pantry.

4. *To thaw and reheat:* Thaw overnight in refrigerator. Pour meat mixture into large saucepan and bring to a simmer over medium heat. Crush gingersnap cookies and add to sauce. Cook, stirring occasionally, for 10 to 12 minutes, until meat is hot and sauce has thickened. Cook noodles according to package directions and serve with sauerbraten.

Beef Barley Stew

To serve immediately, simmer stew with barley added for 30 minutes. Then add frozen green beans, bring back to a simmer, and cook 10 to 15 minutes until barley is tender.

1. Trim beef and cut into 1-inch pieces. Combine flour, salt, pepper, and marjoram on shallow plate and toss with beef to coat. Heat olive oil in large stockpot and brown beef on all sides, 5 to 6 minutes total. Then add onion, leek, and carrots. Cook and stir 4 to 5 minutes until crisp-tender. Add tomato sauce and broth. Bring to a boil, then cover, reduce heat, and simmer for 2 hours.

2. Add barley, stir, and simmer for 30 minutes. Cool stew in ice-water bath or refrigerator, then pack into rigid containers. Attach bag with frozen green beans; then label and freeze.

3. *To thaw and reheat:* Thaw stew overnight in refrigerator. Keep green beans frozen. Place stew in large saucepan and bring to a simmer. After five minutes, add beans, stir, and bring back to a simmer. Simmer, stirring occasionally, for 10 to 15 minutes until stew is thoroughly heated and barley and green beans are tender.

Serves 4–6

1 pound chuck roast
3 tablespoons flour
1 teaspoon salt
¼ teaspoon pepper
1 teaspoon dried marjoram leaves
2 tablespoons olive oil
1 onion, chopped
1 leek, chopped
4 carrots, peeled and chopped
1 (8-ounce) can tomato sauce
2 cups Beef Broth (page 302)
½ cup medium pearl barley
2 cups frozen green beans

Serves 12–18

3 pounds chuck roast
9 tablespoons flour
1 tablespoon salt
¾ teaspoon pepper
1 tablespoon dried marjoram leaves
6 tablespoons olive oil
3 onions, chopped
3 leeks, chopped
12 carrots, peeled and chopped
3 (8-ounce) cans tomato sauce
6 cups Beef Broth (page 302)
1½ cups medium pearl barley
6 cups frozen green beans

Swiss Steak

Serves 6

¼ cup flour
1 teaspoon salt
⅛ teaspoon pepper
1 teaspoon paprika
2 pounds round steak
3 tablespoons olive oil
2 tablespoons butter
1 onion, sliced
2 (14-ounce) cans diced
  tomatoes, undrained
1 (8-ounce) can tomato
  sauce
½ cup Beef Broth (page 302)

Serves 18

¾ cup flour
1 tablespoon salt
⅜ teaspoon pepper
1 tablespoon paprika
6 pounds round steak
9 tablespoons olive oil
6 tablespoons butter
3 onions, sliced
6 (14-ounce) cans diced
  tomatoes, undrained
3 (8-ounce) cans tomato
  sauce
1½ cups Beef Broth (page
  302)

To serve without freezing, just serve the steak when it's tender and the sauce is slightly thickened. The sauce is really perfect served over hot mashed potatoes.

---

1. Combine flour and seasonings in small bowl. Cut steak into 6 pieces. Place meat between two layers of waxed paper and pound with mallet or rolling pin to flatten. Remove top sheet of waxed paper and sprinkle meat with half of flour mixture. Replace waxed paper and pound flour mixture into the meat. Turn meat over and repeat on other side with remaining flour mixture.

2. Heat olive oil and butter in large skillet and add onion. Cook and stir until crisp-tender. Then add floured steaks and cook on one side until golden, about 4 to 5 minutes. Turn steaks over and cook for 2 to 3 minutes. Add tomatoes, tomato sauce, and beef broth to skillet and bring to a boil. Reduce heat, cover pan, and simmer for 1 to 1½ hours until steak is tender.

3. Cool steak and sauce in ice-water bath or refrigerator. Pour into zipper-lock bags, seal, label, and freeze.

4. *To thaw and reheat:* Thaw overnight in refrigerator. Place steak and sauce in large skillet and cook over medium heat until steak is hot and sauce bubbles.

Stuffed Peppers

To serve immediately, don't chill filling. Fill peppers
with hot meat mixture and place in baking dish. Sprinkle with cheese
and pour sauce over. Bake at 350°F for 20 to 25 minutes.

1. Cut the tops off the green peppers and remove veins and seeds. Rinse well, then submerge peppers in boiling water for 2 to 3 minutes. Remove and drain upside down on kitchen towels. Chop pepper tops, discarding stem.

2. Cook barley according to package directions until almost tender. Drain well and set aside.

3. In large skillet, sauté onion and garlic in olive oil until crisp-tender; drain well. Add beef, salt, red pepper, and first can of tomato sauce; simmer for 10 minutes to blend flavors. Cool beef mixture in refrigerator or ice-water bath.

4. Stuff peppers with cooled beef mixture and sprinkle each with shredded cheese. Wrap each pepper, label, and freeze. Reserve remaining tomato sauce in pantry.

5. *To thaw and reheat:* Thaw overnight in refrigerator. Place thawed peppers in 9" × 9" square baking dish and pour tomato sauce over all. Bake at 350°F for 25 to 30 minutes, until thoroughly heated, basting peppers occasionally with sauce.

Serves 4

4 green bell peppers
½ cup medium barley
1 onion, chopped
3 cloves garlic, chopped
2 tablespoons olive oil
2 cups cooked, cubed beef
1 teaspoon salt
¼ teaspoon red pepper flakes
1 (8-ounce) can tomato sauce
1 cup shredded Gruyère cheese
1 (8-ounce) can tomato sauce

Serves 12

12 green bell peppers
1½ cups medium barley
3 onions, chopped
9 cloves garlic, chopped
6 tablespoons olive oil
6 cups cooked, cubed beef
1 tablespoon salt
¾ teaspoon red pepper flakes
3 (8-ounce) cans tomato sauce
3 cups shredded Gruyère cheese
3 (8-ounce) cans tomato sauce

Shredded Beef Tacos

Serves 4

1 pound beef chuck roast
1 teaspoon salt
⅛ teaspoon pepper
5 cloves garlic, slivered
3 cups water
1 (14-ounce) can diced
    tomatoes, undrained
1 (4-ounce) can chopped
    green chilies
8 taco shells

Serves 12

3 pounds beef chuck roast
1 tablespoon salt
⅜ teaspoon pepper
15 cloves garlic, slivered
9 cups water
3 (14-ounce) cans diced
    tomatoes, undrained
3 (4-ounce) cans chopped
    green chilies
24 taco shells

To serve immediately, place shredded beef, tomatoes, and chilies in large skillet. Cook over medium heat until mixture thickens. Heat taco shells in oven; then spoon beef mixture into shells.

1. Sprinkle beef with salt and pepper. Cut small slits in beef and insert garlic slivers. Place in large stockpot. Pour water over; then cover stockpot and bring to a boil. Reduce heat and simmer for 1½ hours, until beef is very tender.

2. Drain beef; then cool in refrigerator. Shred the meat using two forks. Combine with tomatoes and green chilies in zipper-lock bag. Seal bag, attach bagged taco shells, then label and freeze.

3. *To thaw and reheat:* Thaw overnight in refrigerator. Heat beef mixture in heavy skillet until hot, stirring occasionally, about 10 to 15 minutes. Bake taco shells in preheated 400°F oven for 4 to 5 minutes until crisp. Serve beef mixture in taco shells; garnish with lettuce, cheese, taco sauce, and sour cream.

Thai Beef Skewers

To serve skewers without freezing, marinate beef in refrigerator for 2 to 8 hours. Grill or broil 4 to 6 inches from heat, 2 to 3 minutes on each side.

1. Partially freeze meat for 1 hour, then slice thinly across the grain into 1-inch strips. To make marinade, combine remaining ingredients in medium bowl and mix well. Add steak strips to marinade and toss to coat.

2. Thread beef onto 20 metal skewers, then place in quart-size zipper-lock bags and pour remaining marinade into bag. Seal, label, and freeze.

3. *To thaw and reheat:* Thaw beef overnight in refrigerator. Grill or broil 4 to 6 inches from heat source for 2 minutes on each side until beef is medium-done. Discard remaining marinade.

Don't Forget to Thaw!

Designate a special space in your refrigerator just for thawing foods. When you remove that night's dish from the refrigerator, that empty space will remind you to take another dish from the freezer and put it in the fridge for overnight thawing.

Serves 3–4

1 pound beef flank steak
2 shallots, minced
4 cloves garlic, minced
1 teaspoon salt
⅛ teaspoon red pepper flakes
1 tablespoon grated gingerroot
¼ cup teriyaki sauce
3 tablespoons honey
2 tablespoons rice wine vinegar

Serves 12–16

3 pounds beef flank steak
6 shallots, minced
12 cloves garlic, minced
1 tablespoon salt
⅜ teaspoon red pepper flakes
3 tablespoons grated gingerroot
¾ cup teriyaki sauce
9 tablespoons honey
6 tablespoons rice wine vinegar

Beef Rouladen

Serves 4–6

8 ¼-inch-thick slices
   bottom round steak
3 tablespoons brown
   mustard
½ cup brown rice
1½ cups water
4 slices bacon
1 tablespoon butter
1 onion, chopped
3 cloves garlic, chopped
3 tablespoons flour
2 cups Beef Broth (page 302)
2 tablespoons olive oil

Serves 12–18

24 ¼-inch-thick slices
   bottom round steak
9 tablespoons brown
   mustard
1½ cups brown rice
4½ cups water
12 slices bacon
3 tablespoons butter
3 onions, chopped
9 cloves garlic, chopped
9 tablespoons flour
6 cups Beef Broth (page 302)
6 tablespoons olive oil

This twist on the German classic combines bacon and brown rice in creamy beef gravy. You can serve this dish immediately, with some mashed potatoes to soak up the sauce.

1. Spread mustard on steak slices and set aside. Cook brown rice in water for 30 to 40 minutes until almost tender. Drain if necessary and set aside. Cook bacon in large skillet over medium heat until crisp. Remove from skillet and drain on paper towels; crumble and set aside.

2. Add butter to drippings in skillet and add onions and garlic. Cook and stir over medium heat until crisp-tender. Sprinkle flour over onions and cook and stir for 2 to 3 minutes, stirring constantly. Add half of beef broth and cook until mixture thickens, about 4 to 5 minutes. Add brown rice and crumbled bacon to this mixture.

3. Divide rice mixture among the round steak slices. Roll up, enclosing filling. Use toothpicks to hold rolls closed, if necessary. Heat olive oil in skillet and brown beef rolls on all sides over medium heat. Add remaining beef broth to skillet and bring to a boil. Cover skillet, reduce heat, and simmer beef rolls for 30 to 45 minutes, until very tender. Cool beef rolls and sauce in ice-water bath or refrigerator. Pack into rigid containers, label, and freeze.

4. *To thaw and reheat:* Thaw overnight in refrigerator. Place beef and sauce in heavy skillet, cover, and bring to a boil over medium heat. Reduce heat and simmer for 10 to 14 minutes, until rolls are thoroughly hot in the center.

Burgundy Beef

This rich stew is delicious served over
hot cooked egg noodles. To serve without freezing,
simply serve stew after 2 to 3 hours of simmering.

2 onions, chopped
4 cloves garlic, chopped
3 tablespoons olive oil
2 pounds cubed beef
¼ cup flour
½ teaspoon salt
2 (4-ounce) cans sliced
    mushrooms
1 (6-ounce) can tomato
    paste
2 cups burgundy wine
3 cups Beef Broth (page 302)
2 teaspoons dried thyme
    leaves
⅛ teaspoon pepper
1 (9-ounce) package baby
    carrots

1. In heavy stockpot, sauté onions and garlic in olive oil until crisp-tender.
   Remove vegetables from pan. On shallow plate, toss beef with flour
   and salt. Add beef to drippings in pan in batches; sauté each batch
   3 to 4 minutes, until browned.

2. Return onions and garlic to pan along with remaining ingredients,
   except carrots. Bring to a boil, then cover, reduce heat, and simmer for
   2 to 3 hours, until beef is very tender.

3. Cool beef mixture in ice-water bath or in refrigerator. Pack into
   1-gallon-size zipper-lock bag; attach bag with baby carrots; label, seal,
   and freeze.

4. *To thaw and reheat:* Thaw beef mixture and carrots overnight in refrigerator. Pour beef mixture into saucepan and add carrots; bring to a
   boil, then reduce heat and simmer for 15 to 20 minutes until hot.

Serves 18–24

6 onions, chopped
12 cloves garlic, chopped
9 tablespoons olive oil
6 pounds cubed beef
¾ cup flour
1½ teaspoons salt
6 (4-ounce) cans sliced
    mushrooms
3 (6-ounce) cans tomato
    paste
6 cups burgundy wine
9 cups Beef Broth (page 302)
6 teaspoons dried thyme
    leaves
⅜ teaspoon pepper
3 (9-ounce) packages baby
    carrots

Mexican Quiche

Serves 6

½ cup refried beans
1 9-inch Pie Crust (page 299)
1 pound sirloin steak
1 onion, chopped
3 cloves garlic, chopped
2 tablespoons olive oil
1 (4-ounce) can chopped
   green chilies
1½ cups grated pepper jack
   cheese
4 eggs
½ cup sour cream
½ cup grated Parmesan
   cheese

Serves 18

1½ cups refried beans
3 9-inch Pie Crusts (page
   299)
3 pounds sirloin steak
3 onions, chopped
9 cloves garlic, chopped
6 tablespoons olive oil
3 (4-ounce) cans chopped
   green chilies
4½ cups grated pepper jack
   cheese
12 eggs
1½ cups sour cream
1½ cups grated Parmesan
   cheese

This quiche is delicious topped with salsa
and sour cream. To serve immediately, bake at 375°F
for 40 to 45 minutes, until set and golden brown.

1. Preheat oven to 375°F. Spread refried beans in bottom of unbaked pie crust and set aside. Cut steak into ½-inch pieces. In heavy skillet, brown steak with onion and garlic in olive oil. Remove from pan with slotted spoon and place in pie crust. Sprinkle drained green chilies over all. Sprinkle pepper jack cheese over green chilies.

2. In medium bowl, combine eggs and sour cream and beat to mix well. Pour over cheese in pie crust; sprinkle Parmesan cheese on top. Bake at 375°F for 35 to 40 minutes until quiche is set and top is light golden brown. Cool in refrigerator; then wrap in freezer wrap, label, and freeze. Or, slice cooled quiche into slices before freezing and flash freeze individually.

3. *To thaw and reheat:* Thaw quiche overnight in refrigerator. Bake at 350°F for 20 to 25 minutes until heated through.

   To reheat individual slices: Microwave each frozen slice on medium power for 2 to 4 minutes, then 1 minute on high.

Curried Beef Stew

To serve this stew immediately, just add the frozen potatoes and peas to simmering stew and cook over medium heat, stirring occasionally, for 15 to 25 minutes, until vegetables are hot and tender.

1 onion, chopped
2 shallots, minced
2 tablespoons olive oil
1 pound chuck steak
3 tablespoons flour
2 teaspoons curry powder
1 teaspoon salt
4 cups Beef Broth (page 302)
1½ cups frozen potato wedges
1 cup frozen baby peas
2 cups baby carrots

1. Cook onion and shallots in olive oil until crisp-tender, stirring frequently. Remove vegetables from pan with slotted spoon. Cut chuck steak into 1-inch pieces. Combine flour, curry powder, and salt on shallow plate and toss steak cubes to coat.

2. Brown steak in drippings remaining in pan for 3 to 4 minutes, stirring occasionally. Return onion and shallots to pan and add beef broth. Bring to a boil, then cover pan, reduce heat, and simmer for 1½ hours until beef is tender.

3 onions, chopped
6 shallots, minced
6 tablespoons olive oil
3 pounds chuck steak
9 tablespoons flour
6 teaspoons curry powder
1 tablespoon salt
12 cups Beef Broth (page 302)
4½ cups frozen potato wedges
3 cups frozen baby peas
6 cups baby carrots

3. Cool stew in ice-water bath or in refrigerator. Pour stew into gallon-size zipper-lock bags and place frozen potato wedges and peas in quart zipper-lock bag; attach to stew. Attach bag with baby carrots; then label and freeze.

4. *To thaw and reheat:* Thaw stew and carrots overnight in refrigerator. Keep potatoes and peas frozen. Pour stew and carrots into large saucepan and bring to a boil over medium-high heat. Reduce heat, add frozen potatoes and peas, and simmer for 15 to 25 minutes until stew is hot and potatoes are tender.

Marinated Round Steak

Serves 4–6

---

2 pounds bottom round
  steak
⅓ cup red wine vinegar
3 tablespoons olive oil
3 cloves garlic, minced
½ teaspoon salt
⅛ teaspoon pepper
1 teaspoon dried thyme
  leaves
2 tablespoons sugar
½ teaspoon celery salt

Serves 12–18

---

3 (2-pound) bottom round
  steaks
1 cup red wine vinegar
9 tablespoons olive oil
9 cloves garlic, minced
1½ teaspoons salt
⅜ teaspoon pepper
1 tablespoon dried thyme
  leaves
6 tablespoons sugar
1½ teaspoons celery salt

To serve without freezing, let meat marinate 4 to 8 hours,
or overnight, in refrigerator. Then grill or broil steak,
turning once, until desired doneness.

---

1. Trim excess fat off steak and cut into 4 to 6 serving pieces. Pierce steak with fork in several places.

2. In gallon zipper-lock bag, combine remaining ingredients to make marinade. Add steak; then seal and massage bag to work marinade into meat. Label bag and freeze.

3. *To thaw and cook:* Thaw meat overnight in refrigerator. Grill or broil steak for 10 to 20 minutes, turning once, until desired doneness. Let meat stand, covered, for 10 minutes before slicing.

CHAPTER 6

Start with Chicken Breasts

Phyllo Chicken Roll

Serves 4

1 red bell pepper, chopped
1 onion, chopped
2 cloves garlic, minced
1 cup chopped mushrooms
1 tablespoon olive oil
½ cup ricotta cheese
1 egg
1 cup shredded Gruyère
    cheese
¼ cup grated Parmesan
    cheese
2 cups cooked, cubed
    chicken breast
6 sheets thawed phyllo
    dough
¼ cup melted butter

Serves 12

3 red bell peppers, chopped
3 onions, chopped
6 cloves garlic, minced
3 cups chopped mushrooms
3 tablespoons olive oil
1½ cups ricotta cheese
3 eggs
3 cups shredded Gruyère
    cheese
¾ cup grated Parmesan
    cheese
6 cups cooked, cubed
    chicken breast
18 sheets thawed phyllo
    dough
¾ cup melted butter

This elegant entree is perfect for a brunch. To serve immediately, bake roll at 375°F for 40 to 50 minutes, until pastry is crisp and golden brown and filling is thoroughly heated.

1. In large skillet, sauté bell pepper, onion, garlic, and mushrooms in olive oil until crisp-tender, stirring frequently. Let cool for 20 minutes.

2. In large bowl, combine ricotta cheese and egg and beat until combined. Add Gruyère, Parmesan, and cooked chicken and mix well. Stir in cooled vegetable mixture until well blended.

3. Place one sheet phyllo dough on large cookie sheet and brush with butter. Top with remaining five sheets, brushing each lightly with butter. Place chicken mixture along one edge of dough, leaving 1-inch margin. Fold in short ends of phyllo dough, and then roll, starting with side containing filling. Seal edges with butter. Brush entire roll with remaining melted butter. Wrap roll in foil, label, and freeze.

4. *To thaw and cook:* Partially unwrap and thaw chicken roll overnight in refrigerator. Brush with 1 tablespoon melted butter. Bake in preheated 375°F oven for 40 to 50 minutes until pastry is crisp and golden brown and filling is thoroughly heated. Let stand 10 minutes before serving. Slice carefully on the diagonal using a serrated knife.

Chicken Fried Rice

To serve immediately, stir-fry the rice mixture in olive oil until hot. Beat eggs and add to skillet. Cook eggs until set but still moist. Add soy sauce and sesame oil and serve.

1½ cups long-grain white rice
2½ cups water
1 onion, chopped
1 cup frozen soybeans
2 cups cooked, cubed chicken breast
2 tablespoons olive oil
2 tablespoons soy sauce
1 teaspoon toasted sesame oil
3 eggs
½ teaspoon salt
⅛ teaspoon pepper

1. Combine rice and water in heavy saucepan. Bring to boil over high heat. Reduce heat to low, cover pan, and cook rice until almost tender but still firm in the center, about 15 minutes. Gently fluff rice with fork. Spread rice into a thin layer on foil-lined cookie sheet and refrigerate until very cold.

2. Gently break up clumps of rice and mix with chopped onions, frozen soybeans, and cooked, cubed chicken. Package in zipper-lock bag, label, and freeze.

3. Mark olive oil, soy sauce, and toasted sesame oil as reserved ingredients and store in your pantry. Mark eggs as reserved in refrigerator.

4. *To thaw and cook:* Let rice mixture thaw overnight in refrigerator. Heat olive oil in large skillet or wok. Stir-fry rice mixture in oil until thoroughly heated. Push rice mixture to one side of wok and pour in beaten eggs. Stir-fry until eggs are set but still moist. Gently stir the set eggs into rice/chicken mixture. Season with soy sauce, sesame oil, salt, and pepper, and serve immediately.

Serves 12

4½ cups long-grain white rice
7½ cups water
3 onions, chopped
3 cups frozen soybeans
6 cups cooked, cubed chicken breast
6 tablespoons olive oil
6 tablespoons soy sauce
1 tablespoon toasted sesame oil
9 eggs
1½ teaspoons salt
⅜ teaspoon pepper

Chicken Tucson

Serves 4

1 (20-ounce) jar salsa
2 (16-ounce) cans black
    beans
1 red bell pepper, chopped
2 cups cooked, cubed
    chicken breast
6 corn tortillas
2 cups shredded Cheddar
    cheese
½ cup sour cream

Serves 12

3 (20-ounce) jars salsa
6 (16-ounce) cans black
    beans
3 red bell peppers, chopped
6 cups cooked, cubed
    chicken breast
18 corn tortillas
6 cups shredded Cheddar
    cheese
1½ cups sour cream

This easy casserole takes about 10 minutes to assemble. To serve immediately, dollop with sour cream and sprinkle with cheese. Bake at 350°F for 25 to 35 minutes until bubbly and cheese begins to brown.

---

1. Spread ½ cup salsa in 9" × 9" baking dish and set aside. Drain black beans and rinse well; drain again. In large bowl, combine beans, bell pepper, chicken, and remaining salsa and mix well.

2. Place 3 tortillas on salsa in bottom of baking dish. Top with half of chicken mixture and sprinkle with half of cheese. Top with 3 more tortillas, then remaining chicken mixture. Wrap and label. Reserve sour cream in refrigerator. Place remaining cheese in zipper-lock bag, attach to baking dish, and freeze.

3. *To thaw and cook:* Thaw overnight in refrigerator. Place small dollops of sour cream on casserole and top with reserved cheese. Bake at 350°F for 30 to 40 minutes until hot and cheese begins to brown.

Cheesy Chicken Manicotti

To serve immediately, sprinkle casserole with cheese and bake at 350°F for 80 to 90 minutes, until chicken is cooked and casserole is bubbly.

1. In shallow bowl, combine Italian seasoning, minced garlic, and first quantity grated Parmesan cheese. Toss chicken tenders with this mixture until coated. Place one coated chicken tender inside each uncooked manicotti shell.

2. Pour 1 cup tomato pasta sauce in lined 13" × 9" baking dish. Arrange filled manicotti shells in dish. Arrange frozen bell peppers and onions around manicotti shells. Add water to remaining tomato pasta sauce in jar and mix well. Pour over vegetables and manicotti shells. Pour Alfredo sauce over all.

3. Freeze casserole until hard, then remove from dish and wrap again. In zipper-lock bag, combine remaining Parmesan cheese and mozzarella cheese. Attach to casserole, label, and freeze.

4. *To thaw and cook*: Thaw casserole overnight in refrigerator. Sprinkle with cheeses. Cover casserole with foil and bake at 350°F for 80 to 95 minutes until chicken is thoroughly cooked, pasta is tender, cheese is beginning to brown, and casserole is bubbly.

Serves 6

1 teaspoon Italian
seasoning
2 cloves garlic, minced
¼ cup grated Parmesan
cheese
1½ pounds chicken tenders
14 manicotti shells
1 (26-ounce) jar tomato
pasta sauce
2 cups frozen peppers and
onions
½ cup water
1 (14-ounce) jar Alfredo
sauce
½ cup Parmesan cheese
1 cup shredded mozzarella
cheese

Serves 18

1 tablespoon Italian
seasoning
6 cloves garlic, minced
¾ cup grated Parmesan
cheese
4½ pounds chicken tenders
42 manicotti shells
3 (26-ounce) jars tomato
pasta sauce
6 cups frozen peppers and
onions
1½ cups water
3 (14-ounce) jars Alfredo
sauce
1½ cups Parmesan cheese
3 cups shredded mozzarella
cheese

Sweet and Sour Chicken Stew

Serves 4

---

3 boneless, skinless chicken
   breasts
1 onion, chopped
2 cloves garlic, chopped
2 tablespoons olive oil
1 (10-ounce) can pineapple
   chunks
¼ cup apple cider vinegar
¼ cup sugar
3 cups Chicken Broth
   (page 301)
1 red bell pepper, chopped
1 green bell pepper,
   chopped
2 tablespoons cornstarch
¼ cup water

Serves 12

---

9 boneless, skinless chicken
   breasts
3 onions, chopped
6 cloves garlic, chopped
6 tablespoons olive oil
3 (10-ounce) cans pineapple
   chunks
¾ cup apple cider vinegar
¾ cup sugar
9 cups Chicken Broth
   (page 301)
3 red bell peppers, chopped
3 green bell peppers,
   chopped
6 tablespoons cornstarch
¾ cup water

To serve immediately, mix cornstarch and water together and add to simmering stew. Cook 5 to 8 minutes longer, until slightly thickened.

---

1. Cut chicken into 1-inch pieces. In heavy stockpot, sauté chicken, onion, and garlic in olive oil until vegetables are crisp-tender. Add undrained pineapple chunks, vinegar, sugar, and chicken broth and stir well. Simmer for 20 to 30 minutes, stirring occasionally, until chicken is thoroughly cooked.

2. Cool stew in ice-water bath or refrigerator until cold. Pour into rigid quart containers, label, and freeze. Attach bag with chopped green and red peppers. Reserve cornstarch in pantry.

3. *To reheat:* Place frozen chicken mixture in top of double boiler and add bell peppers. Reheat over simmering water, stirring occasionally, until hot. In small bowl, combine cornstarch and water and mix well. Add cornstarch mixture to double boiler and cook over medium heat, stirring frequently, until sauce is thickened.

Chicken Potato Skillet

Serves 4

2 boneless, skinless chicken breasts
2 cups frozen potato wedges
1 cup frozen green beans
1 onion, chopped
1 (10-ounce) can cream of chicken soup
½ cup milk
1 cup grated Swiss cheese
2 tablespoons olive oil

Serves 12

6 boneless, skinless chicken breasts
6 cups frozen potato wedges
3 cups frozen green beans
3 onions, chopped
3 (10-ounce) cans cream of chicken soup
1½ cups milk
3 cups grated Swiss cheese
6 tablespoons olive oil

To serve immediately, sauté chicken in olive oil, then add vegetables. Cook and stir until vegetables are hot. Add soup and milk, cover, and simmer for 10 minutes. Add cheese and serve.

1. Cut chicken breasts into 1-inch pieces and place in zipper-lock bag. Combine frozen potatoes, green beans, and chopped onion and place in another zipper-lock bag. Combine soup and milk in small bowl and pour into a third zipper-lock bag. Place grated cheese in a fourth zipper-lock bag. Place all bags inside a larger bag, label, and freeze. Reserve olive oil in pantry.

2. *To thaw and cook:* Thaw overnight in the refrigerator. Heat 2 table-spoons olive oil in skillet and add chicken. Cook and stir for 5 minutes until almost done. Add thawed vegetables; cook and stir 10 to 15 minutes longer, until vegetables are hot and potatoes start to crisp. Add soup mixture and cover. Simmer 10 minutes until flavors are blended. Sprinkle with cheese and serve.

The Greek Leaf

Phyllo, which literally translates as "leaf" in Greek, is made of finely rolled and stretched sheets of dough. Practically see-through, these paper-thin sheets are stacked, rolled, wrapped, and then frozen. Phyllo dough is available at most supermarkets and at Greek and Middle Eastern specialty food stores (making your own is tricky). Because the dough is already rolled and precut, phyllo is relatively easy to work with.

Fragrant Sticky Chicken

Serves 4

1/3 cup soy sauce
1/2 cup Chicken Broth (page 301)
1 tablespoon grated gingerroot
4 boneless, skinless chicken breasts
3 cloves garlic, minced
1/4 cup honey

Serves 12

1 cup soy sauce
1 1/2 cups Chicken Broth (page 301)
3 tablespoons grated gingerroot
6 cloves garlic, minced
12 boneless, skinless chicken breasts
3/4 cup honey

To serve this delicious chicken without freezing, cook marinated chicken over medium heat for 6 to 8 minutes, then add honey, cover skillet, and cook 7 to 9 minutes longer or until chicken is thoroughly cooked.

1. In medium bowl, combine soy sauce, broth, gingerroot, and garlic. Mix well, then add chicken breasts. Cover and marinate for 1 to 2 hours in the refrigerator; then pack into zipper-lock bag, label, and freeze. Reserve honey in pantry.

2. *To thaw and cook:* Thaw chicken in marinade overnight in the refrigerator. Heat 12-inch skillet over medium heat, then add chicken and marinade. Cook 5 to 8 minutes on one side, then turn chicken, add honey, cover, and cook an additional 8 to 10 minutes until chicken is thoroughly cooked and sauce is reduced.

Citrus Glazed Chicken

To serve immediately, marinate chicken in refrigerator for up to 6 hours. Bake at 350°F for 25 to 30 minutes, until chicken is thoroughly cooked, basting frequently.

---

1. Place chicken in zipper-lock bag. Mix remaining ingredients in medium bowl to make marinade and pour over chicken. Seal bag, label, and freeze.

2. *To thaw and reheat:* Thaw chicken overnight in refrigerator. Uncover and bake chicken at 350°F for 25 to 30 minutes, basting frequently, until chicken is thoroughly cooked and glazed.

Serves 4

4 boneless, skinless chicken breasts
¼ cup honey
3 tablespoons lemon juice
2 tablespoons orange juice
1 teaspoon dried tarragon

Serves 12

12 boneless, skinless chicken breasts
¾ cup honey
9 tablespoons lemon juice
6 tablespoons orange juice
1 tablespoon dried tarragon

Creamy Bacon Chicken

To serve immediately, crumble bacon and sprinkle over casserole. Sprinkle cheese over bacon. Bake at 350°F for 18 to 25 minutes, until chicken is thoroughly cooked and cheese is melted.

---

1. In heavy skillet, cook bacon until crisp. Remove bacon from pan and drain on paper towels. Sauté mushrooms in bacon drippings. Place uncooked chicken in 9" × 9" baking dish; top with mushrooms. Pour Alfredo sauce over all. Cool in refrigerator, then wrap, attach bag with bacon and another bag with cheese, label, and freeze.

2. *To thaw and reheat:* Thaw casserole overnight in refrigerator. Crumble bacon and sprinkle over all. Sprinkle cheese over bacon. Bake at 375°F for 20 to 25 minutes, until thoroughly heated and chicken is thoroughly cooked.

Serves 4

5 slices bacon
8 ounces mushrooms, chopped
4 boneless, skinless chicken breasts
1 (10-ounce) jar Alfredo sauce
1 cup grated Havarti cheese

Serves 12

15 slices bacon
3 (8-ounce) packages mushrooms, chopped
12 boneless, skinless chicken breasts
3 (10-ounce) jars Alfredo sauce
3 cups grated Havarti cheese

Chicken Risotto

Serves 4

---

3 boneless, skinless chicken
    breasts
2 tablespoons olive oil
1 onion, chopped
½ cup chopped leeks
2 cups long-grain white rice
1 cup white wine
1 cup Chicken Broth
    (page 301)
½ cup grated Parmesan
    cheese
1 (10-ounce) can condensed
    chicken broth
3 tablespoons heavy cream
3 tablespoons butter

Serves 12

---

9 boneless, skinless chicken
    breasts
6 tablespoons olive oil
3 onions, chopped
1½ cups chopped leeks
6 cups long-grain white rice
3 cups white wine
3 cups Chicken Broth
    (page 301)
1½ cups grated Parmesan
    cheese
3 (10-ounce) cans condensed
    chicken broth
9 tablespoons heavy cream
9 tablespoons butter

To serve immediately, continue cooking rice mixture, adding 1 cup water and condensed chicken broth, until rice is tender and chicken is cooked through. Add remaining ingredients and cook until hot.

---

1. Cut chicken breasts into 1-inch pieces. Heat olive oil in large stockpot. Add chicken, onion, and leeks; cook and stir for 5 to 7 minutes until onion is crisp-tender and chicken turns white.

2. Add uncooked rice and stir well until rice is coated. Cook for 2 to 3 minutes over medium heat, until rice begins to look translucent. Add white wine and cook, stirring frequently, until liquid is absorbed. Turn heat down to low; add plain chicken broth and cook, stirring frequently, until liquid is absorbed.

3. Remove pan from heat and place mixture in rigid containers. Chill in refrigerator or ice-water bath; then wrap, pack, and freeze. Attach bag with grated cheese. Reserve condensed chicken broth in pantry, and cream and butter in fridge.

4. *To thaw and reheat:* Thaw overnight in refrigerator. Place in saucepan over low heat, stirring occasionally, until hot. Combine reserved condensed chicken broth with 1 cup water and add to rice mixture. Cook and stir over medium heat until liquid is absorbed, rice is tender, and chicken is cooked through. Add cheese, cream, and butter, and stir until cheese and butter are melted.

Chicken Divan Soup

2 boneless, skinless chicken breasts
1 onion, chopped
2 cloves garlic, chopped
2 tablespoons olive oil
3 cups Chicken Broth (page 301)
⅛ teaspoon pepper
1 (10-ounce) can condensed broccoli cheese soup
1 (10-ounce) package frozen chopped broccoli
1 cup grated Swiss cheese

To serve immediately, add broccoli to soup when chicken is cooked through. Cook for 4 to 5 minutes longer, until broccoli is hot. Add grated cheese; cook and stir until cheese melts, about 3 to 4 minutes.

1. Cut chicken breasts into 1-inch pieces. In large saucepan, cook chicken, onion, and garlic in olive oil until vegetables are crisp-tender. Add broth, pepper, and condensed soup; stir well. Simmer for 10 to 15 minutes, until chicken is thoroughly cooked.

2. Chill soup in ice-water bath or refrigerator. Place in rigid containers and attach package of frozen broccoli and bag of grated cheese. Wrap, label, and freeze.

3. *To thaw and reheat:* Thaw everything overnight in refrigerator. Place soup and broccoli in saucepan and heat over medium-low heat until soup simmers. Add cheese and stir for 2 to 3 minutes, until cheese melts.

Organization Makes Thawing Easy

When preparing and packaging your meals, write complete thawing and reheating information on the freezer package. Then follow that information during the reheating process.

Serves 12

6 boneless, skinless chicken breasts
3 onions, chopped
6 cloves garlic, chopped
6 tablespoons olive oil
9 cups Chicken Broth (page 301)
⅜ teaspoon pepper
3 (10-ounce) cans condensed broccoli cheese soup
3 (10-ounce) packages frozen chopped broccoli
3 cups grated Swiss cheese

Cheesy Chicken Supreme

Serves 4

4 slices bacon
4 boneless, skinless chicken
    breasts
1 onion, chopped
2 cloves garlic, chopped
1 (10-ounce) can condensed
    mushroom soup
½ cup milk
1 cup grated Havarti cheese
1 (6-ounce) package
    couscous

Serves 14

12 slices bacon
12 boneless, skinless chicken
    breasts
3 onions, chopped
6 cloves garlic, chopped
3 (10-ounce) cans condensed
    mushroom soup
1½ cups milk
3 cups grated Havarti cheese
3 (6-ounce) packages
    couscous

To serve immediately, don't refrigerate.
Add crumbled bacon and cheese to skillet; cover and
cook over medium-low heat for 4 to 5 minutes, until cheese
is melted and mixture is bubbly. Serve over hot cooked couscous.

1. In large skillet, cook bacon until crisp; remove from pan and drain on paper towels. Add chicken to drippings remaining in skillet; cook 2 to 3 minutes on each side.

2. Add onion and garlic to skillet; cook and stir for 4 to 5 minutes, until crisp-tender. Add soup and milk; stir to blend. Simmer until chicken is thoroughly cooked. Chill chicken mixture in refrigerator or ice-water bath.

3. Crumble bacon and place in zipper-lock bag. Place cheese in zipper-lock bag. Place chilled chicken and sauce in zipper-lock bag. Place all bags inside a larger bag; label and freeze. Reserve couscous in pantry.

4. *To thaw and reheat:* Thaw overnight in refrigerator. Place chicken mixture in skillet and heat for about 10 minutes, until hot. Add bacon and cheese to skillet; cover and cook on low heat for 5 to 6 minutes, until chicken is thoroughly heated. Serve over hot cooked couscous.

Lemon Chicken

To serve immediately, mix cornstarch with water and add to simmering sauce. Cook for 3 to 4 minutes, until thickened. Drain mandarin oranges and add; cook 2 to 3 minutes, until hot.

---

1. Cut chicken breasts in half crosswise. Cook chicken and garlic in olive oil until chicken is browned on both sides. Add orange juice, lemon juice and peel, broth, salt, and pepper to skillet. Simmer until chicken is thoroughly cooked, about 10 to 12 minutes.

2. Pour chicken and sauce into rigid containers and cool in refrigerator. Reserve cornstarch and mandarin oranges in pantry. Wrap chicken, label, and freeze.

3. *To thaw and reheat:* Thaw overnight in refrigerator. Pour chicken and sauce into heavy saucepan and bring to a simmer. Mix cornstarch and water in small bowl and add to saucepan. Cook and stir until thickened, 3 to 4 minutes. Drain mandarin oranges and add to skillet; simmer until heated through. Serve over hot cooked rice.

Serves 4

4 boneless, skinless chicken breasts
2 cloves garlic, chopped
2 tablespoons olive oil
½ cup orange juice
¼ cup lemon juice
2 teaspoons grated lemon peel
½ cup Chicken Broth (page 301)
½ teaspoon salt
⅛ teaspoon pepper
2 tablespoons cornstarch
1 (16-ounce) can mandarin oranges
¼ cup water

Serves 12

12 boneless, skinless chicken breasts
6 cloves garlic, chopped
6 tablespoons olive oil
1½ cups orange juice
¾ cup lemon juice
2 tablespoons grated lemon peel
1½ cups Chicken Broth (page 301)
1½ teaspoons salt
⅜ teaspoon pepper
6 tablespoons cornstarch
3 (16-ounce) cans mandarin oranges
¾ cup water

Orange Curried Chicken

Serves 4

---

4 boneless, skinless chicken breasts
3 tablespoons flour
1 tablespoon curry powder
1 teaspoon salt
3 tablespoons olive oil
1 cup orange juice
½ cup evaporated milk
2 cups frozen peppers and onions

Serves 12

---

12 boneless, skinless chicken breasts
9 tablespoons flour
3 tablespoons curry powder
1 tablespoon salt
9 tablespoons olive oil
3 cups orange juice
1½ cups evaporated milk
6 cups frozen peppers and onions

Serve this delicious Indian dish with extra curry powder for those who like it hot. To serve immediately, add frozen peppers and onions and simmer 5 to 8 minutes until hot; serve over rice.

---

1. Cut chicken breasts into 1-inch pieces. Combine flour, curry powder, and salt on large plate. Add chicken and toss to coat.

2. Heat olive oil in large skillet. Add chicken; cook and stir until chicken is almost cooked. Add orange juice; simmer for 10 to 15 minutes, until chicken is thoroughly cooked. Add evaporated milk, stir, and remove from heat.

3. Chill mixture in refrigerator or ice-water bath until cold. Add frozen vegetables and mix gently. Wrap, label, and freeze.

4. *To thaw and reheat:* Thaw mixture overnight in refrigerator. Place in heavy skillet and cook over medium heat for 10 to 15 minutes, until bubbly and thoroughly heated. Serve over hot cooked rice.

Chicken on Cornbread

Serves 4

To serve immediately, bake the cornbread at 400°F for 20 to 25 minutes until golden brown around edges. Heat chicken in gravy and pour over squares of hot cornbread.

1. Preheat oven to 400°F. Line 8" × 8" pan with foil and grease. In large bowl, combine flour, cornmeal, baking soda, baking powder, and salt. In small bowl, combine green chilies, oil, buttermilk, and egg. Mix with dry ingredients. Pour mixture into prepared pan and bake at 400°F for 15 minutes, until set; cool.

2. Meanwhile, in large saucepan, cook onion in butter for 3 to 4 minutes. Add flour, salt, and pepper; cook and stir 2 to 3 minutes. Add broth and milk; cook and stir 5 to 6 minutes. Cool gravy in ice-water bath or refrigerator.

3. Remove baked cornbread from pan and wrap again in foil. Slice chicken and put in 1-quart zipper-lock bag with gravy. Seal bag, attach to cornbread, then label and freeze.

4. *To thaw and reheat:* Thaw cornbread and chicken overnight in refrigerator. Unwrap cornbread and place in pan; bake at 400°F for 8 to 10 minutes or until hot and golden. Place chicken and gravy in skillet and cook over low heat for 8 to 11 minutes or until hot. Serve chicken and gravy over hot cornbread squares.

Serves 4

½ cup flour
½ cup yellow cornmeal
¼ teaspoon baking soda
½ teaspoon baking powder
½ teaspoon salt
2 tablespoons chopped
    green chilies
3 tablespoons vegetable oil
½ cup buttermilk
1 egg, beaten
¼ cup minced onion
¼ cup butter
¼ cup flour
½ teaspoon salt
⅛ teaspoon pepper
1 cup Chicken Broth (page 301)
½ cup milk
2 cooked chicken breasts

Serves 12

1½ cups flour
1½ cups yellow cornmeal
¾ teaspoons baking soda
1½ teaspoons baking
    powder
1 teaspoon salt
6 tablespoons chopped
    green chilies
9 tablespoons vegetable oil
1½ cups buttermilk
3 eggs, beaten
¾ cup minced onion
¾ cup butter
¾ cup flour
1 teaspoon salt
⅜ teaspoon pepper
3 cups Chicken Broth
    (page 301)
1½ cups milk
6 cooked chicken breasts

Chicken Santa Fe Soup

Serves 4

2 boneless, skinless chicken
  breasts
1 onion, chopped
2 tablespoons olive oil
1 (16-ounce) can black
  beans, drained
1 (4-ounce) can green
  chilies, drained
⅛ teaspoon red pepper
  flakes
1 (16-ounce) can corn,
  drained
3 cups Chicken Broth
  (page 301)

Serves 12

6 boneless, skinless chicken
  breasts
3 onions, chopped
6 tablespoons olive oil
3 (16-ounce) cans black
  beans, drained
3 (4-ounce) cans green
  chilies, drained
⅜ teaspoon red pepper
  flakes
3 (16-ounce) cans corn,
  drained
9 cups Chicken Broth
  (page 301)

To serve immediately, garnish soup with tortilla chips, sour cream, salsa, or chopped tomatoes. Serve with fruit salad and cornbread.

1. Cut chicken breasts into 1-inch pieces. In heavy skillet, sauté chicken and onion in olive oil until onion is crisp-tender. Add remaining ingredients, stir to blend, and simmer for 10 to 15 minutes. Cool soup in refrigerator or ice bath. Pour soup into rigid containers; seal, label, and freeze.

2. *To thaw and reheat:* Thaw soup overnight in refrigerator, then reheat in heavy saucepan until bubbling.

   To reheat from frozen: Place frozen soup in top of double boiler; heat over simmering water, stirring occasionally, until soup is hot. Transfer to saucepan and heat until bubbling.

Grandma's Chicken Soup

Serves 6–8

3-pound stewing chicken,
   cut up
1 teaspoon salt
⅛ teaspoon pepper
2 tablespoons olive oil
1 onion, chopped
4 cloves garlic, chopped
5 cups water
3 carrots, sliced
2 cups frozen pearl onions
1 cup frozen peas
1 cup frozen green beans
1 cup uncooked egg noodles

Serves 18–24

---

3 (3-pound) stewing
   chickens, cut up
1 tablespoon salt
⅜ teaspoon pepper
6 tablespoons olive oil
3 onions, chopped
12 cloves garlic, chopped
15 cups water
9 carrots, sliced
6 cups frozen pearl onions
3 cups frozen peas
3 cups frozen green beans
3 cups uncooked egg
   noodles

To serve immediately, simmer carrots and frozen vegetables in broth for 5 minutes. Add chicken and egg noodles and simmer 4 to 5 minutes longer, until noodles and vegetables are tender.

---

1. Sprinkle chicken with salt and pepper and set aside. Heat olive oil in large stockpot or Dutch oven over medium heat and sauté onion and garlic until crisp-tender. Add chicken pieces and water to pot. Bring to a boil; then cover, reduce heat, and simmer for 70 to 80 minutes, until chicken is thoroughly cooked. Remove chicken from broth, remove and discard skin and bones; strain broth. Wash stockpot and dry thoroughly.

2. Place broth in stockpot and add carrots. Simmer for 5 to 7 minutes, until carrots are tender. Add chicken meat and cool soup in ice-water bath or in refrigerator. Stir in pearl onions, peas, and green beans. Pour soup into rigid container, label, and freeze. Reserve egg noodles in pantry.

3. *To thaw and reheat:* Thaw soup in refrigerator overnight. Place in large stockpot or Dutch oven. Bring to a simmer over medium heat, stirring occasionally. Add egg noodles and cook for 4 to 5 minutes, until tender.

Spanish Chicken and Olives

To serve immediately, bake until chicken pieces are tender,
removing cover for last 10 minutes of cooking time.
Serve with hot cooked rice or mashed potatoes.

1. Sprinkle chicken pieces with salt, pepper, and paprika. Heat olive oil in large skillet. Add chicken in batches, skin-side down. Sauté until skin browns, turning once, about 5–8 minutes. Remove chicken from pan as it browns.

2. When all the chicken is browned, add garlic, diced tomatoes, tomato paste, and broth to skillet. Bring to a boil, scraping up pan drippings.

3. Preheat oven to 350°F. Place chicken in 9" × 13" baking dish. Pour mixture in skillet over chicken. Sprinkle with olives, cover, and bake at 350°F for 60 to 70 minutes, until chicken is tender and thoroughly cooked. Cool in ice-water bath or refrigerator. Place in zipper-lock bags, seal, label, and freeze.

4. *To thaw and reheat:* Thaw in refrigerator overnight. Place mixture in heavy skillet. Bring to a boil, reduce heat, and simmer for 10 to 15 minutes, until chicken is thoroughly heated.

2 pounds chicken pieces
1 teaspoon salt
⅛ teaspoon pepper
1 teaspoon paprika
2 tablespoons olive oil
5 cloves garlic, chopped
1 (14-ounce) can diced
    tomatoes, undrained
1 (6-ounce) can tomato
    paste
1 cup Chicken Broth
    (page 301)
1 cup sliced pimento-stuffed
    olives

Serves 18–24

6 pounds chicken pieces
1 tablespoon salt
⅜ teaspoon pepper
1 tablespoon paprika
6 tablespoons olive oil
15 cloves garlic, chopped
3 (14-ounce) cans diced
    tomatoes, undrained
3 (6-ounce) cans tomato
    paste
3 cups Chicken Broth
    (page 301)
3 cups sliced pimento-
    stuffed olives

Spicy Thai Chicken

Serves 4–6

½ cup orange juice
⅓ cup chunky peanut butter
½ teaspoon crushed red
    pepper
¼ teaspoon ground cumin
1 tablespoon curry powder
2 pounds boned, skinned
    chicken thighs
2 cups frozen peppers and
    onions
2 tablespoons olive oil
1 (6-ounce) package garlic
    couscous

Serves 12–18

1½ cups orange juice
1 cup chunky peanut butter
1½ teaspoons crushed red
    pepper
¾ teaspoon ground cumin
3 tablespoons curry powder
6 pounds boned, skinned
    chicken thighs
6 cups frozen peppers and
    onions
6 tablespoons olive oil
3 (6-ounce) packages garlic
    couscous

To serve this dish without freezing, marinate chicken for 3 to 4 hours in refrigerator. Cook chicken mixture in olive oil for 8 to 10 minutes, then add frozen vegetables; cook 5 to 8 minutes longer, until done.

1. Combine orange juice, peanut butter, and spices in large zipper-lock bag. Cut chicken into 1-inch-wide strips and add to bag; mix by kneading the bag. Attach bag with frozen peppers and onions and place in larger bag. Label chicken and freeze. Reserve olive oil and couscous in pantry.

2. *To thaw and reheat:* Thaw all bags overnight in refrigerator. Heat olive oil in large skillet and add chicken mixture. Cook over medium-high heat, stirring frequently, for 8 to 10 minutes, until chicken is almost cooked. Drain peppers and onions and add to chicken in skillet. Cook and stir 3 to 6 minutes longer, until vegetables are hot and chicken is thoroughly cooked. Serve over prepared couscous.

Chicken Potato Pie

Hash brown potatoes form a crust in this delicious
main-dish pie. To serve immediately, bake as directed.
Let the pie stand 10 minutes before slicing.

1. Preheat oven to 375°F. In heavy skillet, sauté onion in olive oil until tender. Remove from heat. Drain potatoes very well and add to skillet along with first egg. Mix well and press into well-greased 9-inch pie pan. Bake at 375°F for 15 to 20 minutes, until crust begins to brown.

2. Place chicken and peas in potato crust and sprinkle with cheese. In medium bowl, beat eggs, milk, marjoram, salt, and pepper until blended. Pour egg mixture over cheese. Bake at 375°F for 25 to 35 minutes, until filling is puffed and set. Run knife around edge of pie pan to loosen crust. Cool pie in refrigerator until cold, then wrap, label, and freeze.

3. *To thaw and reheat*: Thaw pie overnight in refrigerator. Bake at 375°F, uncovered, for 20 to 25 minutes, until thoroughly heated.

Stay Sharp

If you store your knives in a knife block, always keep them cutting-side up. If the cutting side is down and against the wood, you'll dull them a little bit each time you remove them. This storage method will also save wear and tear on your knife block.

Serves 6

For crust:
½ cup finely chopped onion
1 tablespoon olive oil
2 cups frozen hash brown
   potatoes, thawed
1 egg

For filling:
3 cups cooked, cubed chicken
1 cup frozen peas, thawed
1 cup shredded Gouda
   cheese
3 eggs
½ cup evaporated milk
½ teaspoon dried marjoram
½ teaspoon salt
⅛ teaspoon white pepper

Serves 18

For crust:
1½ cups finely chopped
   onion
3 tablespoons olive oil
6 cups frozen hash brown
   potatoes, thawed
3 eggs

For filling:
9 cups cooked, cubed chicken
3 cups frozen peas, thawed
3 cups shredded Gouda cheese
9 eggs
1½ cups evaporated milk
1½ teaspoons dried
   marjoram
1½ teaspoons salt
⅜ teaspoon white pepper

Chicken Cassoulet

Serves 4–6

2 cups dried Great Northern
beans
½ pound sweet Italian pork
sausage
2 tablespoons olive oil
1 onion, chopped
3 cloves garlic, chopped
1 cup chopped fennel
2 cups baby carrots
1 cup soft bread crumbs
2 tablespoons olive oil
2 cups cooked, cubed
chicken
1 (14-ounce) can diced
tomatoes, undrained
1 (10-ounce) can ready-to-
serve chicken broth
1 teaspoon dried thyme
leaves

Serves 12–18

6 cups dried Great Northern
beans
1½ pounds sweet Italian
pork sausage
6 tablespoons olive oil
3 onions, chopped
9 cloves garlic, chopped
3 cups chopped fennel
6 cups baby carrots
3 cups soft bread crumbs
6 tablespoons olive oil
6 cups cooked, cubed
chicken
3 (14-ounce) cans diced
tomatoes, undrained
3 (10-ounce) cans ready-to-
serve chicken broth
1 tablespoon dried thyme
leaves

To serve immediately, sprinkle casserole with the
bread crumbs and bake at 375°F for 40 to 50 minutes,
until bread crumbs are golden brown and casserole is bubbly.

1. In large stockpot, cover dried beans with water and bring to a boil. Boil for 1 minute, and then remove from heat, cover, and let stand for 1 hour. (Or place beans and 4 cups water in 4-quart slow cooker. Cover and cook on low for 8–10 hours, until beans are tender.) When cooked, drain and set aside.

2. Cut sausages into 1-inch slices. In large skillet, heat olive oil. Add sausages and cook, turning frequently, until browned. Remove from pan to large bowl. In drippings remaining in pan, sauté onion, garlic, and fennel until crisp-tender and remove from pan. Cut baby carrots in half lengthwise.

3. Combine bread crumbs and olive oil in small zipper-lock bag. Combine all other ingredients in large bowl and mix gently. Put meat-and-vegetable mixture in lined 3-quart baking dish. Cool in refrigerator, then wrap. Attach bag of bread crumb mixture to casserole, label, and freeze.

4. *To thaw and reheat:* Thaw casserole in refrigerator overnight. Sprinkle with bread crumbs and bake at 375°F for 45 to 55 minutes until golden brown and casserole is bubbly.

   To heat from frozen: Cover casserole and bake at 375°F for 1 hour. Sprinkle with bread crumb mixture and bake another 25 to 35 minutes until bread crumbs are golden brown.

Lasagna Chicken Rolls

1 onion, chopped
1 tablespoon olive oil
1 cup ricotta cheese
1 (3-ounce) package cream cheese
1 egg
1 cup shredded mozzarella cheese
½ cup grated Parmesan cheese
1 tablespoon cornstarch
2 cups cooked, cubed chicken
1 teaspoon dried basil leaves
6 lasagna noodles
2 cups prepared pasta sauce
1 cup grated mozzarella cheese
¼ cup grated Parmesan cheese

To serve this dish immediately, sprinkle reserved cheese over casserole and bake at 350°F for 40 to 45 minutes, until bubbly and cheese is golden brown.

1. In heavy skillet, sauté onion in olive oil until tender. Remove from heat and cool for 15 minutes. In medium bowl, combine ricotta cheese, cream cheese, egg, 1 cup shredded mozzarella cheese, ½ cup Parmesan cheese, and cornstarch. Mix well until blended and creamy, then stir in sautéed onion, along with chicken and basil leaves.

2. Cook lasagna noodles as directed on package until slightly under-cooked. Drain and rinse with cool water. Place noodles in single layer on kitchen towel. Spread each cooked noodle with chicken mixture. Roll up each noodle, starting at short end.

3. Place ½ cup pasta sauce in bottom of 9" × 9" square baking dish. Place filled lasagna rolls over pasta sauce. Pour remaining sauce over all. Cool in refrigerator, then wrap, seal, and label. Place 1 cup mozzarella cheese and ¼ cup Parmesan cheese in small zipper-lock bag and attach to dish. Wrap and freeze.

4. *To thaw and reheat:* Thaw casserole in refrigerator overnight. Bake at 350°F for 30 to 40 minutes, until hot and bubbly. Sprinkle cheese over all and bake 5 to 10 minutes longer, until cheese begins to brown. Let stand 10 minutes before serving.

Serves 18

3 onions, chopped
3 tablespoons olive oil
3 cups ricotta cheese
1 (8-ounce) package cream cheese
3 eggs
3 cups shredded mozzarella cheese
1½ cups grated Parmesan cheese
3 tablespoons cornstarch
6 cups cooked, cubed chicken
1 tablespoon dried basil leaves
18 lasagna noodles
6 cups prepared pasta sauce
3 cups grated mozzarella cheese
¾ cup grated Parmesan cheese

Tortellini Chicken Cacciatore

Serves 6–8

---

3 tablespoons flour
1 teaspoon paprika
1 teaspoon salt
⅛ teaspoon pepper
2 pounds skinned chicken
    thighs and drumsticks
¼ cup olive oil
1 onion, chopped
5 cloves garlic, chopped
½ cup chopped celery
1 (8-ounce) package
    mushrooms, sliced
2 (14-ounce) cans diced
    tomatoes, undrained
½ cup white wine
1½ cups Chicken Broth
    (page 301)
½ cup sliced ripe olives
1 (9-ounce) package frozen
    chicken tortellini

Serves 18–24

---

9 tablespoons flour
1 tablespoon paprika
1 tablespoon salt
⅜ teaspoon pepper
6 pounds skinned chicken
    thighs and drumsticks
¾ cup olive oil
3 onions, chopped
15 cloves garlic, chopped
1½ cups chopped celery
3 (8-ounce) packages
    mushrooms, sliced
6 (14-ounce) cans diced
    tomatoes, undrained
1½ cups white wine
4½ cups Chicken Broth
    (page 301)
1½ cups sliced ripe olives
3 (9-ounce) packages frozen
    chicken tortellini

You can serve this dish immediately by adding frozen tortellini to chicken mixture in skillet when chicken is thoroughly cooked. Simmer until tortellini are hot and tender.

---

1. Combine flour, paprika, salt, and pepper on shallow plate. Coat chicken pieces in flour mixture and shake off excess. Heat olive oil over medium heat in large skillet and cook chicken pieces, in batches, until browned, about 5 to 6 minutes per batch.

2. As chicken is cooked, remove from pan. When all chicken is browned, add onion, garlic, celery, and mushrooms to drippings remaining in pan. Cook and stir for 4 to 5 minutes, until crisp-tender. Return chicken to pan and add undrained tomatoes, wine, broth, and olives. Cover pan and simmer for 40 to 50 minutes or until chicken is thoroughly cooked.

3. Cool cacciatore in ice-water bath or refrigerator. When cold, pack into zipper-lock bag. Attach frozen tortellini to bag; then label and freeze.

4. *To thaw and reheat:* Thaw overnight in refrigerator. In large skillet, bring chicken mixture to a boil, reduce heat, and simmer for 10 to 12 minutes, until hot. Add tortellini to skillet and stir to make sure pasta is covered with sauce. (Add more broth if necessary to make mixture soupy.) Cover pan and simmer for 3 to 4 minutes, until tortellini is tender and chicken is hot.

Herb Roasted Chicken

4 pounds chicken pieces
2 tablespoons finely minced
   fresh rosemary
2 tablespoons minced fresh
   marjoram leaves
3 cloves garlic, minced
2 teaspoons salt
⅛ teaspoon white pepper
3 tablespoons mayonnaise
½ cup Chicken Broth
   (page 301)
2 tablespoons olive oil

To serve without freezing, put the herb-rubbed chicken
in the refrigerator for 2 to 3 hours, then brown in skillet
and roast as directed in the recipe.

1. Gently loosen the skin from the flesh of the chicken. In small bowl, combine herbs, garlic, salt, pepper, and mayonnaise, and rub this mixture between the skin and flesh of the chicken. Smooth skin back over chicken pieces.

2. Flash freeze chicken in single layer on baking sheet. When frozen solid, pack in zipper-lock bags; attach small bag with chicken broth. Label chicken and freeze. Reserve olive oil in pantry.

3. *To thaw and cook:* Thaw chicken overnight in refrigerator. Preheat oven to 400°F. Meanwhile, heat olive oil in ovenproof skillet over medium heat. Place chicken, skin-side down, in pan and brown for 4 to 5 minutes. Turn chicken over and pour chicken broth into skillet. Place skillet in preheated oven, and roast for 30 to 40 minutes until chicken is thoroughly cooked and tender, basting occasionally with pan juices.

Flavorful, Economical Chicken

Chicken meat will be more tender and flavorful if cooked with the skin on and on the bone. The price per pound will also be cheaper. Remove skin and bones after cooking, and the calories will be the same as boned, skinned chicken.

Serves 18–24

12 pounds chicken pieces
6 tablespoons finely minced
   fresh rosemary
6 tablespoons minced fresh
   marjoram leaves
9 cloves garlic, minced
2 tablespoons salt
⅜ teaspoon white pepper
9 tablespoons mayonnaise
1½ cups Chicken Broth
   (page 301)
6 tablespoons olive oil

Lemon Drumsticks

Serves 6

---

2 pounds chicken drumsticks
3 cloves garlic, minced
¼ cup lemon juice
2 tablespoons olive oil
½ cup Chicken Broth (page 301)
1 teaspoon salt
⅛ teaspoon white pepper
1 teaspoon dried basil

Serves 18

---

6 pounds chicken drumsticks
9 cloves garlic, minced
¾ cup lemon juice
6 tablespoons olive oil
1½ cups Chicken Broth (page 301)
1 tablespoon salt
⅜ teaspoon white pepper
1 tablespoon dried basil

To serve immediately, marinate chicken for 2 to 3 hours in the refrigerator, then bake at 375°F for 35 to 40 minutes, until thoroughly cooked and tender.

---

1. Place drumsticks in 1-gallon zipper-lock freezer bag. In medium bowl, combine remaining ingredients and mix well. Pour over drumsticks, seal bag, and shake gently until chicken is coated; label and freeze.

2. *To thaw and reheat:* Thaw overnight in refrigerator. Preheat oven to 375°F. Pour contents of bag into 13" × 9" baking dish. Bake at 375°F for 35 to 45 minutes, until drumsticks are thoroughly cooked, basting occasionally with sauce.

Sticky Roast Chicken

Serves 4–6

---

4 pounds chicken, cut into
 serving pieces
⅓ cup honey
1 teaspoon salt
3 tablespoons balsamic vinegar
2 tablespoons olive oil
1 teaspoon paprika
⅛ teaspoon pepper
½ teaspoon cayenne pepper
3 cloves garlic, minced

Serves 12–18

---

12 pounds chicken, cut into
 serving pieces
1 cup honey
1 tablespoon salt
9 tablespoons balsamic vinegar
6 tablespoons olive oil
1 tablespoon paprika
⅜ teaspoon pepper
1½ teaspoons cayenne pepper
9 cloves garlic, minced

To serve this delicious dish without freezing, marinate chicken for 4 to 8 hours in the refrigerator, then roast the chicken as directed.

---

1. Place chicken pieces in 1-gallon zipper-lock bag. In medium bowl, mix remaining ingredients and pour over chicken. Seal bag, label, and freeze.

2. *To thaw and cook:* Thaw chicken and sauce overnight in refrigerator. Preheat oven to 325°F. Place chicken pieces and sauce in 9" × 13" baking pan; roast at 325°F for 60 to 75 minutes until instant-read thermometer reads 180°F. To make a sauce from the pan drippings, place pan over medium heat and add ½ cup chicken broth; bring to a boil.

Cannellini Chicken Soup

Serves 4

1 pound boned, skinned chicken thighs
1 onion, chopped
3 cloves garlic, minced
3 tablespoons olive oil
1 tablespoon butter
3 carrots, sliced
4 cups Chicken Broth (page 301)
1 teaspoon salt
⅛ teaspoon white pepper
½ teaspoon dried marjoram leaves
2 (16-ounce) cans cannellini beans
½ cup grated Parmesan cheese

This hearty soup can be served without freezing by simmering for 40 to 45 minutes, then adding drained and rinsed cannellini beans. Simmer soup for another 10 to 15 minutes, until slightly thickened.

1. Cut chicken into 1-inch pieces. Sauté chicken, onion, and garlic in olive oil and butter in large stockpot until chicken is browned and vegetables are crisp-tender. Add carrots; cook and stir 4 to 5 minutes. Add broth, salt, pepper, and marjoram and bring to a boil. Reduce heat, cover, and simmer for 30 to 35 minutes, until chicken is thoroughly cooked.

2. Chill soup in ice-water bath or refrigerator. Drain and rinse beans and add to chilled soup. Pour soup into 1-gallon zipper-lock bag and attach small bag with Parmesan cheese. Label and freeze.

3. *To thaw and reheat:* Let soup thaw overnight in refrigerator. Pour into heavy saucepan or stockpot and simmer for 10 to 15 minutes, until thoroughly heated. Serve topped with Parmesan cheese.

Serves 12

3 pounds boned, skinned chicken thighs
3 onions, chopped
9 cloves garlic, minced
9 tablespoons olive oil
3 tablespoons butter
9 carrots, sliced
12 cups Chicken Broth (page 301)
1 tablespoon salt
⅜ teaspoon white pepper
1½ teaspoons dried marjoram leaves
6 (16-ounce) cans cannellini beans
1½ cups grated Parmesan cheese

White and Green Lasagna

Serves 6

3 tablespoons olive oil
2 tablespoons butter
1 onion, chopped
¼ cup flour
½ cup Chicken Broth (page 301)
1 cup milk
1 cup shredded Monterey jack
    cheese
½ cup grated Romano cheese
3 cups cooked, cubed chicken
1 (9-ounce) package frozen
    cut-leaf spinach
2 cups ricotta cheese
1 egg
1 cup grated Parmesan cheese
1 (4-ounce) jar sliced
    mushrooms, drained
9 lasagna noodles
1 cup grated Parmesan cheese

Serves 18

9 tablespoons olive oil
6 tablespoons butter
3 onions, chopped
¾ cup flour
1½ cups Chicken Broth (page
    301)
3 cups milk
3 cups shredded Monterey
    jack cheese
1½ cups grated Romano
    cheese
9 cups cooked, cubed chicken
3 (9 ounce) packages frozen
    cut leaf spinach
6 cups ricotta cheese
3 eggs
3 cups grated Parmesan cheese
3 (4 ounce) jars sliced
    mushrooms, drained
27 lasagna noodles
3 cups grated Parmesan
    cheese

This easy lasagna doesn't use any tomato products. To serve immediately, sprinkle cheese on casserole and bake at 375°F for 20 to 30 minutes, until bubbly and cheese begins to brown.

1. In large skillet, heat olive oil and butter. Add onion; cook and stir until crisp-tender, about 4 to 5 minutes. Sprinkle flour over onion; cook and stir until bubbly. Add broth and milk; cook and stir until thickened and bubbly. Add Monterey jack cheese, Romano cheese, and cubed chicken. Mix well and set aside.

2. Thaw spinach and drain by pressing between paper towels. In large bowl, combine ricotta cheese, egg, first quantity Parmesan cheese, drained spinach, and mushrooms. Cook lasagna noodles until almost done, according to package directions. Drain well and rinse with cold water.

3. In 13" × 9" baking dish, place ½ cup chicken sauce. Top with three lasagna noodles, then with half of spinach mixture. Then top with more chicken sauce. Repeat layers, ending with chicken sauce. Chill in ice-water bath or in refrigerator, wrap, label, and attach small bag with 1 cup grated Parmesan cheese; then freeze.

4. *To thaw and reheat:* Thaw overnight in refrigerator. Preheat oven to 375°. Sprinkle lasagna with Parmesan cheese. Bake at 375°F for 30 to 40 minutes, until casserole is hot in center, cheese is brown, and sauce bubbles.

Spicy Chicken Pizza

Prebaking the pizza crust makes it stay crisp through freezing and reheating. To serve immediately, bake the pizza as soon as it is assembled at 400°F for 15 to 20 minutes.

1. Preheat oven to 400°F. Prebake pizza crust at 400°F for 10 minutes, until set. Cool on wire rack. In small bowl, combine tomato sauce, tomato paste, and crushed red pepper flakes; spread over cooled crust.

2. Top pizza with chicken and frozen onions and peppers. Drop ricotta cheese by small spoonfuls over chicken. Top with Colby-jack and Parmesan; flash freeze on baking sheet. Wrap frozen pizza in freezer wrap; seal, label, and freeze.

3. *To reheat:* Bake frozen pizza in preheated 400°F oven for 18 to 25 minutes, until thoroughly heated and cheese is melted and bubbly.

Flavorful, Economical Chicken

Chicken meat will be more tender and flavorful if cooked with the skin on and on the bone. The price per pound will also be cheaper. Remove skin and bones after cooking, and the calories will be the same as boned, skinned chicken.

Serves 6

1 12-inch round Pizza Crust (page 298)
1 (8-ounce) can tomato sauce
3 tablespoons tomato paste
¼ teaspoon crushed red pepper flakes
2 cups cooked, cubed chicken
1 cup frozen onions and peppers
½ cup ricotta cheese
2 cups shredded Colby-jack cheese
½ cup grated Parmesan cheese

Serves 18

3 12-inch round Pizza Crusts (page 298)
3 (8-ounce) cans tomato sauce
9 tablespoons tomato paste
¾ teaspoon crushed red pepper flakes
6 cups cooked, cubed chicken
3 cups frozen onions and peppers
1½ cups ricotta cheese
6 cups shredded Colby-jack cheese
1½ cups grated Parmesan cheese

Creamy Peanut Chicken

Serves 4–6

2 pounds boned, skinned
    chicken thighs
1 onion, chopped
2 tablespoons olive oil
2 cups Chicken Broth
    (page 301)
½ cup peanut butter
2 tablespoons soy sauce
½ cup evaporated milk
½ teaspoon salt
⅛ teaspoon pepper
2 tablespoons lemon juice
2 tablespoons honey
½ cup chopped peanuts

Serves 12–18

6 pounds boned, skinned
    chicken thighs
3 onions, chopped
6 tablespoons olive oil
6 cups Chicken Broth
    (page 301)
1½ cups peanut butter
6 tablespoons soy sauce
1½ cups evaporated milk
1½ teaspoons salt
⅜ teaspoon pepper
6 tablespoons lemon juice
6 tablespoons honey
1½ cups chopped peanuts

To serve without freezing, cook chicken and onion mixture in olive oil for 7 to 8 minutes. Add sauce and simmer for another 10 to 15 minutes, until chicken is thoroughly cooked.

1. Freeze chicken for 1 hour so it's easier to slice. Then cut chicken into 1-inch strips and refrigerate. In heavy skillet, sauté onion in olive oil until crisp-tender. Cool in refrigerator. When cool, place chicken strips and sautéed onion in zipper-lock bags and place in freezer.

2. In medium bowl, combine chicken broth, peanut butter, soy sauce, evaporated milk, salt, pepper, lemon juice, and honey and mix well to blend. Pour into another zipper-lock bag and attach to chicken along with small bag of chopped peanuts. Label bags and freeze.

3. *To thaw and reheat:* Thaw all bags overnight in refrigerator. Heat 2 tablespoons olive oil in heavy skillet. Add chicken mixture and cook, stirring frequently, for 7 to 8 minutes. Add sauce mixture and bring to a boil. Simmer chicken and sauce for 10 to 20 minutes, until chicken is thoroughly cooked, stirring frequently. Sprinkle dish with chopped peanuts and serve.

Chicken Pot Pie

To serve this recipe without freezing, heat chicken and vegetables in gravy until bubbly. Pour into 10-inch deep-dish pie pan. Place pastry on top, flute, and cut decorative holes. Bake at 400°F for 30 to 35 minutes, until crust is golden brown and filling is bubbly.

1. Preheat oven to 400°F. In large saucepan, melt butter; add onion, cook and stir over medium heat until crisp-tender, about 4 to 5 minutes. Add flour, salt, and pepper to saucepan. Cook and stir until bubbly, about 3 to 4 minutes. Add broth and milk and stir; cook 5 to 6 minutes, until mixture is thickened and bubbly.

2. Add thyme, chicken, and bell pepper to mixture in saucepan. Cool mixture in refrigerator until cold, and then stir in frozen vegetables and frozen potatoes. Pour gravy with chicken and vegetables into deep-dish 10-inch pie pan.

3. Roll out pastry between pieces of waxed paper into 10-inch circle. Cover pie with pastry round, crimp edges, and cut vent holes. Wrap pie, label, and freeze.

4. *To thaw and reheat:* Thaw pie overnight in refrigerator. Remove wrapping and bake at 400°F for 65 to 85 minutes, or until filling is bubbling in center and crust is golden brown. Let stand 10 minutes before serving.

¼ cup butter
¼ cup minced onion
¼ cup flour
½ teaspoon salt
⅛ teaspoon pepper
1 cup Chicken Broth (page 301)
½ cup milk
½ teaspoon dried thyme leaves
2 cups cooked, cubed chicken
1 cup chopped red bell pepper
2 cups frozen peas and carrots
1 cup frozen Southern-style hash brown potatoes
1 Pie Crust (page 299)

Serves 12–18

¾ cup butter
¾ cup minced onion
¾ cup flour
1 teaspoon salt
⅜ teaspoon pepper
3 cups Chicken Broth (page 301)
1½ cups milk
1½ teaspoons dried thyme leaves
6 cups cooked, cubed chicken
3 cups chopped red bell pepper
6 cups frozen peas and carrots
3 cups frozen Southern-style hash brown potatoes
3 Pie Crusts (page 299)

Pesto Drumsticks

Serves 4–6

---

8 chicken drumsticks
½ teaspoon salt
⅛ teaspoon pepper
¼ cup Pesto Sauce (page 296)
½ cup Chicken Broth (page 301)
2 tablespoons lemon juice

Serves 12–18

---

24 chicken drumsticks
1½ teaspoons salt
¼ teaspoon pepper
¾ cup Pesto Sauce (page 296)
1½ cups Chicken Broth (page 301)
6 tablespoons lemon juice

To serve these tender and juicy drumsticks immediately, bake as directed without freezing. Serve with mashed potatoes and cooked peas drizzled with a little melted butter.

---

1. Sprinkle drumsticks with salt and pepper. Carefully loosen skin of drumsticks and spread pesto over flesh. Smooth skin back into place. In small bowl, combine chicken broth and lemon juice. Place drumsticks in zipperlock bags and pour chicken broth and lemon juice over. Label and freeze.

2. *To thaw and reheat:* Thaw drumsticks overnight in refrigerator. Place drumsticks and sauce in 13" × 9" baking dish. Cover and bake at 350°F for 30 minutes. Uncover casserole and baste drumsticks with liquid in pan. Bake, uncovered, for 20 to 30 minutes longer, until chicken is thoroughly cooked (meat thermometer registers 180°F).

CHAPTER 8
Start with Turkey Pieces

Roasted Turkey Breast

Serves 8–10

1 (5-pound) turkey breast
2 teaspoons seasoned salt
⅛ teaspoon white pepper
1 teaspoon dried marjoram
    leaves
1 teaspoon dried thyme
    leaves
2 tablespoons butter, melted
2 tablespoons olive oil
1 cup Chicken Broth
    (page 301)

Serves 24–30

3 (5-pound) turkey breasts
6 teaspoons seasoned salt
⅜ teaspoon white pepper
1 tablespoon dried
    marjoram leaves
1 tablespoon dried thyme
    leaves
6 tablespoons butter, melted
6 tablespoons olive oil
3 cups Chicken Broth
    (page 301)

To serve immediately, roast turkey breast as directed below. Remove from oven, cover, and let stand 10 minutes before carving. Serve with pan juices.

---

1. Preheat oven to 325°F. Loosen skin from turkey breast, being careful not to tear skin. In small bowl, combine salt, pepper, marjoram, thyme, butter, and olive oil and mix well. Spread this mixture over the turkey flesh. Smooth skin back over turkey.

2. Place turkey on rack in baking pan and pour chicken broth over all. Roast at 325°F for 2½ to 3 hours, until internal temperature registers 180°F, basting occasionally with pan juices.

3. Cool turkey and juices in refrigerator until cold. Slice turkey (leaving skin on slices if desired) and place in zipper-lock bag. Pour juices over, seal bag, label, and freeze.

4. *To thaw and reheat:* Thaw overnight in refrigerator. Place turkey slices and juices in heavy skillet. Heat turkey over medium heat for 8 to 12 minutes, shaking pan occasionally, until slices are thoroughly heated and juices boil.

Turkey Cassoulet

To serve immediately, pour turkey mixture into baking dish after simmering and bake at 375°F for 15 minutes. Sprinkle with bread crumb mixture and bake 15 minutes longer.

1. Cut turkey into 1½-inch pieces. In large stockpot, cook bacon until crisp. Remove from pan and drain on paper towels. Add first quantity of olive oil to pan and cook turkey, in batches, until the cubes begin to brown. Remove from pan as they are browned.

2. Add onion and garlic to pan and cook and stir until crisp-tender. Deglaze pan by pouring in broth and scraping up drippings; then add remaining ingredients except for bread crumbs, 2 tablespoons olive oil, and Parmesan cheese. Cover pan and simmer for 20 to 25 minutes or until turkey is thoroughly cooked and vegetables are tender.

3. Cool cassoulet in ice-water bath or in refrigerator. When cold, package in rigid containers. Combine bread crumbs, olive oil, and cheese and place in small zipper-lock bag. Attach to cassoulet, label, and freeze.

4. *To thaw and reheat:* Thaw overnight in refrigerator. Preheat oven to 375°F. Place turkey mixture in 2-quart baking dish. Cover and bake at 375°F for 30 to 40 minutes or until bubbly. Uncover, sprinkle bread crumb mixture over, and bake 10 to 15 minutes longer, until topping is crisp.

Serves 8–10

2 pounds boneless, skinless turkey breast
4 slices bacon, chopped
3 tablespoons olive oil
2 onions, chopped
4 cloves garlic, chopped
1 cup Chicken Broth (page 301)
2 (16-ounce) cans cannellini beans, drained
3 carrots, sliced
2 (14-ounce) cans diced tomatoes, undrained
1 teaspoon dried thyme leaves
1 teaspoon dried marjoram leaves
⅛ teaspoon pepper
1 cup whole wheat bread crumbs
2 tablespoons olive oil
¼ cup grated Parmesan cheese

Serves 24–30

6 pounds boneless, skinless turkey breast
12 slices bacon, chopped
9 tablespoons olive oil
6 onions, chopped
12 cloves garlic, chopped
3 cups Chicken Broth (page 301)
6 (16-ounce) cans cannellini beans, drained
9 carrots, sliced
6 (14-ounce) cans diced tomatoes, undrained
1 tablespoon dried thyme leaves
1 tablespoon dried marjoram leaves
⅜ teaspoon pepper
3 cups whole wheat bread crumbs
6 tablespoons olive oil
¾ cup grated Parmesan cheese

Orange Glazed Turkey Cutlets

2 pounds turkey cutlets
1 teaspoon salt
⅛ teaspoon white pepper
2 tablespoons olive oil
2 tablespoons butter
1 cup orange juice
1 tablespoon Worcestershire
   sauce
2 tablespoons honey
1 teaspoon dried basil leaves
1 tablespoon white wine
   vinegar

Serves 18–24

6 pounds turkey cutlets
1 tablespoon salt
⅜ teaspoon white pepper
6 tablespoons olive oil
6 tablespoons butter
3 cups orange juice
3 tablespoons
   Worcestershire sauce
6 tablespoons honey
1 tablespoon dried basil
   leaves
3 tablespoons white wine
   vinegar

Turkey cutlets are also known as turkey tenders.
To serve immediately, simmer cutlets in sauce for 5 to 10 minutes, and serve over hot cooked rice or egg noodles.

---

1. Sprinkle cutlets with salt and white pepper. Heat olive oil and butter in large skillet over medium heat until foamy. Add cutlets and cook in batches, turning once, for 3 to 4 minutes per side, until turkey is thoroughly cooked. Remove cutlets as they cook.

2. To make sauce, add remaining ingredients to the pan. Cook and stir over medium heat until bubbly. Chill turkey and sauce in ice-water bath or refrigerator. Pack into zipper-lock bags, label, and freeze.

3. *To thaw and reheat:* Thaw in refrigerator overnight. Place turkey and sauce in heavy skillet. Cook over medium heat, stirring occasionally, about 8 to 9 minutes or until cutlets are hot and sauce bubbles.

Turkey Meatloaf

This tender loaf is full of flavor. To serve without freezing,
let fully cooked meatloaf stand, covered, 10 minutes before slicing.

1. Preheat oven to 350°F. In heavy skillet, cook onions, mushrooms, and garlic in olive oil until vegetables are tender. Remove from heat and set aside.

2. In large bowl, combine bread crumbs, milk, egg, salt, pepper, and marjoram and mix well. Add sautéed vegetable mixture and stir to blend. Add ground turkey and mix gently with hands. Form mixture into oblong loaf and place on baking pan. Bake at 350°F for 50 to 60 minutes, until instant-read thermometer measures 170°F. Cool meatloaf in refrigerator; then wrap, label, and freeze.

3. *To thaw and reheat:* Thaw meatloaf overnight in refrigerator. It can be served cold at this point, or to reheat, place meatloaf on baking pan and brush with chicken broth. Bake at 350°F for 20 to 35 minutes, until thoroughly heated.

How Big Is Your Freezer?

Check the cubic-foot capacity of your freezer and write it down in your freezer notebook. Don't add more than two pounds of food per cubic foot each cooking-and-freezing session. This means that if your freezer has a twenty cubic-foot capacity; add a maximum of forty pounds of food at one time.

Serves 6

1 onion, chopped
2 cups mushrooms, finely chopped
3 cloves garlic, minced
2 tablespoons olive oil
½ cup dry bread crumbs
¼ cup evaporated milk
1 egg
1 teaspoon salt
⅛ teaspoon white pepper
½ teaspoon dried marjoram leaves
2 pounds ground turkey

Serves 18

3 onions, chopped
6 cups mushrooms, finely chopped
9 cloves garlic, minced
6 tablespoons olive oil
1½ cups dry bread crumbs
¾ cup evaporated milk
3 eggs
1 tablespoon salt
⅜ teaspoon white pepper
1½ teaspoons dried marjoram leaves
6 pounds ground turkey

Curried Turkey Casserole

Serves 4–6

2 turkey tenderloins
1 tablespoon curry powder
¼ cup flour
1 teaspoon salt
2 tablespoons olive oil
1½ cups apple juice
1 tablespoon grated
    gingerroot
½ cup sour cream
2 cups Chicken Broth
    (page 301)
⅛ teaspoon saffron
1 cup long-grain rice
3 carrots, sliced

Serves 12–18

6 turkey tenderloins
3 tablespoons curry powder
¾ cup flour
1 tablespoon salt
6 tablespoons olive oil
4½ cups apple juice
3 tablespoons grated
    gingerroot
1½ cups sour cream
6 cups Chicken Broth
    (page 301)
⅜ teaspoon saffron
3 cups long-grain rice
9 carrots, sliced

To serve without freezing, when casserole is assembled, bake at 375°F for 20 to 30 minutes, until thoroughly heated.

1. Cut turkey into 1-inch cubes. On shallow plate, combine curry powder, flour, and salt and mix well. Add turkey cubes and toss to coat well. Heat olive oil in heavy skillet and add coated turkey in batches. Cook and stir turkey until browned, about 4 to 5 minutes. Add apple juice and gingerroot to turkey and simmer 20 minutes. Add sour cream and remove from heat.

2. In saucepan, bring chicken broth and saffron to a boil. Add rice, cover, reduce heat, and simmer for 15 minutes or until almost tender. Add rice to turkey mixture; then add carrots. Place in 2-quart casserole dish, wrap, seal, label, and freeze.

3. *To thaw and reheat:* Thaw casserole overnight in refrigerator. Bake in preheated 375°F oven for 30 to 35 minutes or until thoroughly heated.

Glazed Turkey Breast

To serve without freezing, roast turkey as directed.
When internal temperature reaches 180°F, let turkey stand, covered,
for 10 minutes before slicing. Serve with cooked rice.

1. Preheat oven to 325°F. Loosen skin from turkey breast. In small bowl, combine all remaining ingredients. Brush some of this mixture on the flesh under the skin. Gently smooth skin back into place and brush entire turkey breast with this mixture.

2. Coat roasting pan with nonstick cooking spray. Place breast in roasting pan, skin-side down, and pour half of sauce over. Roast at 325°F for 1 hour. Turn turkey over and cover with remaining sauce. Continue roasting for 60 to 90 minutes, basting occasionally with pan juices, until turkey registers 180°F on instant-read thermometer. Cool turkey in refrigerator and slice. Place slices in zipper-lock bags and pour pan juices over turkey; freeze.

3. *To thaw and reheat:* Thaw overnight in refrigerator. Place turkey slices and pan juices in heavy skillet. Heat turkey over medium heat for 8 to 12 minutes, shaking pan occasionally, until slices are thoroughly heated and juices boil.

Serves 6–8

1 (5-pound) boneless
  turkey breast
1 teaspoon salt
⅛ teaspoon white pepper
⅓ cup honey
1 cup orange juice
3 tablespoons lime juice
2 teaspoons dried basil

Serves 18–24

3 (5-pound) boneless turkey
  breasts
1 tablespoon salt
⅜ teaspoon white pepper
1 cup honey
3 cups orange juice
9 tablespoons lime juice
2 tablespoons dried basil

Turkey Pot Pie

Serves 6–8

1 onion, chopped
1 leek, chopped
2 tablespoons butter
2 tablespoons olive oil
¼ cup flour
1 teaspoon salt
⅛ teaspoon pepper
1 teaspoon dried thyme
 leaves
1 cup Chicken Broth
 (page 301)
1 cup evaporated milk
½ cup grated Parmesan
 cheese
2 cups cubed, cooked turkey
1 cup frozen mixed
 vegetables
1 sheet frozen puff pastry
1 egg

Serves 18–24

3 onions, chopped
3 leeks, chopped
6 tablespoons butter
6 tablespoons olive oil
¾ cup flour
1 tablespoon salt
⅜ teaspoon pepper
1 tablespoon dried thyme
 leaves
3 cups Chicken Broth
 (page 301)
3 cups evaporated milk
1½ cups grated Parmesan
 cheese
6 cups cubed, cooked turkey
3 cups frozen mixed
 vegetables
3 sheets frozen puff pastry
3 eggs

To serve without freezing, do not cool sauce. Add cheese, turkey, and vegetables and pour into pie pan. Add pastry and bake as directed.

1. In heavy skillet, sauté onion and leek in butter and olive oil over medium heat until crisp-tender. Sprinkle with flour, salt, pepper, and thyme. Cook and stir until mixture bubbles, 3 to 4 minutes. Add broth and evaporated milk; cook and stir until sauce thickens. Remove from heat and stir in Parmesan cheese.

2. Cool sauce in ice-water bath or refrigerator. Stir in cooked turkey and frozen vegetables. Pour into lined 9-inch deep-dish pie pan, wrap, seal, and attach wrapped puff pastry; freeze. Reserve egg in refrigerator.

3. *To thaw and reheat:* Thaw pie and pastry overnight in refrigerator. Preheat oven to 400°F. Cut 10-inch circle from puff pastry and place over turkey mixture in pie plate. Seal edges, brush with beaten egg, and bake pie at 400°F for 50 to 60 minutes, until filling bubbles in center and crust is golden brown.

Turkey Tenderloins
with Blueberry Compote

Tender turkey slices are deliciously contrasted with
cold spicy-fruity compote. To serve immediately, marinate turkey
in refrigerator for 2 hours; cook as directed.

1. In small bowl, combine salt, pepper, vinegar, honey, and olive oil. Rub over turkey tenderloins. Place tenderloins in zipper-lock bag and freeze.

2. To make compote, in medium saucepan, combine remaining ingredients. Bring to a boil, reduce heat, and simmer for 5 to 8 minutes until mixture thickens slightly. Cool in ice-water bath or refrigerator, pour into zipper-lock bag, attach to turkey tenderloins, label, and freeze.

3. *To thaw and reheat:* Thaw turkey and compote overnight in refrigerator. Heat 2 more tablespoons olive oil in heavy ovenproof skillet. Brown tenderloins on all sides in hot oil. Place skillet in preheated 400° oven for 25 to 30 minutes, turning turkey once, or until internal temperature registers 170°F. Let stand 10 minutes, then slice and serve with cold compote.

Serves 6

1 teaspoon salt
⅛ teaspoon white pepper
1 tablespoon white wine
   vinegar
1 tablespoon honey
1 tablespoon olive oil
2 turkey tenderloins
2 cups frozen blueberries
¼ cup minced onion
2 cloves garlic, minced
¼ cup orange juice
¼ teaspoons cinnamon
2 tablespoons sugar

Serves 18

1 tablespoon salt
⅜ teaspoon white pepper
3 tablespoons white wine
   vinegar
3 tablespoons honey
3 tablespoons plus
   2 tablespoons olive oil
6 turkey tenderloins
6 cups frozen blueberries
¾ cup minced onion
6 cloves garlic, minced
¾ cup orange juice
¾ teaspoon cinnamon
6 tablespoons sugar

Turkey Spinach Crepes

Serves 6

1 onion, chopped
1 tablespoon olive oil
1 cup frozen cut-leaf spinach
2 strips sun-dried tomatoes
    in oil
½ cup ricotta cheese
1 cup shredded Havarti
    cheese
2 cups cooked, cubed turkey
½ teaspoons dried oregano
    leaves
12 Basic Crepes (page 300)
1 (16-ounce) jar Alfredo
    sauce
½ cup evaporated milk

Serves 18

3 onions, chopped
3 tablespoons olive oil
3 cups frozen cut-leaf
    spinach
6 strips sun-dried tomatoes
    in oil
1½ cups ricotta cheese
3 cups shredded Havarti
    cheese
6 cups cooked, cubed turkey
1½ teaspoons dried oregano
    leaves
36 Basic Crepes (page 300)
3 (16-ounce) jars Alfredo
    sauce
1½ cups evaporated milk

These elegant crepes are perfect for company. To serve without freezing, place in preheated 400°F oven for 55 to 60 minutes, until filling bubbles and crepes begin to brown.

1. In skillet, sauté onion in olive oil until crisp-tender. Add spinach; cook and stir until spinach is thawed and liquid evaporates, about 5 to 6 minutes. Remove from heat and cool completely.

2. Drain sun-dried tomatoes and mince. In large bowl, mix tomatoes with cheeses, turkey, oregano, and cooled spinach mixture.

3. Place crepes, browned-side down, on work surface. Divide turkey mixture evenly among crepes. Roll up crepes and place in 13" × 9" baking dish. Mix Alfredo sauce and evaporated milk and pour over casserole, and then wrap, label, and freeze.

4. *To reheat:* Bake casserole from frozen in preheated 400°F oven for 60 to 80 minutes, until sauce bubbles and tops of crepes brown.

Turkey Meatballs and Couscous

These tender meatballs are low in fat and very delicious.
To serve immediately, combine hot meatballs with sauce and place in casserole. Bake at 350°F for 20 to 25 minutes, until bubbly.

1. In large bowl, combine turkey, bread crumbs, garlic powder, salt, thyme, egg, and evaporated milk and mix to blend. Form into about 24 (or 72) meatballs.

2. Heat olive oil and butter in large skillet and cook meatballs in batches, removing to plate as they brown. Drain off excess fat, and then add chicken broth, return meatballs to skillet, cover, and simmer for 15 minutes or until meatballs are thoroughly cooked.

3. Cool meatballs in refrigerator. When cold, combine with Alfredo sauce, evaporated milk, and Swiss cheese in 2-quart casserole. Wrap casserole, seal, label, and freeze. Reserve couscous in pantry.

4. *To thaw and reheat:* Thaw casserole overnight in refrigerator. Bake at 350°F for 30 to 40 minutes, until casserole is bubbly and thoroughly heated. Cook couscous according to package directions and serve with casserole.

Serves 4–6

1 pound ground turkey
½ cup soft bread crumbs
¼ teaspoon garlic powder
½ teaspoon salt
½ teaspoon dried thyme
  leaves
1 egg
¼ cup evaporated milk
2 tablespoons olive oil
1 tablespoon butter
½ cup Chicken Broth
  (page 301)
1 (16-ounce) jar Alfredo
  sauce
½ cup evaporated milk
1 cup grated Swiss cheese
1 (6-ounce) package
  couscous

Serves 12–18

3 pounds ground turkey
1½ cups soft bread crumbs
¾ teaspoon garlic powder
1½ teaspoons salt
1½ teaspoons dried thyme
  leaves
3 eggs
¾ cup evaporated milk
6 tablespoons olive oil
3 tablespoons butter
1½ cups Chicken Broth
  (page 301)
3 (16-ounce) jars Alfredo
  sauce
1½ cups evaporated milk
3 cups grated Swiss cheese
3 (6-ounce) packages
  couscous

Veggie Turkey Pizza

Serves 4

1 cup ricotta cheese
½ cup grated Parmesan cheese
1 teaspoon dried basil leaves
1 prebaked Pizza Crust (page 298)
2 cups cooked, cubed turkey
2 cups frozen peppers and onions
1 cup shredded mozzarella cheese
1 cup shredded Monterey jack cheese

Serves 12

3 cups ricotta cheese
1½ cups grated Parmesan cheese
1 tablespoon dried basil leaves
3 prebaked Pizza Crusts (page 298)
6 cups cooked, cubed turkey
6 cups frozen peppers and onions
3 cups shredded mozzarella cheese
3 cups shredded Monterey jack cheese

To serve without freezing, sprinkle cheeses over pizza and bake as directed until crust is crisp and cheeses are melted.

1. In small bowl, combine ricotta, Parmesan, and basil. Spread over pizza crust and top with turkey and frozen peppers and onions. Sprinkle with mozzarella and jack cheeses. Wrap pizza in freezer wrap, label, and freeze.

2. *To cook*: Preheat oven to 400°F. Place frozen pizza on baking sheet and bake at 400°F for 18 to 25 minutes or until pizza is hot, crust is crisp, and cheeses are melted and beginning to brown.

Turkey Spinach Casserole

Serves 4–6

1 onion, chopped
1 cup sliced carrots
2 tablespoons olive oil
2 cups cooked, cubed turkey
1 (14-ounce) jar pasta sauce
2 cups frozen cut-leaf spinach, thawed
1 cup ricotta cheese
1 egg
1 cup grated mozzarella cheese
1 cup grated Parmesan cheese
¼ cup dried Italian bread crumbs

Serves 12–18

3 onions, chopped
3 cups sliced carrots
6 tablespoons olive oil
6 cups cooked, cubed turkey
3 (14-ounce) jars pasta sauce
6 cups frozen cut-leaf spinach, thawed
3 cups ricotta cheese
3 eggs
3 cups grated mozzarella cheese
3 cups grated Parmesan cheese
¾ cup dried Italian bread crumbs

To serve this casserole without freezing, combine Parmesan cheese and bread crumbs and sprinkle over turkey mixture. Bake at 375°F for 20 to 25 minutes, until casserole bubbles and cheese browns.

1. In heavy skillet, sauté onion, and carrots in olive oil until crisp-tender. Add turkey and pasta sauce and simmer for 5 minutes.

2. Meanwhile, thoroughly drain spinach and combine with ricotta, egg, and mozzarella. Place spinach mixture in 2-quart casserole and top with turkey mixture. Cool in ice-water bath or refrigerator; then wrap, label, attach small bag with Parmesan cheese and bread crumbs, and freeze.

3. *To thaw and reheat:* Thaw casserole overnight in refrigerator. Sprinkle with Parmesan cheese and bread crumb mixture and bake in preheated 375°F oven for 30 to 40 minutes, until bubbly and thoroughly heated.

Apricot Turkey Steaks

The apricot sauce is delicious served over hot noodles or rice.
To serve without freezing, add apricot preserves to skillet during last
3 to 4 minutes of cooking time and simmer until steaks are glazed.

1. Lightly pound turkey steaks to flatten slightly. On shallow plate, combine flour, salt, and cumin and coat turkey steaks with mixture on both sides. Heat olive oil in heavy skillet and cook steaks in batches until browned on both sides, about 4 to 5 minutes per batch. Remove steaks as they are browned.

2. Return steaks to skillet and add apricot nectar and chopped dried apricots. Bring to a boil, reduce heat, and simmer for 8 to 12 minutes, until turkey is thoroughly cooked. Cool in ice-water bath or refrigerator; then pour into zipper-lock bag. Attach small bag with apricot preserves, label bags, and freeze.

3. *To thaw and reheat:* Thaw overnight in refrigerator. Place steaks, sauce, and apricot preserves in heavy skillet. Bring to a simmer over medium heat and cook until steaks are thoroughly heated and glazed, about 8 to 10 minutes.

Serves 4

4 turkey steaks
3 tablespoons flour
½ teaspoon salt
½ teaspoon cumin
3 tablespoons olive oil
1 cup apricot nectar
½ cup chopped dried
   apricots
¼ cup apricot preserves

Serves 12

12 turkey steaks
9 tablespoons flour
1½ teaspoons salt
1½ teaspoons cumin
9 tablespoons olive oil
3 cups apricot nectar
1½ cups chopped dried
   apricots
¾ cup apricot preserves

Spicy Turkey Meatballs

Serves 4

---

1 pound ground turkey
1 egg
½ cup minced onion
1 jalapeno pepper, minced
¼ cup tomato juice
½ cup dried bread crumbs
½ teaspoon salt
⅛ teaspoon crushed red
    pepper flakes
2 tablespoons olive oil
4 cloves garlic, minced
2 cups Chicken Broth
    (page 301)
1 (10-ounce) jar Alfredo
    sauce
1 cup shredded pepper jack
    cheese

Serves 12

---

3 pounds ground turkey
3 eggs
1½ cups minced onion
3 jalapeno peppers, minced
¾ cup tomato juice
1½ cups dried bread crumbs
1½ teaspoons salt
⅜ teaspoon crushed red
    pepper flakes
6 tablespoons olive oil
12 cloves garlic, minced
6 cups Chicken Broth
    (page 301)
3 (10-ounce) jars Alfredo
    sauce
3 cups shredded pepper jack
    cheese

Try an exotic rice with these spicy meatballs; basmati or jasmine would be wonderful. To serve immediately, simply serve meatballs and sauce when meat is thoroughly cooked.

---

1. In large bowl, combine turkey, egg, onion, jalapeno pepper, tomato juice, bread crumbs, salt, and red pepper flakes and blend well. Form into 24 (or 72) meatballs. Heat olive oil in large skillet and brown meatballs, in batches, on all sides, about 4 to 5 minutes per batch.

2. Drain excess fat from skillet and add garlic. Cook and stir for 1 to 2 minutes. Return meatballs to skillet along with chicken broth. Bring to a boil, reduce heat, cover pan, and simmer meatballs for 15 to 20 minutes until thoroughly cooked. Stir Alfredo sauce and cheese into skillet and simmer 1 to 2 minutes to blend flavors. Cool in ice-water bath or refrigerator. Pack into zipper-lock bags, label, seal, and freeze.

3. *To thaw and reheat:* Thaw meatballs and sauce overnight in refrigerator. Place in heavy skillet and add ¼ cup water if mixture looks dry. Bring to a boil and simmer for 10 to 15 minutes, until meatballs are thoroughly heated.

Italian Turkey Sauce

You can use ground turkey breast or a combination of dark and light meat in this easy sauce. To serve immediately, cook spaghetti as directed on package and serve sauce over pasta.

1. In heavy skillet, sauté turkey, onion, and mushrooms in olive oil until turkey is browned, stirring to break up meat. Drain if necessary; then add remaining ingredients except cheese and pasta. Simmer for 5 to 8 minutes, until turkey is thoroughly cooked and flavors are blended.

2. Cool sauce in ice-water bath or in refrigerator. Pack into zipper-lock bags and attach small bag with Parmesan cheese; label, seal, and freeze. Reserve pasta in pantry.

3. *To thaw and reheat:* Thaw sauce overnight in refrigerator. Pour into heavy skillet and bring to a boil. Reduce heat and simmer for 8 to 10 minutes, until thoroughly heated. Cook spaghetti according to package directions, drain, and serve sauce over pasta. Sprinkle each serving with cheese.

Quick Lid Solution

If you have more pots and pans than you do lids, you can use heavy duty aluminum foil as a temporary lid. Simply tear off a piece of foil slightly larger than the diameter of the pot, and loosely crimp the foil around the top of the pot.

Serves 4

1 pound ground turkey
1 onion, chopped
2 cups mushrooms, chopped
2 tablespoons olive oil
½ teaspoon salt
1 teaspoon Italian seasoning
1 (14-ounce) jar pasta sauce
1 (14-ounce) can diced
    tomatoes, undrained
1 cup grated Parmesan
    cheese
1 (8-ounce) package
    spaghetti

Serves 12

3 pounds ground turkey
3 onions, chopped
6 cups mushrooms, chopped
6 tablespoons olive oil
1½ teaspoons salt
1 tablespoon Italian
    seasoning
3 (14-ounce) jars pasta sauce
3 (14-ounce) cans diced
    tomatoes, undrained
3 cups grated Parmesan
    cheese
3 (8-ounce) packages
    spaghetti

Stuffed Turkey Tenderloins

Serves 4

---

2 turkey tenderloins
1 teaspoon salt
⅛ teaspoon white pepper
½ cup golden raisins
½ cup dried fruit bits
1 (3-ounce) package cream
    cheese
2 tablespoons honey
    mustard
1 tablespoon honey
1 cup dried bread crumbs

Serves 12

---

6 turkey tenderloins
1 tablespoon salt
⅜ teaspoon white pepper
1½ cups golden raisins
1½ cups dried fruit bits
3 (3-ounce) packages cream
    cheese
6 tablespoons honey
    mustard
3 tablespoons honey
3 cups dried bread crumbs

The unusual sweet and spicy filling that stuffs these tenderloins is delicious. To serve without freezing, just serve the rolls after they are thoroughly cooked.

---

1. Cut turkey tenderloins in half crosswise to make four pieces. Cut slit in side of each piece and spread turkey pieces open. Sprinkle with salt and pepper. In small bowl, combine raisins, dried fruit, cream cheese, and honey mustard and mix well. Divide this mixture among turkey pieces and fold to enclose filling. Use toothpicks to secure edges.

2. Preheat oven to 400°F. Coat tenderloins with honey and roll in bread crumbs. Place in 9" × 13" baking pan and bake at 350°F for 40 to 45 minutes, turning once, until internal temperature registers 170°F. Cool rolls in refrigerator, then wrap individually in freezer wrap and place in zipper-lock bags. Label, seal, and freeze.

3. *To thaw and reheat:* Thaw overnight in refrigerator. Preheat oven to 400°F. Place turkey rolls in 9" × 13" baking pan and bake at 400°F for 18 to 25 minutes or until thoroughly heated and bread crumb coating is crisp.

CHAPTER 9
Start with Pork and Sausage

Tex Mex Pork Casserole

Serves 6–8

---

2 pounds boneless pork
    chops
1 cup Beef Broth (page 302)
¼ cup red wine vinegar
½ cup red wine
2 cloves garlic, minced
1 jalapeno pepper, minced
2 tablespoons honey
 ⅛ teaspoon pepper
2 tablespoons olive oil
1 tablespoon butter
1 onion, chopped
½ cup Beef Broth
½ cup taco sauce
2 (16-ounce) cans kidney
    beans

Serves 18–24

---

6 pounds boneless pork
    chops
3 cups Beef Broth (page 302)
¾ cup red wine vinegar
1½ cups red wine
6 cloves garlic, minced
3 jalapeno peppers, minced
6 tablespoons honey
 ⅜ teaspoon pepper
6 tablespoons olive oil
3 tablespoons butter
3 onions, chopped
1½ cups Beef Broth
1½ cups taco sauce
6 (16-ounce) cans kidney
    beans

To serve without freezing, add kidney beans to casserole after 90 minutes of cooking. Simmer another 20 to 30 minutes, until sauce is thickened.

---

1. Cut pork chops into 1-inch cubes. In large bowl, combine first quantity of broth, vinegar, red wine, garlic, peppers, honey, and pepper. Add pork cubes to this mixture, cover, and refrigerate overnight.

2. Drain pork, reserving marinade. Pat pork dry with paper towels. Heat olive oil and butter in heavy skillet and add pork in batches. Cook, stirring frequently, for 4 minutes per batch, removing pork from the pan as it browns. When all pork is browned, return to skillet along with reserved marinade and onion, beef broth, and taco sauce. Bring to a boil, cover pan, reduce heat, and simmer mixture for 1½ hours until pork is tender. Cool mixture in ice-water bath or in refrigerator. Pour mixture into zipper-lock bags, label, and freeze. Reserve kidney beans in pantry.

3. *To thaw and reheat:* Thaw overnight in refrigerator. Pour mixture into heavy skillet and bring to a boil. Drain kidney beans, rinse, drain again, and add to skillet. Reduce heat, cover, and simmer casserole for 15 to 20 minutes, until thoroughly heated.

Citrus Pork Stew

To serve without freezing, serve stew after
pork is thoroughly cooked.

1. Trim excess fat from pork and cut into 1-inch cubes. On shallow plate, combine salt, pepper, orange rind, and flour. Toss pork in this mixture to coat. In heavy skillet, heat olive oil and butter. Add coated pork cubes in batches, and cook until browned, stirring occasionally. Remove pork from pan as it browns.

2. Add onion to pan and cook until crisp-tender, 3 to 4 minutes. Return pork to pan along with all remaining ingredients. Bring to a boil; then reduce heat, cover pan, and simmer stew for 1½ hours, until pork is thoroughly cooked. Cool stew in ice-water bath or in refrigerator. Pour into rigid containers, label, seal, and freeze.

3. *To thaw and reheat:* Thaw stew overnight in refrigerator. Pour into large saucepan and bring to a boil. Simmer over medium-low heat for 15 to 20 minutes, until thoroughly heated.

Is Preheating Necessary?

Always preheat your oven for ten minutes when cooking foods for less than one hour. If the cooking time is one hour or longer, preheating isn't necessary.

Serves 6–8

2 pounds boneless pork
   shoulder
1 teaspoon salt
⅛ teaspoon white pepper
1 teaspoon grated orange
   rind
¼ cup flour
¼ cup olive oil
3 tablespoons butter
1 onion, chopped
5 cups Chicken Broth
   (page 301)
1 cup orange juice
1 cup white wine
1 (9-ounce) bag baby
   carrots
1 cup chopped fennel

Serves 18–24

6 pounds boneless pork
   shoulder
1 tablespoon salt
⅜ teaspoon white pepper
1 tablespoon grated orange
   rind
¾ cup flour
¾ cup olive oil
9 tablespoons butter
3 onions, chopped
15 cups Chicken Broth
   (page 301)
3 cups orange juice
3 cups white wine
3 (9-ounce) bags baby
   carrots
3 cups chopped fennel

Pork and Tomato Farfalle

Serves 6

1 pound pork tenderloin
½ teaspoon salt
⅛ teaspoon pepper
4 cloves garlic, minced
2 tablespoons olive oil
1 onion, chopped
1 (14-ounce) can diced
    tomatoes, undrained
1 (8-ounce) can tomato
    paste
2 tablespoons sugar
½ teaspoon dried basil
    leaves
½ teaspoon dried thyme
    leaves
3 cups farfalle pasta
½ cup evaporated milk

Serves 18

3 pounds pork tenderloin
1½ teaspoons salt
⅜ teaspoon pepper
12 cloves garlic, minced
6 tablespoons olive oil
3 onions, chopped
3 (14-ounce) cans diced
    tomatoes, undrained
3 (8-ounce) cans tomato
    paste
6 tablespoons sugar
1½ teaspoons dried basil
    leaves
1½ teaspoons dried thyme
    leaves
9 cups farfalle pasta
1½ cups evaporated milk

To serve without freezing, marinate pork in the refrigerator for 2 hours. Cook sauce as directed and let simmer while sautéing pork slices. Pour sauce over pork and simmer for 10 minutes; then add milk.

1. Slice pork tenderloin crosswise into ¼-inch slices. In small bowl, combine salt, pepper, and garlic. Using back of spoon, crush garlic into spices until a paste forms. Rub this paste on the pork tenderloin slices. Place pork in zipper-lock bag and set in refrigerator.

2. In heavy skillet, heat olive oil and cook onion until crisp-tender. Add undrained tomatoes, tomato paste, sugar, basil, and thyme. Bring to a boil, reduce heat, cover pan, and simmer for 15 minutes to blend flavors. Cool sauce in ice-water bath or refrigerator. Pour into zipper-lock bag, attach to pork bag, label, and freeze. Reserve pasta and evaporated milk in pantry.

3. *To thaw and reheat:* Thaw pork and sauce overnight in refrigerator. Heat 1 tablespoon olive oil in large skillet. Add pork slices and cook, turning once, until pork is browned, about 5 minutes. Add tomato sauce to pan and bring to a boil. Simmer, covered, for 15 to 20 minutes, until pork is tender, then add evaporated milk and simmer 3 minutes longer. Cook pasta as directed on package, drain, and serve with pork.

Pineapple Pork Chops

To serve without freezing, marinate chops in refrigerator for 4 to 8 hours, then cook as directed below. Be sure to boil marinade before serving.

1. Trim excess fat from pork chops and sprinkle with salt and pepper. Combine all remaining ingredients in large zipper-lock bag and add pork chops. Seal bag and knead to distribute sauce. Label bag and freeze.

2. *To thaw and cook:* Thaw overnight in refrigerator. Remove chops from marinade and broil or grill 4 to 6 inches from heat source for 12 to 15 minutes, until pork chops are no longer pink in center. Place marinade in small saucepan and bring to a boil. Boil for 3 minutes, stirring frequently. Serve marinade with chops.

Serves 6

6 (¾-inch-thick) boneless
   pork chops
1 teaspoon salt
⅛ teaspoon white pepper
2 cloves garlic, chopped
1 (8-ounce) can pineapple
   tidbits, undrained
1 tablespoon honey
2 teaspoons grated gingerroot
½ cup pineapple preserves

Serves 18

18 (¾-inch-thick) boneless
   pork chops
1 tablespoon salt
⅜ teaspoon white pepper
6 cloves garlic, chopped
3 (8-ounce) cans pineapple
   tidbits, undrained
3 tablespoons honey
2 tablespoons grated gingerroot
1½ cups pineapple preserves

Honey Mustard Pork Chops

These easy pork chops are packed full of flavor.
To serve without freezing, marinate pork chops in refrigerator
for 4 to 8 hours, then broil as directed.

1. In zipper-lock bag, combine all ingredients except pork chops and squish bag to mix. Add pork chops, seal bag, label, and freeze.

2. *To thaw and reheat:* Thaw overnight in refrigerator. Broil pork chops 4 to 6 inches from heat source for 18 to 20 minutes, turning once, until internal temperature registers 160°F. Discard any remaining marinade.

Serves 6

¼ cup mustard
¼ cup honey
2 tablespoons apple cider
   vinegar
⅛ teaspoon pepper
¼ teaspoon garlic powder
½ teaspoon dried thyme
½ teaspoon dried marjoram
6 boneless pork loin chops

Serves 18

¾ cup mustard
¾ cup honey
6 tablespoons apple cider
   vinegar
⅜ teaspoon pepper
¾ teaspoon garlic powder
1½ teaspoons dried thyme
1½ teaspoons dried marjoram
18 boneless pork loin chops

Apple Glazed Pork Roast

Serves 6–8

1 (3-pound) boneless pork
   sirloin roast
1 teaspoon salt
⅛ teaspoon pepper
2 tablespoons olive oil
3 cloves garlic, minced
1 cup apple cider
½ cup apple jelly
2 tablespoons apple cider
   vinegar
2 tablespoons brown sugar

Serves 18–24

3 (3-pound) boneless pork
   sirloin roasts
1 tablespoon salt
⅜ teaspoon pepper
6 tablespoons olive oil
9 cloves garlic, minced
3 cups apple cider
1½ cups apple jelly
6 tablespoons apple cider
   vinegar
6 tablespoons brown sugar

To serve without freezing, when pork reaches 160°F,
remove from oven, cover with foil, and let stand for 10 minutes.
Thinly slice and serve with sauce.

1. Preheat oven to 400°F. Trim excess fat from roast. Sprinkle on all sides with salt and pepper. In heavy skillet, brown roast on all sides in olive oil over medium heat. Remove pork from pan and add remaining ingredients to skillet. Cook and stir over medium heat until sugar dissolves and mixture comes to a boil.

2. Place pork in roasting pan and roast at 400°F for 30 minutes. Then pour apple cider mixture over all and roast 35 to 45 minutes longer, basting occasionally with sauce, until instant-read thermometer measures 160°F. Cool pork and sauce in refrigerator. Thinly slice pork and place in zipper-lock bag along with sauce. Seal bag, label, and freeze.

3. *To thaw and reheat:* Thaw overnight in refrigerator. Place pork and sauce in heavy skillet and bring to a simmer over medium heat. Cook for 4 to 5 minutes, until pork is thoroughly heated.

BBQ Ribs

Experience a new variation on your favorite homemade or store-bought barbecue sauce in this recipe. To serve immediately, cook ribs as directed, basting frequently with sauce, until they are very tender.

1. Preheat oven to 400°F. Sprinkle ribs with salt and pepper and place in baking pan. Roast ribs, uncovered, for 1 hour.

2. While ribs are roasting, in heavy skillet, sauté onion and garlic in olive oil until tender. Add remaining ingredients and bring to a boil. Reduce heat and simmer for 15 to 20 minutes, stirring frequently, until slightly thickened.

3. After ribs are roasted, drain fat from pan. Pour sauce over ribs. Reduce oven temperature to 350°F and roast ribs for another 80 to 95 minutes, basting occasionally with sauce, until ribs are very tender. Cool ribs in refrigerator. Pack into zipper-lock bags with sauce, label packages, and freeze.

4. *To thaw and reheat:* Thaw ribs overnight in refrigerator. Place ribs on baking pan and cover with sauce. Bake at 350°F for 20 to 25 minutes, until ribs are glazed and thoroughly heated.

Serves 4

4 pounds meaty pork short ribs
1 teaspoon salt
⅛ teaspoon pepper
1 onion, chopped
5 cloves garlic, chopped
2 tablespoons olive oil
½ cup honey
½ cup barbecue sauce
1 tablespoon mustard
1 cup Beef Broth (page 302)

Serves 12

12 pounds meaty pork short ribs
1 tablespoon salt
⅜ teaspoon pepper
3 onions, chopped
15 cloves garlic, chopped
6 tablespoons olive oil
1½ cups honey
1½ cups barbecue sauce
3 tablespoons mustard
3 cups Beef Broth (page 302)

Pork Medallions in Lemon Sauce

Serves 4–6

2 (¾ pound) pork
  tenderloins
1 teaspoon salt
⅛ teaspoon white pepper
3 tablespoons flour
1 teaspoon grated lemon
  peel
1 cup Chicken Broth
  (page 301)
½ cup white wine
¼ cup lemon juice
2 tablespoons sugar
1 tablespoon cornstarch
1 teaspoon dried thyme
  leaves
2 tablespoons olive oil

Serves 12–18

6 (¾ pound) pork
  tenderloins
1 tablespoon salt
⅜ teaspoon white pepper
9 tablespoons flour
1 tablespoon grated lemon
  peel
3 cups Chicken Broth
  (page 301)
1½ cups white wine
¾ cup lemon juice
6 tablespoons sugar
3 tablespoons cornstarch
1 tablespoon dried thyme
  leaves
6 tablespoons olive oil

This fresh lemon sauce complements the rich pork meat perfectly. To serve without freezing, dredge pork in flour mixture, cook in olive oil, then finish cooking in the lemon sauce.

1. Trim excess fat from tenderloins and cut each into 8 slices. Place pork between two sheets of waxed paper and gently flatten with rolling pin or meat mallet. Place pork into zipper-lock bag, with waxed paper separating each piece, and freeze. Combine salt, pepper, flour, and lemon peel in small bag, attach to pork, and freeze.

2. In heavy skillet, combine remaining ingredients except olive oil and bring to a boil. Simmer for 5 to 6 minutes, then cool in ice-water bath or refrigerator. Pour into third zipper-lock bag. Attach all bags together, label, and freeze. Reserve olive oil in pantry.

3. *To thaw and cook:* Thaw all bags overnight in refrigerator. Dredge pork medallions in flour mixture. Heat 2 tablespoons olive oil in heavy skillet and cook pork, in batches, 2 to 3 minutes per side over medium heat until browned. Remove pork from skillet as it cooks. To drippings remaining in pan, add lemon sauce and bring to a simmer, stirring frequently. Return pork to skillet and simmer for 3 to 4 minutes, until pork is thoroughly cooked.

Pork with Onion Conserve

Onion conserve is a rich mixture made of fruit juices and onions. To serve without freezing, when pork is done, let stand, covered with foil, for 10 minutes before slicing.

1. Preheat oven to 325°F. Sprinkle tenderloin with salt, pepper, and dried herbs. Heat olive oil in heavy skillet and brown tenderloin on all sides over medium high heat, about 4 to 5 minutes. Place tenderloin on baking pan, cover with foil, and bake at 325°F for 20 minutes. Uncover pan and roast 45–70 minutes longer or until internal temperature registers 160°F.

2. Meanwhile, mix raisins with orange juice and set aside. Melt butter in skillet used to brown pork and cook onions until tender. Add sugar, stir, and cook 4 minutes longer. Add raisin mixture and bring to a boil. Reduce heat and simmer until mixture is thickened and liquid is syrupy, about 10 to 15 minutes.

3. Cool pork in refrigerator. Slice pork into ¼-inch slices and place in zipper-lock bag with onion mixture. Seal bag, label, and freeze.

4. *To thaw and reheat:* Thaw overnight in refrigerator. Place pork and onion mixture in heavy skillet. Bring to a simmer over medium heat and cook 4 to 5 minutes until pork is thoroughly heated.

Serves 4–6

1 (2–3 pound) pork tenderloin
½ teaspoon salt
⅛ teaspoon pepper
1 teaspoon dried thyme leaves
½ teaspoon dried marjoram leaves
2 tablespoons olive oil
½ cup raisins
½ cup orange juice
2 tablespoons butter
1 cup chopped red onion
2 teaspoons sugar

Serves 12–18

3 (2–3 pound) pork tenderloins
1½ teaspoons salt
⅜ teaspoon pepper
1 tablespoon dried thyme leaves
1½ teaspoons dried marjoram leaves
6 tablespoons olive oil
1½ cups raisins
1½ cups orange juice
6 tablespoons butter
3 cups chopped red onion
6 teaspoons sugar

Pepperoni Pizza

Serves 4

---

1 onion, chopped
2 cloves garlic, minced
1 tablespoon olive oil
1 (8-ounce) can tomato
   sauce
1 (6-ounce) can tomato
   paste
½ cup Chicken Broth
   (page 301)
1 teaspoon Italian seasoning
1 tablespoon mustard
2 (10-inch) baked Pizza
   Crusts (page 298)
1 (6-ounce) package
   pepperoni slices
1 cup shredded mozzarella
   cheese
1 cup shredded Cheddar
   cheese

Serves 12

---

3 onions, chopped
6 cloves garlic, minced
3 tablespoons olive oil
3 (8-ounce) cans tomato
   sauce
3 (6-ounce) cans tomato
   paste
1½ cups Chicken Broth
   (page 301)
1 tablespoon Italian
   seasoning
3 tablespoons mustard
6 baked Pizza Crusts
   (page 298)
3 (6-ounce) packages
   pepperoni slices
3 cups shredded mozzarella
   cheese
3 cups shredded Cheddar
   cheese

To serve without freezing, simply bake pizza at 400°F for 15 to 20 minutes, until crust is crisp, pizza is hot, and cheese is melted and bubbly.

---

1. In heavy skillet, sauté onion and garlic in olive oil until crisp-tender. Add tomato sauce, tomato paste, chicken broth, and Italian seasoning. Simmer for 8 to 10 minutes to blend flavors. Cool sauce in refrigerator; then stir in mustard.

2. Spread cooled sauce over pizza crusts and top with pepperoni slices. Sprinkle cheeses over pepperoni. Flash freeze pizzas, then when frozen solid, wrap, label, and freeze.

3. *To bake:* Preheat oven to 400°F. Place frozen pizza on baking sheet and bake at 400°F for 20 to 25 minutes, until crust is crisp, pizza is hot, and cheese is melted and beginning to brown.

Reserved Ingredients

An easy way to mark nonperishable ingredients as "reserved" is to place a sticker or colored dot on each. Or, if you have the luxury of extra storage space, think about creating an area for stored ingredients. Let your family know that all foods stored on that shelf or in that cupboard are off-limits.

Sausage Quiche

You can serve this delicious quiche immediately after baking;
let stand 5 minutes before slicing. It's perfect for a spring brunch
served along with a fruit salad and crisp breadsticks.

1. Preheat oven to 375°F. Bake empty pie crust for 5 minutes until set. In heavy skillet, brown sausage links over medium heat. As sausage is cooked, remove from pan and slice into ½-inch pieces. After removing sausage, drain off excess oil, leaving two tablespoons pan drippings, and add onion to pan along with olive oil; cook and stir until crisp-tender. Sprinkle flour and pepper into pan and cook and stir until bubbly, about 3 to 4 minutes.

2. Add evaporated milk to pan and bring to a simmer, stirring constantly, until sauce is thickened. In large bowl, beat eggs with sour cream. Add milk sauce to bowl, along with Gouda cheese. Place sausage links in pie crust and pour egg mixture over. Sprinkle with Parmesan cheese and bake at 375°F for 20 to 30 minutes, until pie is puffed, set, and golden brown. Cool in refrigerator, then flash freeze; wrap, label, and freeze. Or, slice quiche into serving pieces before freezing and flash freeze individually.

3. *To thaw and reheat:* Thaw quiche overnight in refrigerator. Bake at 350°F for 20 to 25 minutes, until heated through.

   To reheat individually: Microwave each frozen slice on medium power for 2 to 4 minutes, then 1 minute on high, until hot.

Serves 6

1 9-inch Pie Crust (page 299)
½ pound sausage links
1 onion, chopped
1 tablespoon olive oil
2 tablespoons flour
⅛ teaspoon pepper
¾ cup evaporated milk
3 eggs
½ cup sour cream
1 cup shredded Gouda cheese
¼ cup grated Parmesan cheese

Serves 18

3 9-inch Pie Crusts (page 299)
1½ pounds sausage links
3 onions, chopped
3 tablespoons olive oil
6 tablespoons flour
⅜ teaspoon pepper
2¼ cups evaporated milk
9 eggs
1½ cups sour cream
3 cups shredded Gouda cheese
¾ cup grated Parmesan cheese

Pork and Apricot Stir-Fry

Serves 4

1 (¾ pound) pork tenderloin
2 cups frozen peppers and
    onions
1 cup frozen asparagus
    pieces
½ cup apricot nectar
2 tablespoons soy sauce
2 tablespoons white wine
    vinegar
⅛ teaspoon pepper
½ cup chopped dried
    apricots
2 tablespoons apricot
    preserves
½ teaspoon dried thyme
    leaves
1 tablespoon cornstarch
2 tablespoons olive oil
1 cup long-grain rice

Serves 12

3 (¾ pound) pork tenderloins
6 cups frozen peppers and
    onions
3 cups frozen asparagus
    pieces
1½ cups apricot nectar
6 tablespoons soy sauce
6 tablespoons white wine
    vinegar
⅜ teaspoon pepper
1½ cups chopped dried
    apricots
6 tablespoons apricot
    preserves
1½ teaspoons dried thyme
    leaves
3 tablespoons cornstarch
6 tablespoons olive oil
3 cups long-grain rice

To serve without freezing, cook pork and frozen vegetables in olive oil until vegetables are crisp-tender, then add sauce. Simmer for 5 to 8 minutes, until pork is thoroughly cooked and sauce is thickened.

---

1. Trim excess fat from tenderloin and cut into 1-inch cubes. Place in zipper-lock bag and freeze. Combine frozen vegetables in another zipper-lock bag and freeze.

2. In a third bag, combine apricot nectar, soy sauce, vinegar, pepper, dried apricots, apricot preserves, and thyme. Place all bags in gallon-size zipper-lock bag, label, and freeze. Reserve cornstarch, olive oil, and rice in pantry.

3. *To thaw and cook:* Thaw bags overnight in refrigerator. Heat olive oil in heavy skillet and add pork cubes. Brown on all sides, stirring frequently. Meanwhile, cook rice according to package directions. Add vegetables to pork, and cook and stir for 2 to 3 minutes, until tender. Combine sauce with cornstarch and add to pan. Bring to a simmer and cook for 5 to 8 minutes, until pork is thoroughly cooked and sauce is thickened. Serve over hot cooked rice.

Spaghetti Casserole

To serve without freezing, don't refrigerate pasta and egg mixture. Top with pork and tomato sauce and bake at 375°F for 30 to 35 minutes, until thoroughly heated and cheese is melted and bubbling.

1. Cook spaghetti as directed on package. Meanwhile, beat eggs, cream, and basil in large bowl. Drain spaghetti and immediately add to egg mixture. Toss spaghetti with egg mixture until coated. Place in 9" × 13" baking dish and put in refrigerator.

2. In heavy skillet, cook pork with onion and garlic until pork is browned. Drain off excess fat. Add remaining ingredients except for cheese and bring to a boil. Reduce heat, cover, and simmer for 15 to 20 minutes to blend flavors. Pour sausage mixture over spaghetti in baking dish. Refrigerate until cold, then wrap, attach bag with Colby-jack cheese, label, and freeze.

3. *To thaw and reheat:* Thaw casserole overnight in refrigerator. Preheat oven to 375°F. Uncover, sprinkle casserole with cheese, and bake at 375°F for 40 to 50 minutes, until thoroughly hot and cheese is melted and beginning to brown.

Serves 8–10

1 (8-ounce) package spaghetti
2 eggs
¼ cup cream
1 teaspoon dried basil leaves
1 pound bulk pork sausage
1 onion, chopped
2 cloves garlic, chopped
1 (14-ounce) can diced tomatoes, undrained
1 (8-ounce) can tomato sauce
1 (6-ounce) can tomato paste
1 cup Beef Broth (page 302)
1 teaspoon dried Italian seasoning
2 cups shredded Colby-jack cheese

Serves 24–30

3 (8-ounce) packages spaghetti
6 eggs
¾ cup cream
1 tablespoon dried basil leaves
3 pounds bulk pork sausage
3 onions, chopped
6 cloves garlic, chopped
3 (14-ounce) cans diced tomatoes, undrained
3 (8-ounce) cans tomato sauce
3 (6-ounce) cans tomato paste
3 cups Beef Broth (page 302)
1 tablespoon dried Italian seasoning
6 cups shredded Colby-jack cheese

Sausage Pie

Serves 6–8

2 9-inch Pie Crusts (page 299)
1 pound bulk pork sausage
1 onion, chopped
3 cloves garlic, minced
1 tablespoon flour
1 cup frozen cut-leaf
   spinach, thawed
1 cup frozen chopped
   broccoli, thawed
5 eggs
⅛ teaspoon pepper
1 (8-ounce) package ricotta
   cheese
1 (3-ounce) package cream
   cheese, softened
2 cups shredded mozzarella
   cheese
1 cup grated Parmesan cheese
1 tablespoon milk

Serves 18–24

6 9-inch Pie Crusts (page 299)
3 pounds bulk pork sausage
3 onions, chopped
9 cloves garlic, minced
3 tablespoons flour
3 cups frozen cut-leaf
   spinach, thawed
3 cups frozen chopped
   broccoli, thawed
15 eggs
⅜ teaspoon pepper
3 (8-ounce) packages ricotta
   cheese
3 (3-ounce) packages cream
   cheese, softened
6 cups shredded mozzarella
   cheese
3 cup grated Parmesan cheese
3 tablespoons milk

*This elegant pie makes a festive entrée for a holiday table.
To serve without freezing, when pie is baked,
let stand for 10 minutes before slicing.*

1. Preheat oven to 375°F. Line a 9-inch pie pan with one crust. In heavy skillet, cook sausage with onion and garlic until sausage is thoroughly cooked. Drain excess fat, then sprinkle flour over sausage. Cook and stir for 2 minutes, then remove from heat and refrigerate until cold.

2. Drain spinach and broccoli by pressing between paper towels. In large bowl, beat eggs, pepper, ricotta cheese, and cream cheese until well mixed. Add vegetables, then add pork mixture, mozzarella cheese, and Parmesan cheese and mix well.

3. Pour sausage mixture into pie crust–lined pan. Top with remaining pie crust, seal and flute edges, and cut vent holes in top of crust. Brush crust with milk and bake at 375°F for 50 to 65 minutes, until crust is browned and pie is set. Cool in refrigerator; then wrap whole pie and freeze, or cut into 8 slices and wrap individually, then freeze.

4. *To thaw and reheat:* Thaw pie overnight in refrigerator. Bake at 375°F for 20 to 25 minutes, until thoroughly heated.

   To reheat individually: Thaw slice overnight in refrigerator, then bake at 375° for 10 to 15 minutes until thoroughly heated.

Pork Adobo

Serve this variation on a traditional Philippine dish with hot rice, sliced avocado, chopped tomato, and warmed flour tortillas. To serve without freezing, simmer pork as directed, then fry in olive oil and garlic until browned.

1. Trim excess fat from pork and cut into 2-inch cubes. Combine in large bowl with vinegar, soy sauce, water, minced garlic, jalapenos, and pepper flakes and refrigerate overnight.

2. Pour marinated pork and sauce into heavy saucepan and bring to a boil. Reduce heat, cover, and simmer pork for 35 to 45 minutes, until pork is done and very tender. Cool in refrigerator, then pack into zipper-lock bag. Label bag and freeze. Reserve rice, olive oil, and garlic cloves in pantry.

3. *To thaw and reheat:* Thaw pork overnight in refrigerator. Pour pork and sauce into heavy saucepan and bring to a simmer; cook for 10 minutes until pork is hot. Mince reserved garlic. In heavy skillet, heat olive oil and garlic until fragrant. Remove pork from sauce with slotted spoon and add to pan with garlic. Cook until cubes are brown, about 10 minutes, stirring frequently. Serve over hot cooked rice with sauce.

Serves 6–8

1 (2-pound) boneless pork shoulder roast
½ cup apple cider vinegar
¼ cup soy sauce
1 cup water
3 garlic cloves, minced
1 jalapeno pepper, minced
⅛ teaspoon crushed red pepper flakes
1 cup long-grain rice
3 tablespoons olive oil
3 cloves garlic

Serves 18–24

3 (2-pound) boneless pork shoulder roasts
1½ cups apple cider vinegar
¾ cup soy sauce
3 cups water
9 garlic cloves, minced
3 jalapeno peppers, minced
⅜ teaspoon crushed red pepper flakes
3 cups long-grain rice
9 tablespoons olive oil
9 cloves garlic

Apricot Pork Chops

Serves 6

½ cup apricot preserves
1 cup apricot nectar
1 onion, finely chopped
2 tablespoons
    Worcestershire sauce
6 (¾-inch-thick) boneless
    pork chops

Serves 18

1½ cups apricot preserves
3 cups apricot nectar
3 onions, finely chopped
6 tablespoons
    Worcestershire sauce
18 (¾-inch-thick) boneless
    pork chops

To serve without freezing, marinate chops for 2 to 8 hours. Broil pork chops 4 to 6 inches from heat for 15 to 20 minutes, turning once, until browned on both sides and internal temperature registers at least 160°F.

---

1. In large bowl, combine all ingredients except pork chops and mix well. Place pork chops in lined 13" × 9" baking pan and pour apricot mixture over all. Freeze casserole until frozen solid, then pop out of pan and wrap, label, and freeze. Pork chops can be wrapped individually if desired.

2. *To thaw and cook:* Unwrap chops and place in 13" × 9" baking pan; thaw overnight in refrigerator. Place 6 inches from heat source and broil for 15 to 20 minutes, turning once and brushing once with thawed marinade, until pork registers 160°F. Discard remaining marinade.

Start with Ham

Wild Rice Ham Rolls

8 (¼-inch-thick) slices deli ham
1½ cups wild rice
4 cups water
2 tablespoons dried parsley
1 bunch green onions, chopped
1 cup finely chopped mushrooms
1 onion, minced
2 tablespoons butter
2 tablespoons olive oil
¼ cup flour
½ teaspoon salt
⅛ teaspoon white pepper
⅛ teaspoon nutmeg
3 tablespoons mustard
½ cup white wine
1 (16-ounce) can evaporated milk
1 cup shredded Gruyère cheese
1 cup grated Parmesan cheese

Serves 18

24 (¼-inch-thick) slices deli ham
4½ cups wild rice
12 cups water
6 tablespoons dried parsley
3 bunches green onions, chopped
3 cups finely chopped mushrooms
3 onions, minced
6 tablespoons butter
6 tablespoons olive oil
¾ cup flour
1½ teaspoons salt
⅜ teaspoon white pepper
⅜ teaspoon nutmeg
9 tablespoons mustard
1½ cups white wine
3 (16-ounce) cans evaporated milk
3 cups shredded Gruyère cheese
3 cups grated Parmesan cheese

This elegant dish is perfect for a company dinner. To serve without freezing, sprinkle with Parmesan cheese and bake at 350° for 30 to 35 minutes or until bubbly.

1. Cook wild rice in water until almost tender; drain if necessary. Add parsley and green onions to rice and mix gently; set aside. In heavy saucepan, sauté mushrooms and onion in butter and olive oil over medium heat. Stir in flour, salt, pepper, and nutmeg and cook until bubbly. Add mustard, wine, evaporated milk, and Gruyère cheese and cook until thickened.

2. Mix 1 cup sauce with 2 cups of the rice mixture. Divide among ham slices and roll up. Place remaining rice in 2-quart baking dish and top with ham rolls. Pour remaining sauce over. Cool casserole in refrigerator; then wrap, attach bag with Parmesan cheese, label, and freeze.

3. *To thaw and reheat:* Thaw casserole overnight in refrigerator. Sprinkle with Parmesan cheese and bake in preheated 350°F oven for 35 to 45 minutes or until thoroughly heated and bubbly.

Sweet and Savory Ham Loaf

To serve without freezing, let cooked loaf
stand, covered with foil, for 10 minutes before slicing.

1. Preheat oven to 350°F. In heavy skillet, heat olive oil and sauté shallots until tender. Let cool slightly. In large bowl, combine shallots with all ingredients except for apricot preserves and second amount of apricot nectar; mix well with hands.

2. Press ham mixture into 9" × 5" loaf pan and top with apricot preserves. Bake at 350°F for 80 to 90 minutes, until browned and set. Cool in refrigerator; wrap, pack, and freeze. Reserve apricot nectar in pantry.

3. *To thaw and reheat:* Thaw overnight in refrigerator. Serve cold, or to reheat, slice loaf and place in baking dish. Pour ½ cup apricot nectar over slices and bake at 375°F for 20 to 25 minutes, until thoroughly heated.

To reheat from frozen: Unwrap loaf and place on broiler pan. Bake at 350°F for 80 to 90 minutes or until internal temperature registers 155°F, basting occasionally with apricot nectar.

Simmering the Day Away

Start long-simmering soups and stews early in the day. Just stir them from time to time as you bustle around preparing your other recipes. At the end of your cooking session, cool, pack, label, seal, and freeze the soup or stew.

Serves 6

1 tablespoon olive oil
3 shallots, chopped
1½ pounds ground ham
½ pound bulk sausage
3 eggs
1 cup cracker crumbs
1 cup apricot nectar
2 tablespoons honey Dijon mustard
¼ teaspoon salt
⅛ teaspoon pepper
½ cup apricot preserves
½ cup apricot nectar

Serves 18

3 tablespoons olive oil
9 shallots, chopped
4½ pounds ground ham
1½ pounds bulk sausage
9 eggs
3 cups cracker crumbs
3 cups apricot nectar
6 tablespoons honey Dijon mustard
¾ teaspoon salt
⅜ teaspoon pepper
1½ cups apricot preserves
1½ cups apricot nectar

Ham and Corn Casserole

Serves 6

1 onion, chopped
1 tablespoon olive oil
4 eggs
1¼ cups milk
2 tablespoons flour
1 cup shredded Swiss cheese
½ cup grated Parmesan
  cheese
1 tablespoon sugar
⅛ teaspoon pepper
2 (10-ounce) packages
  frozen corn, thawed
2 cups chopped smoked
  ham
¼ cup grated Parmesan
  cheese

Serves 18

3 onions, chopped
3 tablespoons olive oil
12 eggs
3¾ cups milk
6 tablespoons flour
3 cups shredded Swiss
  cheese
1½ cups grated Parmesan
  cheese
3 tablespoons sugar
⅜ teaspoon pepper
6 (10-ounce) packages
  frozen corn, thawed
6 cups chopped smoked
  ham
¾ cup grated Parmesan
  cheese

Like a crustless quiche, corn and ham bake in an egg-and-cheese filling. This homey casserole can be served as soon as it's baked. Drizzle with warmed maple syrup if desired.

1. Preheat oven to 350°F. In heavy skillet, sauté onions in olive oil until crisp-tender. Remove from heat and cool 10 minutes.

2. In large bowl, beat eggs until foamy and blended. Add milk and beat well. Add flour, Swiss cheese, first quantity Parmesan cheese, sugar, pepper, corn, and ham and mix to blend. Stir in cooled sautéed onions. Pour into greased 2-quart baking dish and top with remaining Parmesan cheese.

3. Bake at 350°F for 55 to 65 minutes or until casserole is puffed and golden brown. Cool 30 minutes at room temperature, then chill in refrigerator. Wrap, label, and freeze.

4. *To thaw and reheat:* Thaw casserole in refrigerator overnight. Bake at 350°F for 15 to 20 minutes or until heated through.

Ham and Bean Soup

This rich and hearty soup is thickened with dried potato flakes. You can serve it immediately, with crisp crackers and a fruit salad.

1. In a large stockpot, cover beans with cold water. Bring to a boil, then cook for 2 minutes. Remove from heat, cover; let stand for 1 hour. Drain well. Return beans to stockpot; add ham hocks, chicken broth, and water. Bring to a boil; then cover, reduce heat, and simmer for 1½ hours.

2. Add remaining ingredients to soup, stir, and simmer for half an hour. Remove ham hocks from pot and trim meat, then return meat to soup; discard ham bones. Cool soup in ice-water bath or refrigerator. Then pour into rigid containers, label, and freeze.

3. *To thaw and reheat:* Thaw overnight in refrigerator. Pour into large saucepan and bring to a simmer. Cook for 10 to 15 minutes or until thoroughly heated.

Serves 6–8

1 pound dried navy beans
2 pounds ham hocks
4 cups Chicken Broth
    (page 301)
4 cups water
2 tablespoons olive oil
1 onion, chopped
4 garlic cloves, chopped
1 green bell pepper,
    chopped
½ cup chopped celery
½ cup dried potato flakes
1 teaspoon salt
⅛ teaspoon pepper
1 teaspoon Italian seasoning
½ teaspoon ground nutmeg

Serves 18–24

3 pounds dried navy beans
6 pounds ham hocks
12 cups Chicken Broth
    (page 301)
12 cups water
6 tablespoons olive oil
3 onions, chopped
12 garlic cloves, chopped
3 green bell peppers,
    chopped
1½ cups chopped celery
1½ cups dried potato flakes
1 tablespoon salt
⅜ teaspoon pepper
1 tablespoon Italian
    seasoning
1½ teaspoons ground
    nutmeg

Double Corn Chowder

Serves 6–8

---

3 slices bacon
1 tablespoon olive oil
1 onion, chopped
3 cloves garlic, minced
1 green pepper, chopped
3 potatoes, peeled and diced
2 cups water
2 cups cubed ham
⅛ teaspoon pepper
1 (10-ounce) can corn,
    undrained
1 (12-ounce) can creamed
    corn
2 (10-ounce) cans
    evaporated milk

Serves 18–24

---

9 slices bacon
3 tablespoons olive oil
3 onions, chopped
9 cloves garlic, minced
3 green peppers, chopped
9 potatoes, peeled and diced
6 cups water
6 cups cubed ham
⅜ teaspoon pepper
3 (10-ounce) cans corn,
    undrained
3 (12-ounce) cans creamed
    corn
6 (10-ounce) cans
    evaporated milk

You can serve this hearty soup without freezing by adding the crumbled bacon and milk to the soup and cooking over low heat for 5 to 6 minutes or until thoroughly heated.

---

1. In large saucepan, fry bacon until crisp. Remove from pan, crumble, and set aside. To drippings remaining in pan, add olive oil and sauté onion, garlic, and green pepper until crisp-tender. Add potatoes; cook and stir for 3 to 4 minutes.

2. Add water and bring to a boil. Reduce heat, cover pan, and simmer for 8 to 12 minutes, until potatoes are almost tender. Add ham, pepper, and cans of corn and creamed corn, and simmer for 10 minutes. Cool soup in ice-water bath or refrigerator. Transfer to rigid container, attach small bag with crumbled bacon, label, and freeze. Reserve evaporated milk in pantry.

3. *To thaw and reheat:* Thaw overnight in refrigerator. Pour soup into saucepan and bring to a simmer. Add bacon and evaporated milk and cook over low heat for 5 to 8 minutes or until thoroughly heated.

Cheesy Ham Quiche

The filling in this quiche stands up to freezing very well because of the flour and evaporated milk. To serve without freezing, let quiche stand for 5 minutes after baking, then slice.

1. Preheat oven to 375°F. Sprinkle cornmeal evenly over pie crust. Bake pie crust for 5 minutes until set. Cool on wire rack while preparing filling.

2. In heavy skillet, cook onion in olive oil; cook and stir until crisp-tender. Sprinkle flour and pepper into pan and cook and stir until bubbly, about 3 to 4 minutes. Add evaporated milk to pan and bring to a simmer, stirring constantly, until sauce is thickened. Cool sauce in refrigerator.

3. In large bowl, beat eggs with sour cream and hot pepper sauce. Add cooled sauce and Swiss cheese. Place ham in pie crust and pour egg mixture over. Sprinkle with Parmesan cheese and bake at 375°F for 20 to 30 minutes or until pie is puffed, set, and golden brown. Cool in refrigerator, then flash freeze; wrap, label, and freeze. Or, slice quiche into serving pieces before freezing and flash freeze individually.

4. *To thaw and reheat:* Thaw quiche overnight in refrigerator. Bake at 350°F for 20 to 25 minutes or until heated through.

   To reheat individually: Microwave each slice on medium heat for 2 to 4 minutes, then 1 minute on high, or until hot.

Serves 6

1 tablespoon cornmeal
1 9-inch Pie Crust (page 299)
1 onion, chopped
1 tablespoon olive oil
2 tablespoons flour
⅛ teaspoon pepper
¾ cup evaporated milk
3 eggs
½ cup sour cream
3 drops hot pepper sauce
1 cup shredded Swiss cheese
1½ cups chopped ham
¼ cup grated Parmesan cheese

Serves 18

3 tablespoons cornmeal
3 9-inch Pie Crusts (page 299)
3 onions, chopped
3 tablespoons olive oil
6 tablespoons flour
⅜ teaspoon pepper
2¼ cups evaporated milk
9 eggs
1½ cups sour cream
9 drops hot pepper sauce
3 cups shredded Swiss cheese
4½ cups chopped ham
¾ cup grated Parmesan cheese

Ham Phyllo Roll

Serves 4

---

1 green bell pepper,
  chopped
1 onion, chopped
1 tablespoon olive oil
1 cup frozen corn, thawed
½ cup ricotta cheese
1 egg
1 cup shredded Swiss cheese
¼ cup grated Parmesan
  cheese
2 cups cubed smoked ham
8 sheets thawed phyllo
  dough
¼ cup melted butter

Serves 12

---

3 green bell peppers,
  chopped
3 onions, chopped
3 tablespoons olive oil
3 cups frozen corn, thawed
1½ cups ricotta cheese
3 eggs
3 cups shredded Swiss
  cheese
¾ cup grated Parmesan
  cheese
6 cups cubed smoked ham
24 sheets thawed phyllo
  dough
¾ cup melted butter

To serve immediately, bake roll at 375°F for 40 to 50 minutes or until pastry is crisp and golden brown and filling is thoroughly heated.

---

1. In large skillet, sauté bell pepper and onion in olive oil until crisp-tender, stirring frequently. Drain corn, add to skillet, and stir. Remove from heat and let cool for 20 minutes.

2. In large bowl, combine ricotta cheese and egg and beat until combined. Add cheeses and cooked ham and mix well. Stir in cooled sautéed vegetable mixture until well blended.

3. Place one sheet phyllo dough on large cookie sheet and brush with butter. Top with remaining sheets, brushing each lightly with butter. Place ham mixture along one edge of dough, leaving 1-inch margin. Fold in short ends of phyllo dough, and then roll, starting with side containing filling, folding in sides, completely enclosing the filling. Seal edges with butter. Brush entire roll with remaining melted butter. Wrap roll in foil, label, and freeze.

4. *To thaw and cook*: Partially unwrap and thaw roll overnight in refrigerator. Brush with 1 tablespoon melted butter. Bake in preheated 375°F oven for 40 to 50 minutes or until pastry is crisp and golden brown and filling is thoroughly heated. Let stand 10 minutes before serving. Slice carefully on the diagonal using a serrated knife.

Split Pea Soup

Sautéing the ham in butter adds a subtle flavor and
preserves the texture of the meat while it's frozen.
You can serve this soup immediately after it finishes simmering.

Serves 6

1 pound dried split peas
3 cups water
5 cups Chicken Broth (page 301)
1 onion, chopped
3 cloves garlic, chopped
2 carrots, chopped
2 tablespoons olive oil
2 tablespoons butter
2 cups cubed ham
1 teaspoon dried thyme leaves
1 (10-ounce) can creamed corn

1. Carefully pick over peas and discard any wrinkled peas or stones. Place in large stockpot, cover with water and broth, and bring to a boil. Reduce heat and simmer for about 1 hour, until peas are tender.

2. While peas are cooking, in heavy skillet sauté onion, garlic, and carrots in olive oil. Add vegetables to stockpot. In the same skillet, heat butter and add ham. Sauté for 3 to 4 minutes, until ham is slightly browned. Add to stockpot along with thyme and creamed corn. Simmer for 10 to 15 minutes more or until peas begin to dissolve and vegetables are tender. Cool in refrigerator or ice-water bath. Package in rigid container, label, seal, and freeze.

Serves 18

3 pounds dried split peas
9 cups water
15 cups Chicken Broth (page 301)
3 onions, chopped
9 cloves garlic, chopped
6 carrots, chopped
6 tablespoons olive oil
6 tablespoons butter
6 cups cubed ham
1 tablespoon dried thyme leaves
3 (10-ounce) cans creamed corn

3. *To thaw and reheat:* Thaw soup overnight in refrigerator. Pour into saucepan and heat over medium heat for 8 to 12 minutes or until soup is thoroughly heated.

Meat Slicing Tip

Meat is more easily sliced and chopped if it is slightly frozen. Place chicken breasts and cuts of beef and pork in the freezer for about half an hour, just until they become firm.

Cheesy Pasta and Ham

Serves 8

1 tablespoon olive oil
2 tablespoons butter
1 onion, chopped
3 tablespoons flour
⅛ teaspoon white pepper
1 cup milk
½ cup dry white wine
1 (3-ounce) package cream
    cheese
1 cup crumbled blue cheese
2 cups cubed ham
2 cups gemelli pasta
1 cup frozen sugar snap
    peas
¼ cup grated Parmesan
    cheese

Serves 24

3 tablespoons olive oil
6 tablespoons butter
3 onions, chopped
9 tablespoons flour
⅜ teaspoon white pepper
3 cups milk
1½ cups dry white wine
3 (3-ounce) packages cream
    cheese
3 cups crumbled blue cheese
6 cups cubed ham
6 cups gemelli pasta
3 cups frozen sugar snap
    peas
¾ cup grated Parmesan
    cheese

To serve without freezing, do not cool ham mixture. Combine with cooked and drained pasta, pour into casserole, sprinkle with cheese, and bake at 375° for 25 to 30 minutes.

1. In heavy skillet, heat olive oil and butter over medium heat until foamy. Add onions and cook, stirring frequently, until crisp-tender. Sprinkle flour and pepper over onions and cook until bubbly. Add milk and wine to skillet; cook and stir until sauce is blended and thickened.

2. Add cream cheese to sauce and stir until melted and blended. Remove from heat and add blue cheese and ham. Stir to combine, then set aside in refrigerator while cooking pasta.

3. Cook pasta according to package directions until almost tender; drain well, rinse with cold water, drain again, and add to ham mixture along with peas. Pour into 2-quart casserole dish, cover, attach bag with Parmesan cheese; seal, label, and freeze.

4. *To thaw and reheat:* Thaw casserole overnight in refrigerator. Uncover, sprinkle with Parmesan cheese, and bake in preheated 375°F oven for 30 to 45 minutes or until heated and bubbly.

Ham-Stuffed Cannelloni

This elegant dish is perfect for company. To serve without freezing, don't chill sauce; assemble casserole and bake as directed.

1. Cook cannelloni as directed on package until almost done; drain, rinse with cold water, and set aside. In large skillet, heat olive oil and first quantity of butter; sauté leek and mushrooms over medium heat until leek is crisp-tender. Remove from heat and cool in ice-water bath or refrigerator. When cold, stir in frozen peas, ham, and first amount of Parmesan cheese.

2. In large saucepan, melt remaining butter and add flour, salt, and white pepper. Cook over medium heat, stirring frequently, until bubbly. Add milk; cook and stir with wire whisk until thickened. Remove from heat and stir in Gruyère cheese until melted.

3. Fill cannelloni shells with ham mixture and place in 13" × 9" baking dish. Pour cheese sauce over filled shells and sprinkle with Parmesan cheese. Wrap, label, and freeze.

4. *To thaw and reheat:* Let thaw overnight in refrigerator. Bake casserole, covered, in preheated 350°F oven for 40 to 45 minutes, until hot. Uncover and bake 8 to 10 minutes longer, until top begins to brown and casserole is thoroughly heated.

Serves 8–10

14 cannelloni shells
2 tablespoons olive oil
1 tablespoon butter
1 leek, chopped
1 cup chopped mushrooms
1 cup frozen peas
2 cups cubed ham
⅓ cup grated Parmesan cheese
¼ cup butter
¼ cup flour
½ teaspoon salt
⅛ teaspoon white pepper
2 cups milk
1½ cups shredded Gruyère cheese
½ cup grated Parmesan cheese

Serves 24–30

42 cannelloni shells
6 tablespoons olive oil
3 tablespoons butter
3 leeks, chopped
3 cups chopped mushrooms
3 cups frozen peas
6 cups cubed ham
1 cup grated Parmesan cheese
¾ cup butter
¾ cup flour
1½ teaspoons salt
⅜ teaspoon white pepper
6 cups milk
4½ cups shredded Gruyère cheese
1½ cups grated Parmesan cheese

Ham Meatballs in Cheesy Sauce

Serves 6–8

2 eggs
½ cup milk
1 cup Ritz cracker crumbs
1½ pounds ground ham
½ pound ground pork
1 onion, chopped
2 tablespoons butter
1 tablespoon olive oil
3 tablespoons flour
1½ cups milk
½ cup apple juice
½ teaspoon dried thyme
1 cup shredded Gruyère
   cheese
½ cup shredded Muenster
   cheese

Serves 18–24

6 eggs
1½ cups milk
3 cups Ritz cracker crumbs
4½ pounds ground ham
1½ pounds ground pork
3 onions, chopped
6 tablespoons butter
3 tablespoons olive oil
9 tablespoons flour
4½ cups milk
1½ cups apple juice
1½ teaspoons dried thyme
3 cups shredded Gruyère
   cheese
1½ cups shredded Muenster
   cheese

To serve without freezing, add meatballs to sauce
and return to oven. Bake at 350°F for 20 to 25 minutes
until sauce is bubbly and beginning to brown on top.

1. Preheat oven to 350°F. In large bowl, beat eggs and add milk and cracker crumbs. Add ground ham and pork and mix well with hands. Form into 1-inch meatballs and place onto baking sheet. Bake at 350°F for 25 to 30 minutes, until meatballs are thoroughly cooked.

2. Meanwhile, in heavy skillet, cook onion in butter and olive oil until crisp-tender. Sprinkle flour over all and cook and stir until bubbly. Add milk and apple juice; cook and stir over medium heat until thickened. Add thyme and cheeses; remove from heat and stir until cheeses melt and sauce is blended.

3. Fold cooked meatballs into sauce and chill in ice water bath or refrigerator. Pour meatballs and sauce into zipper-lock bag; seal, label, and freeze.

4. *To thaw and reheat:* Thaw overnight in refrigerator. Pour meatballs and sauce into casserole and bake in preheated 350°F oven for 25 to 35 minutes or until sauce is bubbly and meatballs are thoroughly heated.

Ham Chile Rellenos

To serve without freezing, cook rice for 20 minutes, until tender. Then assemble casserole as directed and bake, covered, at 375°F for 20 to 25 minutes, until thoroughly heated.

1. Place ham on work surface. In medium bowl, combine cheeses, red onion, and chili powder. Drain green chilies and stir in. Divide mixture among ham slices, then roll up ham, enclosing filling. Brush rolls with 2 tablespoons melted butter. Refrigerate while preparing rice.

2. In medium saucepan, combine rice, chicken broth, and butter and bring to a boil. Reduce heat, cover pan, and simmer for 15 minutes, until rice is almost tender. Pour rice into a 9" × 9" baking dish, sprinkle with water, and top with ham rolls. Sprinkle Parmesan cheese over all, wrap, seal, label, and freeze.

3. *To thaw and reheat:* Let thaw overnight in refrigerator. Sprinkle two tablespoons water over rice. Cover casserole and bake in preheated 375°F oven for 20 to 25 minutes or until rice is tender and ham rolls are thoroughly heated.

Serves 4

4 (¼-inch-thick) slices deli ham
1 cup shredded Muenster cheese
½ cup ricotta cheese
1 (3-ounce) package cream cheese, softened
3 tablespoons minced red onion
1 teaspoon chili powder
1 (4-ounce) can chopped green chili peppers
2 tablespoons butter
1 cup rice
2 cups Chicken Broth (page 301)
1 tablespoon butter
2 tablespoons water
3 tablespoons grated Parmesan cheese

Serves 12

12 (¼-inch-thick) slices deli ham
3 cups shredded Muenster cheese
1½ cups ricotta cheese
1 (8-ounce) package cream cheese, softened
¾ cup minced red onion
1 tablespoon chili powder
3 (4-ounce) cans chopped green chili peppers
6 tablespoons butter
3 cups rice
6 cups Chicken Broth (page 301)
3 tablespoons butter
6 tablespoons water
9 tablespoons grated Parmesan cheese

Polenta Ham Casserole

Serves 4

---

1 cup cornmeal
3½ cups water
3 tablespoons sun-dried
   tomatoes in oil
1 onion, chopped
3 tablespoons butter
3 tablespoons flour
1½ cups Chicken Broth
   (page 301)
1 cup shredded white
   Cheddar cheese
¼ cup grated Parmesan
   cheese
2 cups cubed ham
1 cup frozen peas

Serves 2

---

3 cups cornmeal
10½ cups water
9 tablespoons sun-dried
   tomatoes in oil
3 onions, chopped
9 tablespoons butter
9 tablespoons flour
4½ cups Chicken Broth
   (page 301)
3 cups shredded white
   Cheddar cheese
¾ cup grated Parmesan
   cheese
6 cups cubed ham
3 cups frozen peas

To serve this casserole without freezing, prepare as directed but do not chill cheese sauce. Slice polenta, top with ham and peas, pour cheese sauce over, and bake at 400°F for 20 to 25 minutes, until bubbly.

---

1. In heavy saucepan, bring water to a boil. Add cornmeal to boiling water; cook over medium heat, stirring constantly, until mixture is thick. Remove from heat. Drain and chop tomatoes; reserving 1 tablespoon of oil. Stir tomatoes and reserved oil into cornmeal. Pour mixture into greased 9" × 9" pan and chill until firm, about 2 hours.

2. In medium saucepan, cook onions in butter until crisp-tender. Sprinkle flour over onions; cook and stir until bubbly. Add chicken broth; cook and stir until thickened. Remove from heat and stir in cheeses until melted. Chill in refrigerator.

3. Slice chilled polenta into 3-inch squares and place in greased 9" × 9" pan. Top with ham and frozen peas and pour cheese sauce over all. Wrap pan in freezer wrap, seal, label, and freeze.

4. *To thaw and reheat:* Let casserole thaw overnight in refrigerator. Bake, covered, in preheated 400°F oven for 20 to 25 minutes, until bubbly. Uncover and bake for 8 to 10 minutes longer or until cheese sauce begins to brown.

Creamy Ham Broccoli Casserole

To serve without freezing, do not cool sauce.
Stir in pasta, ham, and broccoli and pour into casserole.
Sprinkle with cheese and bread crumbs and bake as directed.

2 cups radiatore pasta
¼ cup butter
1 onion, chopped
¼ cup flour
1 teaspoon salt
⅛ teaspoon pepper
1 cup whole milk
1 cup Chicken Broth
    (page 301)
1 cup grated Gruyère cheese
½ cup mayonnaise
2 cups cubed ham
2 cups frozen broccoli florets
¼ cup grated Parmesan
    cheese
3 tablespoons dry bread
    crumbs

1. Cook pasta according to package directions until almost tender; drain and rinse with cold water. Set aside. In heavy saucepan, melt butter and add onion. Cook and stir until crisp-tender. Sprinkle with flour, salt, and pepper; cook and stir until bubbly. Add milk and broth; cook and stir until sauce is thickened. Remove from heat and add Gruyère cheese and mayonnaise; stir until blended.

2. Cool cheese sauce in ice-water bath or refrigerator. When cold, add cooled pasta, ham, and broccoli. Stir well and pour into 2-quart casserole. Wrap casserole, seal, and attach zipper-lock bag with Parmesan cheese and bread crumbs; label and freeze.

3. *To thaw and reheat:* Let thaw overnight in refrigerator. Preheat oven to 375°F. Sprinkle casserole with Parmesan cheese and bread crumb mixture. Bake casserole, uncovered, at 375°F for 30 to 40 minutes or until casserole is bubbly and thoroughly heated and topping begins to brown.

Serves 18–24

6 cups radiatore pasta
¾ cup butter
3 onions, chopped
¾ cup flour
2 teaspoons salt
⅜ teaspoon pepper
3 cups whole milk
3 cups Chicken Broth
    (page 301)
3 cups grated Gruyère
    cheese
1½ cups mayonnaise
6 cups cubed ham
6 cups frozen broccoli florets
¾ cup grated Parmesan
    cheese
9 tablespoons dry bread
    crumbs

Ham Lasagna

9 lasagna noodles
2 tablespoons oil
1 onion, chopped
3 cloves garlic, minced
1 (25-ounce) jar pasta sauce
1 (8-ounce) can tomato sauce
2 cups ricotta cheese
1 egg
½ cup grated Parmesan
 cheese
1 cup shredded mozzarella
 cheese
2 cups cubed ham
1 teaspoon dried basil leaves
½ teaspoon dried oregano
 leaves
⅛ teaspoon pepper
1 cup grated Parmesan
 cheese

Serves 24–30

27 lasagna noodles
6 tablespoons oil
3 onions, chopped
9 cloves garlic, minced
3 (25-ounce) jars pasta
 sauce
3 (8-ounce) cans tomato
 sauce
6 cups ricotta cheese
3 eggs
1½ cups grated Parmesan
 cheese
3 cups shredded mozzarella
 cheese
6 cups cubed ham
1 tablespoon dried basil leaves
1½ teaspoons dried oregano
 leaves
⅜ teaspoon pepper
3 cups grated Parmesan
 cheese

To serve without freezing, do not cool casserole. Bake, covered, in preheated 375°F oven for 15 minutes; uncover and bake 20 to 25 minutes longer, until thoroughly heated and bubbly.

1. Cook lasagna noodles as directed on package until almost al dente. Drain, rinse with cold water, drain again, and set aside on kitchen towels. Meanwhile, heat oil in heavy skillet and cook onion and garlic until crisp-tender.

2. In large bowl, combine pasta sauce and tomato sauce; add cooked onion and garlic and stir to combine. In medium bowl, combine ricotta and egg and beat well. Stir in first quantity Parmesan cheese, mozzarella cheese, ham, basil, oregano, and pepper and mix well.

3. Pour about ½ cup tomato sauce mixture in bottom of 9" × 13" baking dish and top with 3 cooked lasagna noodles. Spread one third of the ricotta mixture over noodles and top with one third of the sauce. Repeat layers twice. Sprinkle with 1 cup Parmesan cheese. Cool lasagna in refrigerator, then wrap in freezer wrap, label, seal, and freeze.

4. *To thaw and reheat:* Thaw lasagna overnight in refrigerator. Bake, covered, in preheated 375°F oven for 30 minutes. Uncover dish and bake an additional 25 to 35 minutes or until lasagna is thoroughly heated and bubbly.

CHAPTER 11
Start with Fish

Fish Tacos with Freezer Coleslaw

Serves 4 to 6

---

1 pound frozen breaded
   fish sticks
1 teaspoon chili powder
½ teaspoon paprika
⅛ teaspoon cayenne
   pepper
½ head cabbage, shredded
1 red bell pepper, chopped
1 red onion, finely chopped
1 cup sugar
½ teaspoon salt
½ teaspoon celery salt
¼ cup apple cider vinegar
½ cup water
8 taco shells
1 (8-ounce) jar salsa

Serves 12–18

---

3 pounds frozen breaded
   fish sticks
1 tablespoon chili powder
1½ teaspoons paprika
⅜ teaspoon cayenne
   pepper
1½ heads cabbage,
   shredded
3 red bell peppers, chopped
3 red onions, finely chopped
3 cups sugar
1½ teaspoons salt
1½ teaspoons celery salt
¾ cup apple cider vinegar
1½ cups water
24 taco shells
3 (8-ounce) jars salsa

To serve these tacos without freezing, let cabbage mixture marinate in refrigerator for 1 to 2 hours. Bake spiced fish sticks as directed, then serve with coleslaw and salsa in the heated taco shells.

---

1. Remove fish sticks from package. Combine chili powder, paprika, and cayenne pepper on shallow plate and toss fish sticks in this mixture. Place fish sticks in zipper-lock bag and freeze.

2. For Freezer Coleslaw, toss cabbage, red pepper, and onion in a large bowl and set aside. In medium saucepan, combine sugar, salt, celery salt, vinegar, and water and bring to a boil. Boil vigorously for 3 minutes, then cool completely in refrigerator. Pour liquid over vegetables and place in rigid container. Attach to fish sticks along with taco shells; label and freeze. Reserve salsa in pantry.

3. *To thaw and reheat:* Thaw Freezer Coleslaw overnight in refrigerator. Keep fish sticks and taco shells in freezer. Preheat oven to 400°F. Place frozen fish sticks on baking sheet and bake for 10 to 15 minutes, until thoroughly heated. Add frozen taco shells to baking sheet for last 4 to 5 minutes of baking time. Serve slaw and fish sticks in taco shells along with salsa.

Madras Shrimp Tart

To serve this tart without freezing, let it cool for 10 minutes when it comes out of the oven, then slice and serve with more chutney.

1. In large skillet, heat oil over medium heat. Add frozen corn, onion, and red pepper; cook and stir for 1 minute. Add curry powder and cook 1 minute more. Stir in shrimp, yogurt, sour cream, flour, and 1 tablespoon each of the raisins and almonds. Remove pan from heat and cool 15 minutes.

2. Preheat oven to 400°F. Beat eggs in small bowl and add to filling in skillet; mix well until combined.

3. Place 1 crust in 10-inch tart pan with removable bottom. Spread chutney over crust, then spoon shrimp filling over chutney. Sprinkle remaining raisins and almonds over filling. Make a lattice top with remaining crust and place over filling, sealing edges. Bake at 400°F for 20 to 35 minutes, until filling is set and crust is golden brown. Cool tart in refrigerator, uncovered, until completely cold. Wrap in heavy duty freezer wrap, label, and freeze. Or, slice the tart into wedges and wrap individually to freeze.

4. *To thaw and reheat:* Thaw tart overnight in refrigerator. Bake in preheated 400°F oven for 15 to 20 minutes, until thoroughly heated.

   To reheat individually: Reheat from frozen in 400°F oven for 15 to 25 minutes.

Serves 6–8

2 tablespoons oil
¼ cup frozen corn
½ cup finely chopped onion
¼ cup chopped red pepper
1 tablespoon curry powder
2½ cups small cooked shrimp
¼ cup plain yogurt
¼ cup sour cream
2 tablespoons flour
3 tablespoons golden raisins
3 tablespoons chopped almonds
2 eggs
2 9-inch Pie Crusts (page 299)
2 tablespoons mango chutney

Serves 18–24

6 tablespoons oil
¾ cup frozen corn
1½ cups finely chopped onion
¾ cup chopped red pepper
3 tablespoons curry powder
7½ cups small cooked shrimp
¾ cup plain yogurt
¾ cup sour cream
6 tablespoons flour
9 tablespoons golden raisins
9 tablespoons chopped almonds
6 eggs
6 9-inch Pie Crusts (page 299)
6 tablespoons mango chutney

Salmon in Curry Sauce

Serves 6

2 pounds salmon fillets
1 tablespoon oil
2 tablespoons butter
2 onions, chopped
2 tablespoons flour
2 teaspoons curry powder
¼ teaspoon garlic salt
1 teaspoon sugar
¼ cup evaporated milk
1½ cups Fish Broth (page
    304)
1 (6-ounce) package
    couscous
1 (8-ounce) jar mango
    chutney

Serves 18

6 pounds salmon fillets
3 tablespoons oil
6 tablespoons butter
6 onions, chopped
6 tablespoons flour
6 teaspoons curry powder
¾ teaspoon garlic salt
1 tablespoon sugar
¾ cup evaporated milk
4½ cups Fish Broth (page
    304)
3 (6-ounce) packages
    couscous
3 (8-ounce) jars mango
    chutney

To serve without freezing, do not cool sauce;
prepare salmon and add to sauce. Simmer for 10 to 15 minutes,
until salmon is thoroughly heated.

1. Place salmon on broiler pan and brush with oil. Broil 4 to 6 inches from heat source, turning once, for 10 to 12 minutes, until fish flakes easily when tested with fork. Remove salmon from oven and refrigerate.

2. Meanwhile, heat butter in large saucepan until foamy. Add onions; cook and stir until crisp-tender. Sprinkle flour, curry powder, garlic salt, and sugar into pan; cook and stir for 2 to 3 minutes, until bubbly. Add evaporated milk and broth; stir well to combine. Cover and simmer for 30 minutes, until sauce is thickened and blended. Cool sauce in ice-water bath or refrigerator until cold.

3. Remove skin from cooked salmon fillets and gently break into large chunks. Add to cooled sauce and pack into zipper-lock bags. Seal bags, label, and freeze. Reserve couscous and chutney in pantry.

4. *To thaw and reheat:* Thaw mixture overnight in refrigerator. Pour into large saucepan and bring to a simmer, stirring occasionally. Simmer for 8 to 12 minutes, until salmon is hot and sauce is thoroughly heated. Serve over couscous and top with chutney.

Shrimp Newburg

This dish is perfect for company. To serve without freezing, thaw shrimp. When sauce is thickened, add shrimp and cook until heated, then serve over hot cooked rice or couscous.

1. In large skillet, melt butter with olive oil. Add garlic and shallots; cook and stir for 3 to 4 minutes, until crisp-tender. Sprinkle flour into skillet; cook and stir until bubbly. Add evaporated milk, cocktail sauce, salt, pepper, and Worcestershire sauce and cook until thickened. Cool sauce in ice-water bath or in refrigerator.

2. Pour cooled sauce into zipper-lock bag and attach frozen shrimp (do not thaw shrimp). Label package, seal, and freeze. Reserve sherry in pantry.

3. *To thaw and reheat:* Thaw sauce overnight in refrigerator. Thaw shrimp according to package directions. Pour sauce into saucepan and bring to a simmer. Add thawed shrimp and cook, stirring frequently, about 3 to 7 minutes or until shrimp are pink and cooked. Add sherry just before serving. Serve with hot cooked rice or couscous.

Flash Freezing

When flash freezing, make sure that the pieces of food do not touch each other. Leave a space of ½ to 1 inch between the individual pieces of food so cold air can circulate freely.

Serves 4

1 tablespoon butter
1 tablespoon olive oil
4 cloves garlic, minced
1 shallot, minced
2 tablespoons flour
1 cup evaporated milk
¼ cup cocktail sauce
½ teaspoon salt
⅛ teaspoon white pepper
1 tablespoon Worcestershire sauce
1 pound frozen uncooked shrimp
2 tablespoons sherry

Serves 12

3 tablespoons butter
3 tablespoons olive oil
12 cloves garlic, minced
3 shallots, minced
6 tablespoons flour
3 cups evaporated milk
¾ cup cocktail sauce
1½ teaspoons salt
⅜ teaspoon white pepper
3 tablespoons Worcestershire sauce
3 pounds frozen uncooked shrimp
6 tablespoons sherry

Spinach Stuffed Fillets

Serves 8

½ cup minced onion
1 tablespoon olive oil
2 cups frozen spinach,
    thawed
1 cup soft bread crumbs
1 egg
½ cup ricotta cheese
1 cup grated Havarti cheese
½ teaspoon dried basil
    leaves
8 (6-ounce) thin red snapper
    fillets
½ cup grated Parmesan
    cheese

Serves 24

1½ cups minced onion
3 tablespoons olive oil
6 cups frozen spinach,
    thawed
3 cups soft bread crumbs
3 eggs
1½ cups ricotta cheese
3 cups grated Havarti cheese
1½ teaspoons dried basil
    leaves
24 (6-ounce) thin red
    snapper fillets
1½ cups grated Parmesan
    cheese

These pretty fillets are good for company and so easy to make. You can serve the cooked fish without freezing.

1. In heavy skillet, cook onion in olive oil until crisp-tender. Drain spinach thoroughly, pressing between paper towels to remove moisture. Add to skillet and cook for 1 to 2 minutes longer. Remove skillet from heat.

2. Preheat oven to 350°F. In medium bowl, combine bread crumbs, egg, cheeses, and basil. Add spinach and onion; mix to combine. Spread spinach mixture on each fillet and roll up to enclose filling; fasten with toothpicks.

3. Roll each fillet in Parmesan cheese to coat. Place rolled fillets on parchment paper–lined baking sheets and bake at 350°F for 25 to 30 minutes, until fish flakes when tested with fork. Cool completely in refrigerator; then place in rigid containers, wrap, seal, and freeze.

4. *To thaw and reheat:* Thaw fish in refrigerator overnight. Bake at 400°F for 12 to 18 minutes, until fish is thoroughly heated.

Salmon Quiche

Apple juice adds a sweet note and complements the salmon and Havarti in this special quiche. To serve without freezing, let quiche stand for 5 to 10 minutes after baking, then slice and serve.

1. Preheat oven to 400°F. Cook onions and garlic in butter and olive oil in heavy skillet until crisp-tender. Sprinkle flour, salt, and pepper over onions; cook and stir for 3 to 4 minutes. Stir in apple juice and evaporated milk; cook and stir for 4 to 5 minutes, until thick. Remove from heat and cool for 10 minutes.

2. Meanwhile, in medium bowl, beat eggs until foamy; add dill weed. Stir egg mixture into onion mixture and blend well. Sprinkle half of the Havarti cheese into bottom of pie crust.

3. Drain salmon and remove and discard skin and bones. Break salmon into chunks and scatter over cheese. Pour onion/egg mixture over salmon and top with remaining Havarti cheese. Sprinkle with Parmesan cheese. Bake at 400°F for 30 to 35 minutes, until golden brown and set. Cool in refrigerator, then flash freeze; wrap, label, and freeze. Or, slice quiche into serving pieces before freezing and flash freeze individually.

4. *To thaw and reheat:* Thaw quiche overnight in refrigerator. Bake at 350°F for 20 to 25 minutes, until heated through.

   To reheat individually: Microwave each frozen slice on medium for 2 to 4 minutes, then 1 minute on high, until hot.

Serves 6

1 onion, chopped
1 clove garlic, minced
2 tablespoons butter
2 tablespoons olive oil
¼ cup flour
½ teaspoon salt
⅛ teaspoon pepper
½ cup apple juice
1 cup evaporated milk
3 eggs, beaten
½ teaspoon dried dill weed
1½ cups shredded Havarti cheese
1 9-inch unbaked Pie Crust (page 299)
1 (14-ounce) can red salmon
¼ cup grated Parmesan cheese

Serves 18

3 onions, chopped
3 cloves garlic, minced
6 tablespoons butter
6 tablespoons olive oil
¾ cup flour
1½ teaspoons salt
⅜ teaspoon pepper
1½ cups apple juice
3 cups evaporated milk
9 eggs, beaten
1½ teaspoons dried dill weed
4½ cups shredded Havarti cheese
3 9-inch unbaked Pie Crusts (page 299)
3 (14-ounce) cans red salmon
¾ cup grated Parmesan cheese

Seafood Chowder

Serves 8

---

1 tablespoon olive oil
1 onion, chopped
1 green pepper, chopped
1 carrot, chopped
2 cloves garlic, minced
½ teaspoon dried thyme
    leaves
½ teaspoon salt
⅛ teaspoon white pepper
¼ cup flour
1 cup dry white wine
3 cups Fish Broth (page 304)
½ pound frozen uncooked
    medium shrimp
1 (6-ounce) can crabmeat
1 pound red snapper fillets,
    cubed
1 cup uncooked shell pasta
1 (13-ounce) can evaporated
    milk

Serves 24

---

3 tablespoons olive oil
3 onions, chopped
3 green peppers, chopped
3 carrots, chopped
6 cloves garlic, minced
1½ teaspoons dried thyme
    leaves
1½ teaspoons salt
⅜ teaspoon white pepper
¾ cup flour
3 cups dry white wine
9 cups Fish Broth (page 304)
1½ pounds frozen uncooked
    medium shrimp
3 (6-ounce) cans crabmeat
3 pounds red snapper fillets,
    cubed
3 cups uncooked shell pasta
3 (13-ounce) cans
    evaporated milk

You can use any fresh seafood you'd like in this easy chowder. To serve without freezing, cook pasta and add to chowder with evaporated milk; simmer until hot.

---

1. In large stockpot, heat olive oil and add onion, green pepper, carrot, and garlic. Cook and stir over medium heat until almost tender. Add thyme, salt, pepper, and flour to pot; cook and stir for 3 minutes, until bubbly. Add wine and broth; cover and simmer for 15 minutes, stirring twice.

2. Uncover pot and add seafood. Bring to a simmer and cook for 5 to 10 minutes, until fillets flake when tested with fork and shrimp curl and turn pink. Chill soup in ice-water bath or refrigerator. Pour into rigid container, attach bag with pasta, label, and freeze. Reserve evaporated milk in pantry.

3. *To thaw and reheat:* Thaw soup overnight in refrigerator. Cook pasta according to package directions until al dente; drain and reserve. Pour soup into stockpot and bring to a simmer. Add evaporated milk and pasta; simmer for 4 to 5 minutes, until heated through.

Freezing Soups and Stews

Use heavy-duty zipper-lock bags to store soups and stews. To make stackable packages, set the bag upright in a square container; fill with the soup, and then freeze. Remove the bag from the container, seal, and store.

Sweet and Sour Shrimp

To serve this dish without freezing, after sauce has simmered, add thawed shrimp and cook as directed in recipe. Thicken as directed with cornstarch mixture.

---

1. In large skillet, cook onion and garlic in olive oil until crisp-tender. Add green pepper and cook 1 to 2 minutes longer. Drain pineapple, reserving juice. Set pineapple aside. Add pineapple juice to skillet, along with broth, ketchup, vinegar, sugar, ginger, and soy sauce. Bring to a boil, reduce heat, and simmer for 5 to 7 minutes; then add pineapple tidbits. Cool in ice-water bath or in refrigerator.

2. Place frozen shrimp in zipper-lock bag. Pour cooled sauce into large zipper-lock bag and attach shrimp; label, seal, and freeze. Reserve cornstarch in pantry.

3. *To thaw and reheat:* Thaw sauce overnight in refrigerator; keep shrimp frozen. Pour sauce into saucepan and bring to a simmer over medium heat. Add shrimp and cook for 4 to 7 minutes, until shrimp turn pink and are thoroughly cooked. Meanwhile, dissolve cornstarch in ¼ cup water and add to skillet. Simmer for 1 to 2 minutes, until sauce thickens. Serve over hot cooked rice.

Serves 4–6

---

1 onion, chopped
3 cloves garlic, minced
2 tablespoons olive oil
1 green pepper, chopped
1 (8-ounce) can pineapple tidbits
1 cup Fish Broth (page 304)
¼ cup ketchup
¼ cup apple cider vinegar
¼ cup sugar
1 teaspoon ground ginger
2 tablespoons soy sauce
1 pound frozen uncooked shrimp
2 tablespoons cornstarch
¼ cup water

Serves 12–18

---

3 onions, chopped
9 cloves garlic, minced
6 tablespoons olive oil
3 green peppers, chopped
3 (8-ounce) cans pineapple tidbits
3 cups Fish Broth (page 304)
¾ cup ketchup
¾ cup apple cider vinegar
¾ cup sugar
1 tablespoon ground ginger
6 tablespoons soy sauce
3 pounds frozen uncooked shrimp
6 tablespoons cornstarch
¾ cup water

Thai Fish with Rice

Serves 4

½ cup coconut milk
¼ cup peanut butter
1 teaspoon minced fresh
    gingerroot
⅛ teaspoon cayenne
    pepper
⅛ teaspoon white pepper
1 tablespoon olive oil
½ cup minced onion
3 cloves garlic, minced
1 cup rice
2 cups Chicken Broth
    (page 301)
4 frozen fish fillets
¼ cup chopped peanuts

Serves 12

1½ cups coconut milk
¾ cup peanut butter
1 tablespoon minced fresh
    gingerroot
⅜ teaspoon cayenne
    pepper
⅜ teaspoon white pepper
3 tablespoons olive oil
1½ cups minced onion
9 cloves garlic, minced
3 cups rice
6 cups Chicken Broth
    (page 301)
12 frozen fish fillets
¾ cup chopped peanuts

To serve without freezing, thaw fish fillets and combine as directed without chilling sauce or rice. Bake, covered, at 375°F for 15 to 25 minutes or until fish flakes when tested with fork.

1. In small bowl, combine coconut milk, peanut butter, gingerroot, cayenne, and white pepper and mix until blended. In heavy skillet, heat olive oil and sauté onion and garlic until crisp-tender. Add coconut milk mixture and cook and stir for 2 to 3 minutes to blend. Chill sauce in ice-water bath or refrigerator.

2. In heavy saucepan, combine rice and chicken broth. Bring to a boil, then reduce heat, cover, and simmer for 15 minutes, until almost tender. Cool rice in refrigerator until cold. Place rice in 9" × 9" baking dish and sprinkle with 2 tablespoons water. Top rice with frozen fish fillets (do not thaw) and pour coconut sauce over fish. Sprinkle with peanuts, wrap casserole, seal, label, and freeze.

3. *To thaw and reheat:* Thaw overnight in refrigerator. Bake in preheated 375°F oven for 20 to 35 minutes or until fish flakes easily when tested with fork.

Tuna Pot Pie

To serve this pie without freezing, do not cool sauce or refreeze pastry. Bake and assemble pastry as directed.

1. Place thawed puff pastry on lightly floured surface and cut a 10-inch round from the center. Cut out small decorative shapes from center of pastry. Wrap pastry in freezer wrap and freeze.

2. In heavy saucepan, sauté onion and garlic in olive oil and butter until crisp-tender. Sprinkle flour, salt, and pepper over onion mixture; cook and stir until bubbly. Stir in half-and-half; cook and stir until slightly thickened. Remove from heat and stir in cheese until melted. Cool sauce in ice-water bath or refrigerator.

3. When sauce is cold, stir in frozen vegetables and drained tuna. Place in 2-quart baking dish, and then wrap dish in freezer wrap, attach puff pastry top, label, seal, and freeze.

4. *To thaw and reheat:* Thaw dish overnight in refrigerator; keep puff pastry frozen. Bake in preheated 375°F oven for 20 minutes or until filling is hot. Top with frozen puff pastry round. If desired, brush puff pastry with mixture of 1 beaten egg and 1 tablespoon water. Bake 20 to 25 minutes longer or until pastry is puffed and golden brown and filling bubbles.

Serves 6–8

1 sheet puff pastry, thawed
1 onion, chopped
3 cloves garlic, minced
2 tablespoons olive oil
2 tablespoons butter
4 tablespoons flour
½ teaspoon salt
⅛ teaspoon pepper
2 cups half-and-half
1 cup shredded Havarti cheese
1 cup frozen peas
2 cups frozen hash brown potatoes
1 cup frozen broccoli
1 (12-ounce) can chunk tuna, drained

Serves 18–24

3 sheets puff pastry, thawed
3 onions, chopped
9 cloves garlic, minced
6 tablespoons olive oil
6 tablespoons butter
12 tablespoons flour
1½ teaspoons salt
⅜ teaspoon pepper
6 cups half-and-half
3 cups shredded Havarti cheese
3 cups frozen peas
6 cups frozen hash brown potatoes
3 cups frozen broccoli
3 (12-ounce) cans chunk tuna, drained

Fisherman's Stew

Serves 8–10

1 onion, chopped
1 leek, chopped
1 red bell pepper, chopped
4 cloves garlic, chopped
3 tablespoons olive oil
3 tablespoons flour
1 teaspoon salt
⅛ teaspoon white pepper
5 cups Fish Broth (page 304)
1 (10-ounce) bottle clam
    juice
2 (14-ounce) cans diced
    tomatoes
2 cups frozen corn
2 cups frozen medium
    uncooked shrimp
1 cup frozen bay scallops
1 (6-ounce) can crabmeat
1 pound frozen fish fillets

Serves 24–30

3 onions, chopped
3 leeks, chopped
3 red bell peppers, chopped
12 cloves garlic, chopped
9 tablespoons olive oil
9 tablespoons flour
1 tablespoon salt
⅜ teaspoon white pepper
15 cups Fish Broth (page
    304)
3 (10-ounce) bottles clam
    juice
6 (14-ounce) cans diced
    tomatoes
6 cups frozen corn
6 cups frozen medium
    uncooked shrimp
3 cups frozen bay scallops
3 (6-ounce) cans crabmeat
3 pounds frozen fish fillets

To serve without freezing, thaw seafood.
Do not cool tomato mixture. Cook as directed below,
adding thawed seafood to simmering soup and stirring gently.

1. In heavy saucepan, sauté onion, leek, bell pepper, and garlic in olive oil until crisp-tender. Sprinkle flour, salt, and pepper over vegetables; cook and stir until bubbly, about 3 minutes. Add broth, clam juice, and undrained tomatoes; cook and stir for 10 to 12 minutes, until slightly thickened. Cool this mixture in ice-water bath or refrigerator; pour into rigid containers and label.

2. Combine frozen corn, frozen shrimp, and frozen scallops in another bag and attach to soup. Cut frozen fish fillets into 2-inch pieces and place in another bag; attach to soup and freeze. Reserve crabmeat in pantry.

3. *To thaw and reheat:* Thaw in refrigerator overnight. Pour tomato mixture into large saucepan and bring to a simmer over medium heat. Simmer for 5 to 8 minutes, then add fish fillets; simmer for 3 minutes. Add corn, shrimp, and scallops; simmer for 3 minutes. Drain crabmeat and add; simmer for 2 to 3 minutes or until fish flakes easily with fork, scallops are opaque, and shrimp are curled and pink.

Shrimp Quiche

To serve without freezing, bake quiche as directed below; let stand 10 minutes. If you like, substitute bay scallops or chunks of fresh crabmeat for shrimp.

1. Preheat oven to 375°F. Bake empty pie crust for 5 minutes until set. In heavy skillet, heat olive oil and butter and add shrimp; cook and stir for 2 to 3 minutes until shrimp just turn pink. Remove shrimp from pan and set aside in refrigerator.

2. Add onion to pan; cook and stir until crisp-tender. Sprinkle flour and pepper into pan and cook and stir until bubbly, about 3 to 4 minutes. Add milk to pan and bring to a simmer, stirring constantly, until sauce is thickened. Cool sauce in refrigerator.

3. In large bowl, beat eggs with sour cream. Add cooled sauce along with Havarti cheese. Place cooled, cooked shrimp and frozen peas in pie crust and pour egg mixture over. Sprinkle with Parmesan cheese and bake at 375°F for 20 to 30 minutes, until pie is puffed, set, and golden brown. Cool in refrigerator, then flash freeze; wrap, label, and freeze. Or, slice quiche into serving pieces before freezing and flash freeze individually.

4. *To thaw and reheat:* Thaw quiche overnight in refrigerator. Bake at 350°F for 20 to 25 minutes, until heated through.

   To reheat individually: Microwave each frozen slice on medium for 2 to 4 minutes, then 1 minute on high, until hot.

Serves 6

1 9-inch Pie Crust (page 299)
2 tablespoons olive oil
1 tablespoon butter
1 pound uncooked medium shrimp
1 onion, chopped
2 tablespoons flour
⅛ teaspoon white pepper
¾ cup evaporated milk
3 eggs
½ cup sour cream
1 cup shredded Havarti cheese
1 cup frozen peas
¼ cup grated Parmesan cheese

Serves 18

3 9-inch Pie Crusts (page 299)
6 tablespoons olive oil
3 tablespoons butter
3 pounds uncooked medium shrimp
3 onions, chopped
6 tablespoons flour
⅜ teaspoon white pepper
2¼ cups evaporated milk
9 eggs
1½ cups sour cream
3 cups shredded Havarti cheese
3 cups frozen peas
¾ cup grated Parmesan cheese

Tex Mex Shrimp

Serves 6

---

2 pounds frozen uncooked
    shrimp
2 tablespoons olive oil
1 onion, chopped
5 cloves garlic, minced
1 red bell pepper, chopped
1 jalapeno pepper, minced
2 (14-ounce) cans diced
    tomatoes
1 (6-ounce) can tomato
    paste
1 cup Fish Broth (page 304)
2 teaspoons sugar
⅛ teaspoon cayenne
    pepper
¼ teaspoon hot sauce
1 cup frozen corn

Serves 18

---

6 pounds frozen uncooked
    shrimp
6 tablespoons olive oil
3 onions, chopped
15 cloves garlic, minced
3 red bell peppers, chopped
3 jalapeno peppers, minced
6 (14-ounce) cans diced
    tomatoes
3 (6-ounce) cans tomato
    paste
3 cups Fish Broth (page 304)
6 teaspoons sugar
⅜ teaspoon cayenne
    pepper
¾ teaspoons hot sauce
3 cups frozen corn

To serve without freezing, thaw shrimp as directed and add to simmering sauce along with frozen corn. Simmer for 3 to 5 minutes or until shrimp are cooked and tender.

---

1. Place shrimp in zipper-lock bag and freeze. In heavy skillet, heat olive oil; sauté onion and garlic until almost crisp-tender. Add bell pepper and jalapeno pepper; cook and stir 2 minutes longer. Add undrained tomatoes, tomato paste, broth, sugar, cayenne pepper, and hot sauce; simmer 10 minutes to blend flavors.

2. Cool sauce in ice-water bath or refrigerator. When sauce is cold, add frozen corn, mix well, and pour into zipper-lock bag. Attach bag of frozen shrimp, seal, label, and freeze.

3. *To thaw and cook:* Place frozen sauce in heavy saucepan and cook over low heat until thawed. Increase heat to medium and bring the sauce to a simmer. Meanwhile, place frozen shrimp in a colander or strainer and place under cold running water for 3 to 4 minutes, until thawed. Add thawed and drained shrimp to simmering sauce and cook for 3 to 4 minutes or until shrimp are curled, pink, and firm, stirring once during cooking.

Fish and Shrimp in Parchment

To serve without freezing, simply bake the assembled packages in a preheated 450°F oven for 15 to 22 minutes or until fish is thoroughly cooked.

1. Cut four 14" × 10" pieces of heavy duty foil or parchment paper. Place one frozen fish fillet in center of each piece and top with frozen shrimp. Remove seeds from lemon slices and divide among packets. Sprinkle with garlic and top with sugar snap peas. Drizzle each with olive oil and sprinkle with salt, pepper, and marjoram.

2. Fold sides of foil or parchment around fish and vegetables and seal with a double fold. Wrap again in freezer paper or heavy duty foil, label, seal, and freeze.

3. *To thaw and cook:* Preheat oven to 450°F. Remove top layer of paper or foil from packages and place packages on cookie sheet. Bake packages for 18 to 25 minutes, until shrimp are pink and curled, fish flakes easily when tested with fork, and snap peas are hot. Open carefully at the table.

Don't Pack It in Too Tightly!

While the packages of food are freezing, leave some air space around each package so the cold air can circulate and freeze the food quickly. Once the food is frozen solid, you can safely stack packages right next to each other.

Serves 4

4 (6-ounce) frozen fish fillets
2 cups medium frozen uncooked shrimp
1 lemon, thinly sliced
2 cloves garlic, minced
2 cups frozen sugar snap peas
2 tablespoons extra-virgin olive oil
½ teaspoon salt
⅛ teaspoon white pepper
½ teaspoon dried marjoram leaves

Serves 12

12 (6-ounce) frozen fish fillets
6 cups medium frozen uncooked shrimp
3 lemons, thinly sliced
6 cloves garlic, minced
6 cups frozen sugar snap peas
6 tablespoons extra-virgin olive oil
1½ teaspoons salt
⅜ teaspoon white pepper
1½ teaspoons dried marjoram leaves

Shrimp Pesto Linguine

Serves 6

4 squares frozen Pesto
    Sauce (page 296)
2 pounds frozen uncooked
    medium shrimp
2 tablespoons oil
1 onion, chopped
2 cloves garlic, minced
2 cups frozen green beans
½ cup grated Parmesan
    cheese
1 (15-ounce) can evaporated
    milk
½ pound linguine pasta

Serves 18

12 squares frozen Pesto
    Sauce (page 296)
6 pounds frozen uncooked
    medium shrimp
6 tablespoons oil
3 onions, chopped
6 cloves garlic, minced
6 cups frozen green beans
1½ cups grated Parmesan
    cheese
3 (15-ounce) cans
    evaporated milk
1½ pounds linguine pasta

To serve without freezing, thaw pesto, shrimp, and green beans. Cook shrimp in oil with sautéed vegetables. Bring milk to a boil, add pesto, cooked pasta, and remaining ingredients; toss and serve with cheese.

1. Place frozen pesto in zipper-lock bag and place in freezer. Place shrimp in another zipper-lock bag and freeze.

2. In heavy skillet, heat oil and add onion and garlic. Cook and stir until crisp-tender; cool in refrigerator or ice-water bath. When cold, mix with frozen green beans and place in another zipper-lock bag. Place cheese in another bag; place all bags in large zipper-lock bag; label, seal, and freeze. Reserve evaporated milk and pasta in pantry.

3. *To thaw and reheat:* Thaw packages overnight in refrigerator. Place onion mixture in heavy saucepan and heat over medium heat until sizzling. Add shrimp; cook and stir until shrimp are pink and beans are hot. Cook pasta according to package directions. Meanwhile, in another saucepan, bring milk to a boil. Add pesto to boiling milk and stir in shrimp mixture and pasta. Toss together over medium heat for 3 to 4 minutes; then serve topped with Parmesan cheese.

Vegetable Crepes

Serves 6

---

12 Basic Crepes (page 300)
1 tablespoon butter
1 tablespoon oil
1 onion, chopped
2 carrots, minced
1 teaspoon salt
3 cups frozen hash brown
  potatoes
1 cup frozen green beans
1 teaspoon dried thyme leaves
2 cups shredded Cheddar
  cheese
¼ cup grated Parmesan
  cheese
1 tablespoon flour
1 cup sour cream
½ cup grated Parmesan cheese
1 cup sour cream

Serves 18

---

36 Basic Crepes (page 300)
3 tablespoons butter
3 tablespoons oil
3 onions, chopped
6 carrots, minced
1 tablespoon salt
9 cups frozen hash brown
  potatoes
3 cups frozen green beans
1 tablespoon dried thyme
  leaves
6 cups shredded Cheddar
  cheese
¾ cup grated Parmesan
  cheese
3 tablespoons flour
3 cups sour cream
1½ cups grated Parmesan
  cheese
3 cups sour cream

To serve without freezing, do not cool onion and carrot mixture; add potatoes and green beans to saucepan and cook until thawed. Fill and roll crepes, then top and bake as directed.

---

1. Cook crepes and let cool. In heavy saucepan, heat butter and oil and add onion and carrots. Cook and stir until crisp-tender. Sprinkle with salt and cool in ice-water bath or refrigerator until cold. Stir in potatoes, green beans, thyme, and cheeses. Add flour and first amount of sour cream and mix gently until combined.

2. Place 2 tablespoons of this mixture onto each crepe and roll up. Flash freeze crepes in single layer on baking pan, then place in rigid container, with layers separated by waxed paper; do not allow crepes to touch each other. Attach bag with ½ cup grated Parmesan cheese. Wrap, label, and freeze. Reserve remaining sour cream in refrigerator.

3. *To thaw and reheat:* Thaw overnight in refrigerator. Place crepes in 9" × 13" pan and spread 1 cup sour cream over; sprinkle with ½ cup grated Parmesan cheese. Bake in preheated 375°F oven for 20 to 30 minutes or until top browns and crepes are thoroughly heated.

Hearty Root Vegetable Soup

You can replace the vegetable broth with chicken or beef broth for a nonvegetarian soup. To serve immediately, sprinkle with cheese, and serve with toasted French bread.

1. Combine the olive oil and butter in a heavy stockpot and add onions and garlic. Cook and stir over medium heat until onions and garlic begin to turn brown, stirring frequently, about 20 to 30 minutes.

2. Peel potatoes and sweet potatoes. Cut potatoes into 2-inch chunks. Cut sweet potatoes into 1-inch chunks. Add potatoes along with all remaining ingredients except cheese to stockpot and bring to a simmer. Cover and cook for 25 to 35 minutes or until potatoes are almost tender when pierced with a fork.

3. Cool soup in ice-water bath or refrigerator until cold. Pour into 2 rigid containers, attach bag with cheese, label, and freeze.

4. *To thaw and reheat:* Thaw soup overnight in refrigerator. Place in large saucepan and bring to a simmer. Cover pan and let simmer for 10 to 15 minutes or until thoroughly heated. Serve with Romano cheese.

How to Flash Freeze

When a recipe calls for flash freezing, place food in freezer in a single layer on baking sheet and freeze until solid. Then wrap or package food, label, and store in freezer.

Serves 6

4 tablespoons olive oil
2 tablespoons butter
3 onions, chopped
6 cloves garlic, minced
½ pound potatoes
½ pound sweet potatoes
2 cups chopped carrots
6 cups Vegetable Broth
   (page 305)
2 teaspoons dried basil
   leaves
1½ teaspoons salt
⅛ teaspoon pepper
½ cup grated Romano
   cheese

Serves 18

12 tablespoons olive oil
6 tablespoons butter
9 onions, chopped
18 cloves garlic, minced
1½ pounds potatoes
1½ pounds sweet potatoes
6 cups chopped carrots
18 cups Vegetable Broth
   (page 305)
2 tablespoons dried basil
   leaves
4½ teaspoons salt
⅜ teaspoon pepper
1½ cups grated Romano
   cheese

Spinach Lasagna

1 (8-ounce) package
  lasagna noodles
2 tablespoons olive oil
1 tablespoon butter
1 onion, chopped
4 cloves garlic, minced
1 teaspoon dried fennel seed
1 teaspoon salt
⅛ teaspoon white pepper
1 (26-ounce) jar spaghetti sauce
1 (16-ounce) package frozen
  cut-leaf spinach
2 cups ricotta cheese
1 egg
1 cup shredded mozzarella
  cheese
1 cup shredded Monterey
  jack cheese
½ cup grated Parmesan cheese

Serves 24

3 (8-ounce) packages
  lasagna noodles
6 tablespoons olive oil
3 tablespoons butter
3 onions, chopped
12 cloves garlic, minced
1 tablespoon dried fennel seed
1 tablespoon salt
⅜ teaspoon white pepper
3 (26-ounce) jars spaghetti
  sauce
3 (16-ounce) packages
  frozen cut-leaf spinach
6 cups ricotta cheese
3 eggs
3 cups shredded mozzarella
  cheese
3 cups shredded Monterey
  jack cheese
1½ cups grated Parmesan
  cheese

To serve immediately, after layering ingredients in pan, bake at 375°F for 25 to 30 minutes or until thoroughly heated and bubbly.

1. Cook pasta according to package directions until almost tender. Remove from pan, rinse with cold water, and set aside on kitchen towels.

2. In large saucepan, heat olive oil and butter. When foamy, add onion and garlic and cook, stirring, until tender. Add fennel seed, salt, pepper, and spaghetti sauce to pan. Bring to a boil, then reduce heat, cover pan, and simmer for 15 to 20 minutes.

3. Meanwhile, drain spinach thoroughly and combine with ricotta and egg in medium bowl. Beat well until combined. Add mozzarella and Monterey jack cheeses.

4. Line 13" × 9" pan with freezer paper and place 1 cup of sauce in pan. Top with three lasagna noodles and half of the ricotta mixture. Top with half of the remaining sauce, three lasagna noodles, and rest of ricotta mixture. Finish layering with three remaining lasagna noodles and remaining sauce. Sprinkle with Parmesan cheese. Cool lasagna in ice-water bath or refrigerator, then wrap well, label, and freeze.

5. *To thaw and reheat:* Thaw overnight in refrigerator. Bake in preheated 375°F oven for 30 to 45 minutes or until thoroughly heated and bubbly.

Pizza Fondue

To serve without freezing, add cheese to blended sauce, toast English muffins, and bake breadsticks as directed. Place sauce in fondue pot and serve with dippers.

1. In heavy skillet, heat olive oil and add frozen crumbles, onion, and garlic. Cook over medium heat, stirring frequently, until vegetables are crisp-tender and crumbles are thawed. Add pizza sauce, oregano, tomato juice, and diced tomatoes. Bring to a boil, then simmer for 15 minutes, stirring occasionally, until blended.

2. Cool sauce in ice-water bath or in refrigerator. Pour into rigid container and attach bag with shredded cheese. Attach bag with English muffins, label, seal, and freeze. Reserve breadsticks in refrigerator.

3. *To thaw and reheat:* Thaw overnight in refrigerator. Pour sauce into saucepan and bring to a simmer; simmer 5 to 10 minutes or until thoroughly heated. Pour into fondue pot and add shredded cheese; stir to melt cheese. Toast English muffins and cut each into quarters. Prepare breadsticks and bake according to package directions. Serve with fondue.

Serves 6

2 tablespoons olive oil
1 (12-ounce) package frozen meatless crumbles
1 onion, chopped
2 cloves garlic, chopped
1 (24-ounce) can pizza sauce
½ teaspoon dried oregano
½ cup tomato juice
1 (14-ounce) can diced tomatoes, undrained
2 cups shredded Colby-jack cheese
6 English muffins
2 (8-ounce) cans refrigerated breadsticks

Serves 18

6 tablespoons olive oil
3 (12-ounce) packages frozen meatless crumbles
3 onions, chopped
6 cloves garlic, chopped
3 (24-ounce) cans pizza sauce
1½ teaspoons dried oregano
1½ cups tomato juice
3 (14-ounce) cans diced tomatoes, undrained
6 cups shredded Colby-jack cheese
18 English muffins
6 (8-ounce) cans refrigerated breadsticks

Lentil Soup

Add your favorite vegetables to this hearty
and warming soup. To serve without freezing, simmer
for 30 minutes after adding all ingredients to lentils.

Serves 4–6

2 cups lentils
4 cups Vegetable Broth
    (page 303)
2 cups water
2 onions, chopped
3 cloves garlic, chopped
2 carrots, chopped
2 tablespoons olive oil
1 tablespoon butter
1 (14-ounce) can diced
    tomatoes, undrained
1 teaspoon salt
⅛ teaspoon white pepper
1 teaspoon dried oregano

Serves 12–18

6 cups lentils
12 cups Vegetable Broth
    (page 303)
6 cups water
6 onions, chopped
9 cloves garlic, chopped
6 carrots, chopped
6 tablespoons olive oil
3 tablespoons butter
3 (14-ounce) cans diced
    tomatoes, undrained
1 tablespoon salt
⅜ teaspoon white pepper
1 tablespoon dried oregano

1. Sort lentils to remove small pebbles and damaged pieces; rinse well. Place lentils in saucepan along with broth and water. Bring to a boil; then reduce heat, cover, and simmer for 30 minutes. Meanwhile, in heavy skillet, cook onions, garlic, and carrots in olive oil and butter until crisp-tender.

2. When lentils are tender, add all ingredients, including sautéed vegetables, to saucepan and simmer 5 minutes longer. Cool soup in ice-water bath or refrigerator. Pour into rigid container, label, seal, and freeze.

3. *To thaw and reheat:* Let soup thaw overnight in refrigerator. Pour into saucepan and bring to a simmer over medium heat. Simmer for 10 to 15 minutes or until thoroughly heated.

Be Careful with Those Peppers!

When working with jalapeno peppers or green chilies, be careful to avoid touching your face, mouth, or eyes. Wash your hands thoroughly, using lots of soap, after you're done processing the peppers, or wear rubber gloves.

Wild Rice Quiche

Wild rice adds a wonderful nutty flavor and a great chewy texture to this classic quiche. To serve immediately, let stand for 10 minutes after baking, then cut into wedges.

1. Preheat oven to 400°F. Bake unfilled pie shell for 8 to 10 minutes, until light golden brown. Set aside on wire rack to cool.

2. Combine wild rice and pimientos in medium bowl. In heavy saucepan, cook onion and garlic in olive oil until tender, stirring frequently. Add to wild rice mixture and set aside. In another bowl, combine eggs, sour cream, mustard, and pepper and beat well to blend. Add to wild rice mixture and stir gently to combine.

3. Combine Havarti and Monterey jack cheeses in a small bowl. Sprinkle 1 cup mixed cheeses in bottom of cooled pie shell. Pour wild rice mixture over cheese and sprinkle remaining cheese on top. Sprinkle Parmesan cheese over all. Bake at 400°F for 30 to 35 minutes or until filling is set and golden brown. Cool in refrigerator, then flash freeze; wrap, label, and freeze. Or, slice quiche into serving pieces before freezing and flash freeze individually.

4. *To thaw and reheat:* Thaw quiche overnight in refrigerator. Bake at 350°F for 20 to 25 minutes or until heated through.

   To reheat individually: Microwave each slice on medium for 2 to 4 minutes, then 1 minute on high, or until hot.

Serves 6

1 9-inch Pie Crust (page 299)
1 cup cooked wild rice
2 tablespoons minced pimientos
1 onion, chopped
3 cloves garlic, minced
1 tablespoon olive oil
3 eggs
1 cup sour cream
1 tablespoon Dijon mustard
⅛ teaspoon white pepper
1 cup shredded Havarti cheese
1 cup shredded Monterey jack cheese
¼ cup grated Parmesan cheese

Serves 18

3 9-inch Pie Crusts (page 299)
3 cups cooked wild rice
6 tablespoons minced pimientos
3 onions, chopped
9 cloves garlic, minced
3 tablespoons olive oil
9 eggs
3 cups sour cream
3 tablespoons Dijon mustard
⅜ teaspoon white pepper
3 cups shredded Havarti cheese
3 cups shredded Monterey jack cheese
¾ cup grated Parmesan cheese

Mexican Quiche

Serves 6

---

2 tablespoons olive oil
2 tablespoons butter
1 onion, chopped
4 cloves garlic, minced
2 tablespoons flour
½ cup half-and-half
4 eggs
½ cup sour cream
½ cup shredded Muenster
  cheese
1 9-inch Pie Crust (page 299)
1 (16-ounce) can black
  beans, rinsed and
  drained
2 tablespoons chopped
  green chilies
1 cup shredded pepper jack
  cheese
¼ cup grated Parmesan
  cheese

Serves 18

---

6 tablespoons olive oil
6 tablespoons butter
3 onions, chopped
12 cloves garlic, minced
6 tablespoons flour
1½ cups half-and-half
12 eggs
1½ cups sour cream
1½ cups shredded Muenster
  cheese
3 9-inch Pie Crusts (page
  299)
3 (16-ounce) cans black
  beans, rinsed and drained
6 tablespoons chopped
  green chilies
3 cups shredded pepper jack
  cheese
¾ cup grated Parmesan
  cheese

If you like your food really spicy, use chopped jalapenos or habanero peppers instead of the green peppers. To serve without freezing, let quiche stand for 5 minutes after baking, then slice.

---

1. Preheat oven to 350°F. In large skillet, heat olive oil and butter until melted. Add onion and garlic; cook and stir until tender. Sprinkle flour over onions and cook and stir 3 to 4 minutes longer. Add half-and-half to skillet and cook, stirring constantly, until thickened.

2. In large bowl, beat eggs until foamy. Add sour cream and mix well with wire whisk. Add onion mixture and beat well.

3. Place Muenster cheese in bottom of unbaked pie crust and top with black beans and green chilies. Top with pepper jack cheese and slowly pour egg mixture into crust. Sprinkle with Parmesan cheese and bake at 350°F for 40 to 45 minutes or until quiche is brown, puffy, and set. Cool quiche in refrigerator, then flash freeze; wrap, label, and freeze. Or, slice quiche into serving pieces before freezing and flash freeze individually.

4. *To thaw and reheat:* Thaw quiche overnight in refrigerator. Bake at 350°F for 20 to 25 minutes or until heated through.

   To reheat individually: Microwave each slice on medium for 2 to 4 minutes, then 1 minute on high, or until hot.

Taco Salad

To serve without freezing, add cheese to
vegetable mixture and let melt, then serve as directed.

1. In heavy skillet, heat olive oil and add onions. Cook and stir for 4 to 5 minutes, until crisp-tender. Add green pepper; cook 2 minutes longer. Add seasonings, tomatoes, and kidney beans; stir. Simmer mixture, stirring occasionally, for 10 minutes. Remove from heat and chill in ice-water bath or refrigerator.

2. Pour mixture into heavy-duty freezer bag and attach small bag with Cheddar cheese. Label, seal, and freeze. Reserve chips and salsa in pantry and greens in refrigerator (or purchase them the day before serving this salad).

3. *To thaw and reheat:* Thaw overnight in refrigerator. Pour vegetable mixture into heavy skillet; heat over medium heat, stirring frequently, until mixture simmers, about 8 to 10 minutes. Add cheese, remove from heat, cover, and let stand until cheese is melted. Place corn chips and greens on serving plates and top with vegetable mixture. Garnish with salsa and serve.

Serves 6

2 tablespoons olive oil
2 onions, chopped
1 green pepper, chopped
1 teaspoon cumin
1 tablespoon chili powder
½ teaspoon Tabasco sauce
1 (14-ounce) can diced
  tomatoes, undrained
2 (14-ounce) cans kidney
  beans, rinsed and
  drained
1 cup diced Cheddar cheese
2 cups corn chips
1 (10 ounce) jar salsa
1 (10-ounce) bag mixed
  salad greens

Serves 18

6 tablespoons olive oil
6 onions, chopped
3 green peppers, chopped
1 tablespoon cumin
3 tablespoons chili powder
1½ teaspoons Tabasco sauce
3 (14-ounce) cans diced
  tomatoes, undrained
6 (14-ounce) cans kidney
  beans, rinsed and
  drained
3 cups diced Cheddar cheese
6 cups corn chips
3 (10 ounce) jars salsa
3 (10-ounce) bags mixed
  salad greens

Tortilla Soup

Serves 4

1 onion, chopped
3 cloves garlic, minced
2 tablespoons olive oil
1 (14-ounce) can diced
    tomatoes, undrained
3 ripe tomatoes, chopped
1 (6-ounce) can tomato
    paste
4 cups Vegetable Broth
    (page 303)
½ teaspoon salt
2 teaspoons sugar
¼ teaspoon red pepper
    flakes
½ teaspoon ground
    coriander
Tortilla chips

Serves 12

3 onions, chopped
9 cloves garlic, minced
6 tablespoons olive oil
3 (14-ounce) cans diced
    tomatoes, undrained
9 ripe tomatoes, chopped
3 (6-ounce) cans tomato
    paste
12 cups Vegetable Broth
    (page 303)
1½ teaspoons salt
6 teaspoons sugar
¾ teaspoon red pepper
    flakes
1½ teaspoons ground
    coriander
Tortilla chips

Three different forms of tomatoes builds a rich flavor base in this easy soup. To serve it immediately, heat and garnish as directed.

1. In large saucepan, cook onion and garlic in olive oil until crisp-tender. Add remaining ingredients except tortilla chips, bring to a boil; then reduce heat and simmer for 10 minutes. Cool the soup in ice-water bath or refrigerator. Pour into rigid container, label, seal, and freeze.

2. *To thaw and reheat:* Place frozen soup in large saucepan and cook over low heat until thawed. Bring to a simmer and serve, garnished with tortilla chips and your favorite toppings, such as chopped avocado and cilantro, sour cream, and shredded cheese.

Measure Carefully

When measuring flavored extracts, spices, and herbs, do not hold the measuring spoon over the mixing bowl. Your hand may slip while measuring and add far too much of the ingredient.

Many Bean Chili

You can use any kind of canned bean in this recipe.
To serve immediately, add corn with beans and simmer
for 15 to 20 minutes, until blended.

1. In large stockpot, cook onion, garlic, and carrots in olive oil until crisp-tender. Drain rinsed beans well and add to stockpot with remaining ingredients except corn. Bring to a boil; then reduce heat and simmer for 5 minutes.

2. Cool in ice-water bath or refrigerator; then pour into rigid container. Label, seal container, and freeze. Reserve canned corn in pantry.

3. *To thaw and reheat:* Let chili thaw overnight in refrigerator. Remove bay leaf. Pour into large saucepan and bring to a simmer. Add undrained corn and simmer for 15 to 20 minutes or until thoroughly heated, stirring occasionally.

Serves 6–8

1 onion, chopped
5 cloves garlic, minced
3 carrots, sliced
3 tablespoons olive oil
2 (15-ounce) cans black beans, rinsed
1 can cannellini beans, rinsed
1 can red kidney beans, rinsed
2 (14-ounce) cans diced tomatoes, undrained
1 bay leaf
½ teaspoon dried basil leaves
1 tablespoon chili powder
½ teaspoon dried marjoram leaves
1 teaspoon salt
¼ teaspoon red pepper flakes
1 (12-ounce) can corn

Serves 18–24

3 onions, chopped
15 cloves garlic, minced
9 carrots, sliced
9 tablespoons olive oil
6 (15-ounce) cans black beans, rinsed
3 cans cannellini beans, rinsed
3 cans red kidney beans, rinsed
6 (14-ounce) cans diced tomatoes, undrained
3 bay leaves
1½ teaspoons dried basil leaves
3 tablespoons chili powder
1½ teaspoons dried marjoram leaves
1 tablespoon salt
¾ teaspoon red pepper flakes
3 (12-ounce) cans corn

Black Bean Lasagna

Serves 8

1 onion, chopped
2 cloves garlic, minced
2 tablespoons olive oil
1 (14-ounce) can diced tomatoes
1 (6-ounce) can tomato paste
1 cup Vegetable Broth (page 303)
½ teaspoon dried thyme leaves
½ teaspoon dried oregano leaves
½ teaspoon salt
⅛ teaspoon pepper
2 cups ricotta cheese
2 eggs, beaten
1 cup shredded Muenster cheese
1 cup shredded mozzarella cheese
9 lasagna noodles
2 (14-ounce) cans black beans, drained and rinsed
2 cups shredded mozzarella cheese
½ cup grated Parmesan cheese

Serves 24

3 onions, chopped
6 cloves garlic, minced
6 tablespoons olive oil
3 (14-ounce) cans diced tomatoes
3 (6-ounce) cans tomato paste
3 cups Vegetable Broth (page 303)
1½ teaspoons dried thyme leaves
1½ teaspoons dried oregano leaves
1½ teaspoons salt
⅜ teaspoon pepper
6 cups ricotta cheese
6 eggs, beaten
3 cups shredded Muenster cheese
3 cups shredded mozzarella cheese
27 lasagna noodles
6 (14-ounce) cans black beans, drained and rinsed
6 cups shredded mozzarella cheese
1½ cups grated Parmesan cheese

To serve without freezing, bake covered in a preheated 350°F oven for 50 to 55 minutes or until noodles are softened. Uncover and bake 10 to 15 minutes longer.

1. In heavy skillet, cook onion and garlic in olive oil until crisp-tender. Add undrained tomatoes, tomato paste, broth, thyme, oregano, salt, and pepper. Simmer, covered, for 10 to 12 minutes, until flavors are blended. In large bowl, combine ricotta, eggs, Muenster, and first quantity mozzarella, and blend well.

2. In 13" × 9" pan, place 1 cup tomato sauce. Cover with 3 uncooked lasagna noodles. Pour half of tomato sauce over noodles. Top with 3 more noodles. Spread half of ricotta mixture over noodles and top with black beans. Spread remaining ricotta mixture over black beans and top with 3 noodles. Pour remaining tomato sauce over and sprinkle with remaining mozzarella and Parmesan. Cool completely in refrigerator; then wrap, seal, label, and freeze.

3. *To thaw and cook:* Thaw lasagna overnight in refrigerator. Bake, covered, in preheated 375° oven for 55 to 60 minutes. Uncover and bake 10 to 15 minutes longer or until cheese is melted and browned.

Spicy Cheese Tortellini

To serve without freezing, add frozen tortellini to simmering sauce and cook for 3 to 4 minutes until tortellini is hot and tender. Serve with Parmesan cheese.

1. Heat olive oil in large skillet and sauté onion and garlic until crisp-tender. Add jalapeno pepper; cook and stir for 1 to 2 minutes, until fragrant. Add remaining ingredients except for tortellini and Parmesan cheese and stir to blend. Simmer for 5 to 6 minutes, until flavors are blended.

2. Cool sauce in ice-water bath or in refrigerator until cold. Pour into rigid container and attach bag of frozen tortellini. Place Parmesan cheese in small zipper-lock bag and attach to sauce. Label, seal, and freeze.

3. *To thaw and reheat:* Thaw sauce and cheese overnight in refrigerator. Do not thaw tortellini. Pour sauce into saucepan and bring to a simmer. Add frozen tortellini, bring back to a simmer, and cook for 3 to 4 minutes or until tortellini is hot and tender. Serve with Parmesan cheese.

Freezing Rice and Pasta

Slightly undercook pasta and rice when these foods are going to be frozen. They will soften slightly during freezing and will cook to perfection when the food is reheated.

Serves 4–6

2 tablespoons olive oil
1 onion, chopped
2 cloves garlic, minced
1 jalapeno pepper, minced
1 (14-ounce) can diced tomatoes, undrained
1 (8-ounce) can tomato sauce
1 (6-ounce) can tomato paste
2 cups Vegetable Broth (page 303)
½ teaspoon salt
⅛ teaspoon white pepper
1 (9-ounce) package frozen cheese tortellini
½ cup grated Parmesan cheese

Serves 12–18

6 tablespoons olive oil
3 onions, chopped
6 cloves garlic, minced
3 jalapeno peppers, minced
3 (14-ounce) cans diced tomatoes, undrained
3 (8-ounce) cans tomato sauce
3 (6-ounce) cans tomato paste
6 cups Vegetable Broth (page 303)
1½ teaspoons salt
⅜ teaspoon white pepper
3 (9-ounce) packages frozen cheese tortellini
1½ cups grated Parmesan cheese

Spinach Pie

You won't miss the meat in this delicious, cheesy pie. To serve without freezing, when pie is baked, let stand for 10 minutes before slicing.

Serves 6–8

2 onions, chopped
5 cloves garlic, minced
2 tablespoons olive oil
1 tablespoon flour
2 cups frozen cut-leaf
    spinach, thawed
1 cup frozen chopped
    broccoli, thawed
5 eggs
⅛ teaspoon pepper
1 cup ricotta cheese
1 (3-ounce) package cream
    cheese, softened
2 cups shredded mozzarella
    cheese
1 cup grated Parmesan
    cheese
2 9-inch Pie Crusts (page
    299)
1 tablespoon milk

Serves 18–24

6 onions, chopped
15 cloves garlic, minced
6 tablespoons olive oil
3 tablespoons flour
6 cups frozen cut-leaf
    spinach, thawed
3 cups frozen chopped
    broccoli, thawed
15 eggs
⅜ teaspoon pepper
3 cups ricotta cheese
3 (3-ounce) packages cream
    cheese, softened
6 cups shredded mozzarella
    cheese
3 cups grated Parmesan
    cheese
6 9-inch Pie Crusts (page 299)
3 tablespoons milk

1. Preheat oven to 375°F. In heavy skillet, cook onion and garlic in olive oil until crisp-tender. Sprinkle flour over vegetables. Cook and stir for 2 minutes; then remove from heat and refrigerate until cold.

2. Drain spinach and broccoli by pressing between paper towels. In large bowl, beat eggs, pepper, ricotta cheese, and cream cheese until well mixed. Add vegetables, mozzarella cheese, and Parmesan cheese and mix well.

3. Pour spinach mixture into pie crust–lined pan. Top with remaining pie crust, seal and flute edges, and cut vent holes in top of crust. Brush crust with milk and bake at 375°F for 50 to 65 minutes or until crust is browned and pie is set. Cool in refrigerator, then wrap whole pie and freeze, or cut pie into 8 slices and wrap individually, then freeze.

4. *To thaw and reheat whole pie:* Thaw overnight in refrigerator. Bake at 375°F for 25 to 35 minutes or until thoroughly heated.

   To thaw and reheat individually: Thaw slice overnight in refrigerator, then bake at 375°F for 10 to 15 minutes or until thoroughly heated.

Crisp Phyllo Burritos

These delicious little bundles are a cross between a French pastry and a Mexican burrito. To serve without freezing, bake as directed below.

1. In heavy skillet, heat olive oil and add crumbles, onion, and garlic. Cook and stir over medium heat until vegetables are crisp-tender. Stir in taco seasoning, water, and refried beans and mix to blend. Simmer for 5 minutes; then add salsa. Cool this mixture completely in refrigerator or ice-water bath.

2. When filling is cold, spread one sheet phyllo dough on work surface and brush with butter. Layer another phyllo sheet on top of first and brush with butter. Add a third sheet and cut the stack of sheets in half crosswise, making two rectangles. Place a spoonful of chilled filling at short end of the phyllo stack and top with cheese. Roll phyllo dough over filling, folding in ends and sealing edges with butter. Repeat with second phyllo stack.

3. Repeat with remaining phyllo sheets, butter, and filling, making six bundles altogether. Brush bundles with butter. Wrap each bundle in freezer paper and place all in heavy-duty zipper-lock bag. Label, seal, and freeze. Reserve paprika in pantry.

4. *To thaw and bake:* Let thaw overnight in refrigerator. Preheat oven to 375°F. Place unwrapped bundles on cookie sheet, sprinkle each with paprika, and bake at 375°F for 20 to 25 minutes or until filling is thoroughly heated, cheese is melted, and phyllo dough is browned and crisp. Serve with sour cream and salsa.

Serves 6

1 tablespoon olive oil
1¼ cups frozen meatless crumbles
½ cup chopped onion
2 cloves garlic, minced
2 tablespoons Taco Seasoning Mix (page 297)
¼ cup water
½ cup refried beans
⅓ cup salsa
9 sheets phyllo dough, thawed
¼ cup melted butter
1 cup shredded pepper jack cheese
1 teaspoon smoked paprika

Serves 18

3 tablespoons olive oil
3¾ cups frozen meatless crumbles
1½ cups chopped onion
6 cloves garlic, minced
6 tablespoons Taco Seasoning Mix (page 297)
¾ cup water
1½ cups refried beans
1 cup salsa
27 sheets phyllo dough, thawed
¾ cup melted butter
3 cups shredded pepper jack cheese
1 tablespoon smoked paprika

Hash Brown Potato Bake

Serves 4

1 tablespoon olive oil
1 shallot, chopped
1 clove garlic, chopped
1 green chili, chopped
½ cup milk
1 (3-ounce) package cream
   cheese
½ teaspoon salt
⅛ teaspoon white pepper
2 cups frozen hash brown
   potatoes
1 cup frozen corn
¼ cup grated Parmesan
   cheese

Serves 12

3 tablespoons olive oil
3 shallots, chopped
3 cloves garlic, chopped
3 green chilies, chopped
1½ cups milk
3 (3-ounce) packages cream
   cheese
1½ teaspoons salt
⅜ teaspoon white pepper
6 cups frozen hash brown
   potatoes
3 cups frozen corn
¾ cup grated Parmesan
   cheese

Look for different types of hash brown potatoes; some come packaged with vegetables like onions and peppers. To serve this dish without freezing, bake, covered, at 375°F for 35 to 40 minutes.

1. In heavy skillet, heat olive oil and cook shallot and garlic until crisp-tender, about 3 to 4 minutes. Add green chili, cook and stir for 1 minute, then add milk, cream cheese, salt, and pepper. Cook and stir over medium heat until cream cheese is melted and sauce is blended. Remove from heat and chill in ice-water bath or refrigerator.

2. When sauce is cold, fold in frozen potatoes and frozen corn. Place in 8" × 8" pan lined with freezer paper and sprinkle with Parmesan cheese. Wrap and freeze casserole until frozen solid, then remove from pan, wrap again, and freeze.

3. *To thaw and reheat:* Unwrap casserole and place in 8" × 8" baking dish; let thaw overnight in refrigerator. Bake, covered, in preheated 375°F oven for 20 to 30 minutes or until casserole is bubbly and hot in center. Uncover and bake 5 to 10 minutes longer, until top is browned.

Beef Stew

Serves 6

1 pound beef stew meat
2 cups baby carrots
2 onions, chopped
3 cloves garlic, minced
1 teaspoon dried thyme
⅛ teaspoon pepper
2 cups frozen baby peas
1 (16-ounce) package frozen
    potato wedges
2 (10-ounce) cans condensed
    beef broth
2 tablespoons cornstarch

Serves 18

3 pounds beef stew meat
6 cups baby carrots
6 onions, chopped
9 cloves garlic, minced
1 tablespoon dried thyme
⅜ teaspoon pepper
6 cups frozen baby peas
3 (16-ounce) packages
    frozen potato wedges
6 (10-ounce) cans condensed
    beef broth
6 tablespoons cornstarch

To cook without freezing, combine all ingredients except peas, potatoes, and cornstarch in slow cooker; cook for 8 to 10 hours on low. Follow directions below for adding these ingredients.

1. Place meat in zipper-lock bag. Combine carrots, onions, garlic, thyme, and pepper in another zipper-lock bag and seal. Place baby peas in another zipper-lock bag and potato wedges in yet another bag. Place all four bags in large zipper-lock bag, label, seal, and freeze. Reserve beef broth and cornstarch in pantry.

2. *To thaw and cook:* Thaw meat and bag of carrot mixture overnight in refrigerator. Keep potatoes and peas frozen. In the morning, combine meat, carrot mixture, beef broth, and 2 cups water in 3- to 4-quart Slow Cooker. Cover and cook on low for 8 to 10 hours, until beef and vegetables are tender. Put potatoes and peas in refrigerator.

3. Half an hour before serving, add peas and potato wedges to slow cooker. Remove ½ cup liquid from slow cooker and mix with cornstarch until smooth; return to slow cooker. Cover and cook on high for 25 to 30 more minutes, until peas and potatoes are hot.

Chicken Supreme

To serve without freezing, do not cool onion mixture. Place chicken, carrots, onion, garlic, apple juice, and soup in slow cooker and cook on low for 7 to 8 hours. Top with bacon and cheese and let melt.

1. In heavy skillet, cook bacon until crisp. Remove bacon from pan and let drain on paper towels; crumble and refrigerate. Pour off half of the fat from skillet. Cook and stir onions and garlic in remaining drippings for 2 to 3 minutes, until onions begin to soften. Remove pan from heat and set aside to cool for 25 to 30 minutes.

2. Add apple juice to skillet; stir to combine. Add chicken breasts and turn over in onion mixture to coat. Pour all into a zipper-lock bag and seal. Attach bag with baby carrots and another bag with crumbled bacon and cubed cheese; label, seal, and freeze. Reserve soup, milk, and couscous in pantry.

3. *To thaw and cook:* Thaw all ingredients overnight in refrigerator. In small bowl, combine soup and evaporated milk and mix to blend. Place chicken mixture in 4- to 5-quart slow cooker and top with soup mixture and carrots. Cover slow cooker and cook on low for 6 to 7 hours or until chicken and carrots are tender. Top with Gouda cheese and bacon, cover, and cook on high for 5 to 10 minutes, until cheese is melted. Cook couscous as directed on package and serve with chicken and sauce.

Serves 6

4 slices bacon
1 onion, chopped
2 cloves garlic, chopped
½ cup apple juice
6 boneless, skinless chicken breasts
2 cups baby carrots
1 cup cubed Gouda cheese
1 (10-ounce) can condensed mushroom soup
½ cup evaporated milk
1 (10-ounce) package couscous

Serves 18

12 slices bacon
3 onions, chopped
6 cloves garlic, chopped
1½ cups apple juice
18 boneless, skinless chicken breasts
6 cups baby carrots
3 cups cubed Gouda cheese
3 (10-ounce) cans condensed mushroom soup
1½ cups evaporated milk
3 (10-ounce) packages couscous

Southwest Chicken Stew

Serves 6

---

2 pounds boned, skinned
    chicken thighs
2 tablespoons Taco
    Seasoning Mix (page
    297)
1 onion, chopped
4 cloves garlic, minced
1 jalapeno pepper, minced
2 cups frozen corn
2 (14-ounce) cans diced
    tomatoes
2 (16-ounce) cans cannellini
    beans
1 (14-ounce) can condensed
    chicken broth
1 (10-ounce) jar green chili
    salsa

Serves 18

---

6 pounds boned, skinned
    chicken thighs
6 tablespoons Taco
    Seasoning Mix (page
    297)
3 onions, chopped
12 cloves garlic, minced
3 jalapeno peppers, minced
6 cups frozen corn
6 (14-ounce) cans diced
    tomatoes
6 (16-ounce) cans cannellini
    beans
3 (14-ounce) cans condensed
    chicken broth
3 (10-ounce) jars green chili
    salsa

You can also purchase taco seasoning mix instead of making your own. To serve immediately, combine in slow cooker and cook as directed.

---

1. Cut chicken thighs into 1-inch pieces and toss with taco seasoning to coat. Flash freeze in single layer on cookie sheet. When frozen solid, place coated chicken in zipper-lock bag and place in freezer.

2. In another zipper-lock bag, place onions, garlic, peppers, and corn; seal bag, label, and attach to bag with chicken. Reserve canned tomatoes, beans, broth, and salsa in pantry.

3. *To thaw and cook:* Thaw chicken and vegetables overnight in refrigerator. Combine in 4- to 5-quart slow cooker and top with undrained tomatoes, drained beans, chicken broth, salsa, and 1 cup water. Cover and cook on low for 8 to 9 hours, until chicken is tender and thoroughly cooked.

Heat Up that Slow Cooker

You can add ¼ cup of warm water to the slow cooker to help the food get to a safe temperature more quickly. If you are at home for the first hour of slow cooker cooking time, set the appliance to high for 1 hour to get the food up to cooking temperature quickly. Then remember to turn it to low before you leave for the day. Put a Post-it note on your front door as a reminder to turn that slow cooker to low before leaving.

Slow Cooker Fajitas

Fajitas are Mexican sandwiches, using tortillas as the bread. To cook without freezing, place everything except tortillas and sour cream in the slow cooker and cook as directed.

1. Cut steak into four pieces, and sprinkle with taco seasoning. Place in zipper-lock bag. Cut peppers into large chunks and combine with onions and garlic in another zipper-lock bag. Place tortillas in another zipper-lock bag. Place all bags in a large bag, label, seal, and freeze. Reserve salsa in pantry and sour cream in refrigerator.

2. *To thaw and cook:* Thaw all ingredients overnight in refrigerator. Place steak in 4- to 5-quart slow cooker and top with vegetables. Pour salsa over all, cover slow cooker, and cook on low for 8 hours until beef and vegetables are tender.

3. Remove meat from slow cooker and shred. Return to slow cooker and mix well. Cook on low for 30 minutes. Serve with flour tortillas, sour cream, and your favorite garnishes.

Serves 6

2 pounds bottom round steak
3 tablespoons Taco Seasoning Mix (page 297)
2 green bell peppers
1 red bell pepper
2 onions, chopped
4 cloves garlic, minced
8 flour tortillas
1 (16-ounce) jar salsa
1 cup sour cream

Serves 18

6 pounds bottom round steak
9 tablespoons Taco Seasoning Mix (page 297)
6 green bell peppers
3 red bell peppers
6 onions, chopped
12 cloves garlic, minced
24 flour tortillas
3 (16-ounce) jars salsa
3 cups sour cream

Beef with Broccoli

Serves 4

1 pound beef stew meat
1 teaspoon ground ginger
1 teaspoon salt
⅛ teaspoon cayenne
    pepper
2 cloves garlic, minced
¼ cup minced onion
¼ cup soy sauce
1 (16-ounce) package frozen
    broccoli florets
1 (8-ounce) bag frozen pearl
    onions
1 (6-ounce) can water
    chestnuts
¼ cup cornstarch
1 cup rice
1 (10-ounce) can condensed
    beef broth

Serves 12

3 pounds beef stew meat
1 tablespoon ground ginger
1 tablespoon salt
⅜ teaspoon cayenne
    pepper
6 cloves garlic, minced
¾ cup minced onion
¾ cup soy sauce
3 (16-ounce) packages
    frozen broccoli florets
3 (8-ounce) bags frozen
    pearl onions
3 (6-ounce) cans water
    chestnuts
¾ cup cornstarch
3 cups rice
3 (10-ounce) cans condensed
    beef broth

To serve without freezing, combine beef and marinade
with water chestnuts in slow cooker; cook as directed below.

1. Cut beef into 1½-inch cubes. In shallow bowl, combine ginger, salt, pepper, garlic, onion, and soy sauce and blend. Add beef cubes and stir to coat. Flash freeze beef in single layer on parchment paper–covered cookie sheets.

2. When beef is frozen solid, pack into zipper-lock bag. Attach bag of broccoli and bag of pearl onions; seal, label, and freeze. Reserve water chestnuts, cornstarch, rice, and beef broth in pantry.

3. *To thaw and cook:* Thaw beef, broccoli, and pearl onions overnight in refrigerator. In 3- to 4-quart slow cooker, combine beef, any remaining marinade, drained water chestnuts, ½ cup water, and half of the can of beef broth. Cover and cook on low for 7 to 8 hours until beef is tender, adding thawed pearl onions and broccoli during last hour of cooking time. During last 30 minutes of cooking time, combine cornstarch with ½ cup water and add to slow cooker; stir well, cover, and cook until thickened.

4. Combine remaining beef broth with enough water to make two cups. Cook rice in this mixture, covered, over medium heat for 15 to 20 minutes, until tender. Serve Beef with Broccoli over rice.

Slow Cooker Beef Stroganoff

This elegant dish is a variation on traditional beef Stroganoff.
To cook without freezing, toss steak cubes with flour mixture and
cook as directed. Serve with cooked egg noodles.

1. Cut steak into 1½-inch pieces and flash freeze in single layer on cookie sheet. When frozen solid, pack into 1-quart zipper-lock bag, seal, label, and place in freezer.

2. Combine onions, garlic, olive oil, mustard, broth, and Worcestershire sauce in another zipper-lock bag; label and seal. Combine flour, salt, pepper, and marjoram in third zipper-lock bag, label, seal, and place in gallon zipper-lock bag along with beef and sauce mixture. Reserve canned mushrooms and egg noodles in pantry. Reserve sour cream in refrigerator.

3. *To thaw and cook:* Thaw beef and sauce mixture overnight in refrigerator. Toss beef with flour mixture. Place thawed sauce mixture into 3- to 4-quart Slow Cooker along with undrained mushrooms and coated beef. Cover Slow Cooker and cook on low for 8 to 9 hours, until beef and vegetables are tender.

4. In medium bowl, combine sour cream with 1 cup of the hot liquid from the Slow Cooker and mix well with wire whisk. Stir into Slow Cooker until blended; cook on high for 25 to 30 minutes, until mixture is thickened. Meanwhile, cook egg noodles as directed on package, drain, and serve with Stroganoff.

Serves 6–8

2 pounds sirloin tip steak
2 onions, chopped
4 cloves garlic, chopped
1 tablespoon olive oil
1 tablespoon mustard
3 cups Beef Broth (page 302)
2 tablespoons
    Worcestershire sauce
¼ cup flour
1 teaspoon salt
⅛ teaspoon pepper
½ teaspoon dried marjoram
1 (10-ounce) can sliced
    mushrooms
1 (12-ounce) package egg
    noodles
1 cup sour cream

Serves 18–24

6 pounds sirloin tip steak
6 onions, chopped
12 cloves garlic, chopped
3 tablespoons olive oil
3 tablespoons mustard
9 cups Beef Broth (page 302)
6 tablespoons
    Worcestershire sauce
¾ cup flour
1 tablespoon salt
⅜ teaspoon pepper
1½ teaspoons dried
    marjoram
3 (10-ounce) cans sliced
    mushrooms
3 (12-ounce) packages egg
    noodles
3 cups sour cream

Beef Chili with Beans

Serves 6

2 pounds flank steak
3 tablespoons Taco
    Seasoning Mix (page
    297)
1 onion, chopped
4 cloves garlic, chopped
1 jalapeno pepper, chopped
⅛ teaspoon cayenne
    pepper
1 teaspoon salt
1 cup tomato juice
1 cup Beef Broth (page 302)
2 (16-ounce) cans black
    beans
1 (8-ounce) can tomato
    sauce
1 (16-ounce) jar salsa

Serves 18

6 pounds flank steak
9 tablespoons Taco
    Seasoning Mix (page
    297)
3 onions, chopped
12 cloves garlic, chopped
3 jalapeno peppers,
    chopped
⅜ teaspoon cayenne
    pepper
1 tablespoon salt
3 cups tomato juice
3 cups Beef Broth (page 302)
6 (16-ounce) cans black
    beans
3 (8-ounce) cans tomato
    sauce
3 (16-ounce) jars salsa

This hearty chili is perfect for a cold winter evening. To serve without freezing, combine all ingredients as directed and cook in slow cooker on low for 8 to 9 hours.

1. Cut flank steak into 1-inch cubes and toss with taco seasoning. Flash freeze beef in single layer on parchment paper–lined cookie sheets. When frozen, combine with onion, garlic, jalapeno, cayenne pepper, and salt in zipper-lock bag. Pour tomato juice and broth into another bag. Seal bags, combine in a larger bag, label, and freeze. Store beans, tomato sauce, and salsa in pantry.

2. *To thaw and reheat:* Thaw beef mixture overnight in refrigerator. In the morning, place in 4- or 5-quart slow cooker. Drain black beans, rinse, and drain again. Pour into slow cooker along with tomato sauce, salsa, and ½ cup water.

3. Cover slow cooker and cook on low for 8 to 9 hours, until beef is tender. Remove about one-third of the beans from the slow cooker, mash, and return to pot. Cook for an additional 20 to 30 minutes, until mixture is thickened.

Chicken and Rice Stew

A "stewp" is like a stew and a soup combined. To serve this hearty meal without freezing, combine all ingredients except rice in slow cooker and cook as directed. Stir in rice for last hour of cooking.

---

1. Cut chicken thighs into 1-inch pieces and sprinkle with flour, paprika, salt, and pepper. Toss well to coat evenly. Flash freeze chicken in single layer on cookie sheet. When frozen solid, pack into zipper-lock bags.

2. In zipper-lock bag, place carrots, frozen beans, frozen onions, and garlic; label, seal, and attach to bag with chicken. Reserve broth, tomatoes, and rice in pantry. Freeze bags with chicken and vegetables.

3. *To thaw and cook:* Thaw chicken and vegetables overnight in refrigerator. In the morning, combine contents of both bags in 4- to 5-quart slow cooker along with chicken broth, water, and undrained tomatoes and mix well. Cover slow cooker and cook on low for 8 hours. Turn slow cooker to high, add rice, and cook for 60 to 80 minutes longer until chicken is done and rice and vegetables are tender.

Serves 6–8

2 pounds boned, skinned chicken thighs
¼ cup flour
1 teaspoon smoked paprika
1 teaspoon salt
⅛ teaspoon pepper
3 carrots, sliced
2 cups frozen green beans
2 cups frozen pearl onions
2 cloves garlic, minced
2 (10-ounce) cans chicken broth
1 (14-ounce) can diced tomatoes
1 cup long-grain rice
1 cup water

Serves 18–24

6 pounds boned, skinned chicken thighs
¾ cup flour
1 tablespoon smoked paprika
1 tablespoon salt
⅜ teaspoon pepper
9 carrots, sliced
6 cups frozen green beans
6 cups frozen pearl onions
6 cloves garlic, minced
6 (10-ounce) cans chicken broth
3 (14-ounce) cans diced tomatoes
3 cups long-grain rice
3 cups water

Swiss Steak

Serves 6–8

2 pounds round steak
1 teaspoon salt
⅛ teaspoon pepper
2 tablespoons flour
3 carrots, sliced
2 onions, chopped
2 cloves garlic, chopped
1 (14-ounce) can diced
    tomatoes
1 (8-ounce) can tomato
    sauce
1 tablespoon Dijon mustard
½ teaspoon dried thyme
    leaves

Serves 18–24

6 pounds round steak
1 tablespoon salt
⅜ teaspoon pepper
6 tablespoons flour
9 carrots, sliced
6 onions, chopped
6 cloves garlic, chopped
3 (14-ounce) cans diced
    tomatoes
3 (8-ounce) cans tomato
    sauce
3 tablespoons Dijon mustard
1½ teaspoons dried thyme
    leaves

Traditionally, Swiss Steak is made from tougher meat that must be cooked slowly to tenderize. Your slow cooker is the perfect appliance for this homey meal. To serve without freezing, cook as directed.

1. Cut steak into serving-size pieces and place on waxed paper. In small bowl, combine salt, pepper, and flour and mix well. Sprinkle half of this mixture over steak pieces and, using meat mallet or rolling pin, pound flour mixture into steak. Turn meat over and repeat process on second side with remaining seasoning. Flash freeze steak in single layer on cookie sheet; then, when frozen solid, place in large zipper-lock bags and freeze.

2. In zipper-lock bag, combine carrots, onions, garlic, undrained tomatoes, tomato sauce, mustard, and thyme leaves. Attach to bag of meat, label, seal, and freeze.

3. *To thaw and cook:* Thaw all ingredients overnight in refrigerator. In the morning, place steak pieces in Slow Cooker and top with vegetables and sauce. Cover and cook on low for 8 to 10 hours, until meat and vegetables are very tender.

Slow Cooker Spaghetti and Meatballs

You can purchased frozen fully cooked meatballs instead of homemade if you prefer. To serve without freezing, cook in slow cooker as directed. Cook pasta according to package directions, drain, and serve with sauce.

1. In large zipper-lock bag, combine cooled meatballs, onion, garlic, carrot, basil, and red pepper flakes; attach small bag with grated cheese and another small zipper-lock bag filled with chicken broth; label, seal, and freeze. Reserve pasta sauce, tomato sauce, and spaghetti in pantry.

2. *To thaw and cook:* Thaw frozen bags overnight in refrigerator. Pour into 3- to 4-quart slow cooker and cover with pasta sauce and tomato sauce. Cover and cook on low for 7 to 8 hours, until sauce is bubbling and meatballs are thawed and hot. Cook pasta according to package directions, drain, and serve with spaghetti sauce and meatballs; top with Parmesan cheese.

Leaving out Onion and Garlic

If you don't like onions or garlic, simply leave them out of the recipe. You can increase the amounts of other vegetables accordingly so the volume of the recipe remains the same.

Serves 8

1 batch Italian Meatballs (page 52)
1 onion, chopped
3 cloves garlic, chopped
1 carrot, coarsely grated
1 teaspoon dried basil leaves
¼ teaspoon dried red pepper flakes
1 cup grated Parmesan cheese
½ cup Chicken Broth (page 301)
1 (26-ounce) jar pasta sauce
1 (8-ounce) can tomato sauce
1 (8-ounce) package spaghetti pasta

Serves 24

3 batches Italian Meatballs (page 52)
3 onions, chopped
9 cloves garlic, chopped
3 carrots, coarsely grated
1 tablespoon dried basil leaves
¾ teaspoon dried red pepper flakes
3 cups grated Parmesan cheese
1½ cups Chicken Broth (page 301)
3 (26-ounce) jars pasta sauce
3 (8-ounce) cans tomato sauce
3 (8-ounce) packages spaghetti pasta

Slow Cooker Pork Chops and Beans

Serves 8

8 boneless center-cut pork
  chops
1 teaspoon salt
1 teaspoon smoked paprika
⅛ teaspoon pepper
1 onion, chopped
2 (16-ounce) cans pork and
  beans
¼ cup ketchup
¼ cup mustard
¼ cup honey

Serves 24

24 boneless center-cut pork
  chops
1 tablespoon salt
1 tablespoon smoked
  paprika
⅜ teaspoon pepper
3 onions, chopped
6 (16-ounce) cans pork and
  beans
¾ cup ketchup
¾ cup mustard
¾ cup honey

To cook without freezing, place all ingredients
in slow cooker and cook on low for 8 to 9 hours,
until pork chops are thoroughly cooked and tender.

1. Sprinkle pork chops with salt, paprika, and pepper; rub into meat. Flash freeze meat in single layer on cookie sheet. When frozen solid, pack into rigid containers, separating chops with waxed paper. Attach bag with chopped onion, seal, label, and freeze. Reserve pork and beans, ketchup, mustard, and honey in pantry.

2. *To thaw and cook:* Thaw meat overnight in refrigerator. Open pork and beans and drain off half of the thick liquid. Pour 1 can into 4- to 5-quart slow cooker and add onions, ketchup, mustard, and honey; mix well. Place half of thawed pork chops in slow cooker and top with remaining can of slightly drained pork and beans, then top with remaining pork chops. Cover slow cooker and cook on low for 8 to 9 hours, until meat is thoroughly cooked and tender.

Slow Cooker Rotisserie Chicken

Serves 6

The spice flavors go deep within the chicken in this easy recipe. To serve without freezing, marinate chicken in its dry rub for at least 8 hours in refrigerator, then cook as directed.

3 pounds chicken breasts, thighs, and drumsticks
2 teaspoons salt
2 teaspoons smoked paprika
1 teaspoon onion salt
1 teaspoon garlic powder
½ teaspoon dried rosemary
½ teaspoon dried thyme leaves
1 tablespoon sugar
⅛ teaspoon pepper
⅛ teaspoon cayenne pepper

1. Rinse chicken pieces and dry with paper towel. Loosen skin from flesh and place chicken on large cookie sheet. In small bowl, combine remaining ingredients and mix well. Sprinkle half this mixture under the chicken skin and rub in well. Sprinkle remaining mixture on the chicken skin and rub in well. Place chicken in rigid container, separating pieces with waxed paper; seal, label, and freeze.

2. *To thaw and cook:* Thaw chicken overnight in refrigerator. Use aluminum foil to make 5 balls about 2 inches in diameter and place these in the bottom of a 4- to 5-quart slow cooker. Place chicken in slow cooker, resting on the aluminum balls. Cover and cook on low for 8 to 10 hours, until chicken is very tender and glazed.

Serves 18

9 pounds chicken breasts, thighs, and drumsticks
6 teaspoons salt
6 teaspoons smoked paprika
1 tablespoon onion salt
1 tablespoon garlic powder
1½ teaspoons dried rosemary
1½ teaspoons dried thyme leaves
3 tablespoons sugar
⅜ teaspoon pepper
⅜ teaspoon cayenne pepper

No Peeking!

Don't lift the lid on your slow cooker while it is cooking. If you're cooking on low, every time you lift the lid, you'll need to cook for an additional 20 to 30 minutes to make up for the escaped heat.

Slow Cooker Turkey Breast

Serves 6

---

1 (3–5-pound) bone-in
    frozen turkey breast
¼ cup lemon juice
3 tablespoons olive oil
¼ cup Chicken Broth
    (page 301)
3 cloves garlic, minced
1 tablespoon sugar
⅛ teaspoon pepper
1 teaspoon dried basil
½ teaspoon dried sage
2 onions, sliced
2 cups baby carrots

Serves 18

---

3 (3–5-pound) bone-in
    frozen turkey breasts
¾ cup lemon juice
9 tablespoons olive oil
¾ cup Chicken Broth
    (page 301)
9 cloves garlic, minced
3 tablespoons sugar
⅜ teaspoon pepper
1 tablespoon dried basil
1½ teaspoons dried sage
6 onions, sliced
6 cups baby carrots

To cook without freezing, thaw turkey, place vegetables in slow cooker, top with turkey, pour marinade over; cook as directed.

---

1. Place turkey breast in large zipper-lock bag. In small bowl, combine lemon juice, oil, broth, garlic, sugar, pepper, basil, and sage and mix well to combine. Pour over turkey in bag, seal bag, and squish to distribute marinade. Place onions and baby carrots in zipper-lock bag, attach to turkey, label, seal, and freeze.

2. *To thaw and cook:* Thaw turkey and vegetables overnight in refrigerator. Place vegetables in bottom of 4- to 5-quart slow cooker and place turkey on top. Pour any marinade remaining in bag over turkey. Cover and cook on low for 8 to 10 hours or until turkey is thoroughly cooked and tender. Slice and serve with vegetables.

Slow Cooker Lasagna

That's right—lasagna in the Slow Cooker!
To serve without freezing, layer the sauce and cheese mixtures
as directed below, then cook on low for 5 to 7 hours.

1. In heavy skillet, sauté sausage until almost cooked. Drain off excess fat and add onion and garlic. Cook and stir until sausage is cooked and vegetables are crisp-tender. Add tomato sauce, and paste, Italian seasoning, and broth. Simmer sauce, stirring frequently, for 5 to 10 minutes to blend flavors. Cool in ice-water bath or refrigerator.

2. Meanwhile, in large bowl, beat cream cheese and ricotta cheese until blended. Add egg, then stir in mozzarella cheese, pepper, and parsley. Place cheese mixture in zipper-lock bag. Pour cooled sauce into zipper-lock bag and attach to bag with cheese; seal, label, and freeze. Reserve lasagna noodles in pantry.

3. *To thaw and cook:* Let sauce and cheese mixture thaw overnight in refrigerator. (If the cheese mixture seems to separate after thawing, just squish the bag to remix.) In the morning, place one-third of the sauce in the bottom of a 4- to 5-quart slow cooker. Top with 3 lasagna noodles, breaking them as necessary to fit. Top with one-half of the cheese mixture, then one-third of meat mixture. Top with 3 more lasagna noodles, then remaining cheese mixture. Finally, add remaining lasagna noodles and remaining meat mixture. Cover slow cooker and cook on low for 6 to 8 hours until noodles are tender.

Serves 6–8

1 pound bulk Italian sausage
1 onion, chopped
3 cloves garlic, minced
2 (8-ounce) cans tomato sauce
1 (6-ounce) can tomato paste
2 teaspoons dried Italian seasoning
1 cup Chicken Broth (page 301)
1 (3-ounce) package cream cheese, softened
2 cups ricotta cheese
1 egg
1½ cups shredded mozzarella cheese
⅛ teaspoon pepper
1 tablespoon dried parsley flakes
9 uncooked lasagna noodles

Serves 18–24

3 pounds bulk Italian sausage
3 onions, chopped
9 cloves garlic, minced
6 (8-ounce) cans tomato sauce
3 (6-ounce) cans tomato paste
2 tablespoons dried Italian seasoning
3 cups Chicken Broth (page 301)
3 (3-ounce) packages cream cheese, softened
6 cups ricotta cheese
3 eggs
4½ cups shredded mozzarella cheese
⅜ teaspoon pepper
3 tablespoons dried parsley flakes
27 uncooked lasagna noodles

Teriyaki Pork Chops

Serves 6

6 boneless center-cut pork
    chops
½ cup soy sauce
½ cup pineapple juice
¼ cup rice wine
2 tablespoons sugar
1 tablespoon grated
    gingerroot
2 cups frozen broccoli florets
2 cups long-grain rice
4 cups Chicken Broth
    (page 301)

Serves 18

18 boneless center-cut pork
    chops
1½ cups soy sauce
1½ cups pineapple juice
¾ cup rice wine
6 tablespoons sugar
3 tablespoons grated
    gingerroot
6 cups frozen broccoli florets
6 cups long-grain rice
12 cups Chicken Broth
    (page 301)

You could substitute 2 tablespoons rice wine vinegar or apple cider vinegar and 2 tablespoons chicken broth for the rice wine. To serve this dish without freezing, combine all ingredients except rice and chicken broth in slow cooker and cook as directed.

1. Place pork chops in zipper-lock bag and add remaining ingredients except broccoli, rice, and broth. Seal bag and knead it to mix thoroughly. Attach bag with frozen broccoli and a rigid container with the broth. Label and freeze. Store rice in pantry.

2. *To thaw and cook:* Thaw meat, broccoli, and broth overnight in refrigerator. Place meat and marinade in 3- to 4-quart slow cooker, cover, and cook on low for 7 hours. Add broccoli and cook for 1 hour longer or until broccoli and chops are hot and tender.

3. During last half hour of cooking, combine rice and broth in heavy saucepan, bring to a boil, then cover pan, reduce heat to low, and simmer for 15 to 20 minutes, until rice is tender and liquid is absorbed. Serve pork chops and broccoli over rice.

Slow Cooker Spicy Peanut Chicken

To serve without freezing, combine all ingredients except couscous in a 3- to 4-quart slow cooker. Cook on low for 7 to 8 hours, until chicken is tender and fully cooked. Served with prepared couscous.

---

1. Cut chicken thighs into 2-inch pieces. Place in 1-quart zipper-lock bag, seal, and refrigerate.

2. In medium bowl, combine peanut butter, soy sauce, orange juice, onion, and jalapenos and mix well. Pour into zipper-lock bag and seal. Attach to bag with chicken, label, and freeze. Reserve couscous in pantry.

3. *To thaw and cook:* Thaw chicken and sauce overnight in refrigerator. In the morning, combine all ingredients except couscous in 3- to 4-quart slow cooker. Cook on low for 7 to 8 hours, until done. Prepare couscous according to package directions and serve with chicken and sauce.

Serves 4

---

2 pounds boned, skinless chicken thighs
½ cup chunky peanut butter
3 tablespoons soy sauce
¼ cup orange juice
1 onion, chopped
2 tablespoons chopped jalapenos
1 (10-ounce) package couscous

Serves 12

---

6 pounds boned, skinless chicken thighs
1½ cups chunky peanut butter
½ cup soy sauce
¾ cup orange juice
3 onions, chopped
6 tablespoons chopped jalapenos
3 (10-ounce) packages couscous

Italian Slow Cooker Chicken

Serves 4

2 pounds boneless, skinless chicken breasts
½ cup Italian salad dressing
2 cups frozen peppers and onions
3 cloves garlic, chopped
3 cups frozen potato wedges

Serves 12

6 pounds boneless, skinless chicken breasts
1½ cups Italian salad dressing
6 cups frozen peppers and onions
9 cloves garlic, chopped
9 cups frozen potato wedges

To serve this dish without freezing, combine all ingredients in 3- to 4-quart slow cooker. Cover and cook on low for 6 to 7 hours

1. Cut chicken breasts in half and combine with salad dressing in zipper-lock bag. Combine peppers, onions, and garlic in zipper-lock bag. Place potatoes in a third zipper-lock bag. Seal bags, label, place all three bags in 1-gallon zipper-lock bag, and freeze.

2. *To thaw and cook:* Thaw chicken, vegetables, and potatoes overnight in refrigerator. In the morning, place vegetables (except potatoes) in the slow cooker. Pour chicken and salad dressing over all. Cover and cook on low for 7 to 8 hours, until chicken is thoroughly cooked and vegetables are tender, adding potatoes after 6 hours of cooking.

Slow Cooker Apricot Pork Chops

Serves 4

4 center-cut boneless pork chops
1 cup dried apricots, chopped
1 cup apricot nectar
2 cloves garlic, minced
1 tablespoon Dijon mustard
3 tablespoons honey
1 teaspoon salt
⅛ teaspoon white pepper
2 cups baby carrots

Serves 12

12 center-cut boneless pork chops
3 cups dried apricots, chopped
3 cups apricot nectar
6 cloves garlic, minced
3 tablespoons Dijon mustard
9 tablespoons honey
1 tablespoon salt
⅜ teaspoon white pepper
6 cups baby carrots

The combination of sweet apricots with mustard and garlic is really delicious with pork. To serve without freezing, simply combine all ingredients in slow cooker and cook as directed.

1. In large zipper-lock bag, combine all ingredients. Seal bag and knead with hands to mix. Label, seal, and freeze.

2. *To thaw and cook:* Thaw overnight in refrigerator. Place all ingredients in 3- to 4-quart slow cooker, cover, and cook on low for 8 hours or until pork chops and carrots are tender. Serve with hot cooked rice.

Red Snapper and Veggies

Serves 4

4 (6-ounce) fillets red
snapper
½ cup sliced carrots
1 onion, chopped
1 cup chopped leeks
2 cloves garlic, minced
2 tablespoons butter
2 tablespoons olive oil
2 teaspoons lemon juice
½ teaspoon dried thyme
leaves
½ teaspoon salt
⅛ teaspoon pepper

Serves 12

12 (6-ounce) fillets red
snapper
1½ cups sliced carrots
3 onions, chopped
3 cups chopped leeks
6 cloves garlic, minced
6 tablespoons butter
6 tablespoons olive oil
6 teaspoons lemon juice
1½ teaspoons dried thyme
leaves
1½ teaspoons salt
⅜ teaspoon pepper

Any firm-fleshed fish can be used in this simple recipe. To serve without freezing, simply cook the packets immediately, as directed in recipe.

1. Tear off four 12" × 18" pieces of heavy-duty aluminum foil. Place one fillet in the center of each piece of foil, skin-side down. In medium bowl, combine carrots, onion, leeks, and garlic and mix to combine. Spoon this mixture over fillets and dot each with butter. Drizzle olive oil over all and sprinkle with lemon juice, thyme, salt, and pepper.

2. Bring short edges of foil together and fold twice. Fold long edges over twice and seal. Label packages and freeze.

3. *To thaw and cook:* Thaw packages overnight in refrigerator. When ready to eat, prepare and heat grill. Place packets on grill 4 to 6 inches from medium coals. Cover grill and cook for 15 to 18 minutes, turning once, until vegetables are tender and fillets flake easily when tested with fork.

BBQ Ribs

6 pounds pork ribs
2 onions, chopped
4 garlic cloves, chopped
1 cup ketchup
1 cup cocktail sauce
2 tablespoons mustard
¼ cup lemon juice
2 teaspoons salt
¼ teaspoon pepper

To grill without freezing, just omit the freezing
and thawing steps. If desired, cook the ribs in the oven at 350°
for 90 minutes instead of using the slow cooker.

1. Wrap pork ribs in freezer paper, label, and freeze. In large saucepan, mix remaining ingredients and bring to a simmer. Cook for 10 to 15 minutes to blend flavors, stirring frequently. Cool sauce in ice-water bath or refrigerator. Place in rigid container, attach to ribs package, label, and freeze.

2. *To thaw and cook:* Let thaw overnight in refrigerator. In the morning, place ribs in Slow Cooker and add 2 cups water. Cover and cook on low for 8 hours. Drain ribs and prepare and preheat grill.

3. Place ribs on grill and brush with sauce. Cover grill and cook, brushing frequently with sauce and turning once, for 20 to 25 minutes until ribs are glazed. Bring remaining sauce to a boil. After boiling for 3 to 4 minutes, serve with ribs.

Serves 24–30

18 pounds pork ribs
6 onions, chopped
12 garlic cloves, chopped
3 cups ketchup
3 cups cocktail sauce
6 tablespoons mustard
¾ cup lemon juice
2 tablespoons salt
¾ teaspoon pepper

Cooking with Charcoal

A charcoal grill takes about 30 to 45 minutes to reach the correct cooking temperature after the coals are lit. Gray ash will form on the coals and flames will disappear when the coals are ready.

Mexican Chicken Packets

Serves 4

---

4 boneless, skinless chicken
    breasts
½ teaspoon salt
⅛ teaspoon pepper
2 tablespoons olive oil
1 onion, chopped
½ cup golden raisins
½ cup sliced black olives
1 jalapeno pepper, seeded
    and minced
½ cup canned diced
    tomatoes, drained
½ cup chunky salsa

Serves 12

---

12 boneless, skinless chicken
    breasts
1½ teaspoons salt
⅜ teaspoon pepper
6 tablespoons olive oil
3 onions, chopped
1½ cups golden raisins
1½ cups sliced black olives
3 jalapeno peppers, seeded
    and minced
1½ cups canned diced
    tomatoes, drained
1½ cups chunky salsa

To serve without freezing, cook packets on a medium grill, covered, for 18 to 24 minutes, until chicken is thoroughly cooked.

---

1. Tear off four 18" × 12" pieces of heavy-duty aluminum foil and spray one side of each with nonstick cooking spray. Place 1 chicken breast in center of each piece of foil and sprinkle with salt and pepper.

2. In heavy skillet, heat olive oil and add onion. Cook and stir until crisp-tender, about 3 to 4 minutes. Remove from heat. In medium bowl, combine onion with remaining ingredients and mix well. Divide onion mixture over chicken breasts and seal packages using double folds, leaving room for expansion. Wrap again in foil, label packets, and freeze.

3. *To thaw and reheat:* Thaw packets overnight in refrigerator. After preheating grill, cook packets, covered, 4 to 6 inches from medium coals for 20 to 25 minutes, until chicken is thoroughly cooked.

Beef Kabobs

To serve without freezing, marinate beef cubes in garlic sauce for 1 to 2 hours in the refrigerator. Prepare carrots as directed. Grill as directed in recipe.

1. In medium bowl, combine olive oil, garlic, vinegar, honey, Worcestershire sauce, and pepper and mix with wire whisk to blend. Cut steaks into 1½-inch cubes and place in bowl with marinade. Stir thoroughly until cubes are well coated. Thread steak onto metal skewers, allowing 4 cubes per skewer, and place in zipper-lock bag. Pour remaining marinade over skewers, and then seal and freeze.

2. Place baby carrots in medium saucepan and cover with water. Bring to a boil over medium heat; cook for 2 to 3 minutes or until slightly tender. Drain carrots and rinse under cold water to cool.

3. Thread onions and cooked baby carrots carefully onto another set of metal skewers, place in zipper-lock bag, and attach to bag of beef kabobs; label and freeze. Reserve butter in refrigerator.

4. *To thaw and cook:* Thaw kabobs overnight in refrigerator. Prepare and preheat grill. Melt butter in small saucepan. Cook vegetable kabobs 4 to 6 inches from medium coals for 4 to 6 minutes, until crisp-tender, brushing with melted butter and turning once. Cook beef kabobs 4 to 6 inches from medium coals for 8 to 12 minutes, until meat thermometer registers 145°F to 160°F, turning once. Serve kabobs with hot cooked rice, if desired.

Serves 4

2 tablespoons olive oil
3 cloves garlic, minced
2 tablespoons apple cider vinegar
2 tablespoons honey
1 tablespoon Worcestershire sauce
⅛ teaspoon pepper
2 boneless ribeye steaks
2 cups baby carrots
2 onions, cut into wedges
2 tablespoons butter

Serves 12

6 tablespoons olive oil
9 cloves garlic, minced
6 tablespoons apple cider vinegar
6 tablespoons honey
3 tablespoons Worcestershire sauce
⅜ teaspoon pepper
6 boneless ribeye steaks
6 cups baby carrots
6 onions, cut into wedges
6 tablespoons butter

Blue Cheese Burgers

Serves 8

2 pounds lean ground beef
4 cloves garlic, minced
½ cup minced onion
1 tablespoon Worcestershire
  sauce
⅛ teaspoon black pepper
⅛ teaspoon white pepper
¼ cup water
¼ cup sour cream
1 cup crumbled blue cheese
2 red onions, peeled and
  sliced
3 tablespoons butter
8 English muffins, split
Blue cheese salad dressing

Serves 24

6 pounds lean ground beef
12 cloves garlic, minced
1½ cups minced onion
3 tablespoons
  Worcestershire sauce
⅜ teaspoon black pepper
⅜ teaspoon white pepper
¾ cup water
¾ cup sour cream
3 cups crumbled blue cheese
6 red onions, peeled and
  sliced
9 tablespoons butter
24 English muffins, split
Blue cheese salad dressing

To serve immediately, grill patties as directed. Be sure to cook them to well done; ground meat must be thoroughly cooked before serving.

1. In large bowl, place ground beef, garlic, minced onion, Worcestershire sauce, and black and white pepper. In small bowl, combine water, sour cream, and crumbled blue cheese and mix well. Add to ground beef and mix gently but thoroughly.

2. Form meat into 8 patties. Flash freeze patties in single layer on parchment paper–lined cookie sheets. When frozen solid, pack into rigid containers with waxed paper separating patties. Place onions in zipper-lock bag and attach to meat container. Spread butter thinly on split sides of English muffins, place in zipper-lock bag, attach to meat container, label, seal, and freeze. Reserve blue cheese dressing in pantry.

3. *To thaw and cook:* Let patties thaw overnight in refrigerator. Keep onions frozen. Prepare and preheat grill. Cook patties 4 to 5 minutes on each side, turning carefully once, until well done. Grill frozen onion slices 2 to 3 minutes per side, until lightly charred. Place English muffins, split-side down, on grill for last 1 to 3 minutes of cooking time, until light golden brown. Serve burgers on English muffins with onions and blue cheese salad dressing.

Peachy Ham Steaks

The salty, smoky flavor of ham combined with the sweetness of peaches is really delicious. To serve without freezing, marinate ham for 1 to 2 hours in the refrigerator, then grill as directed.

1. In large zipper-lock bag, combine nectar, vinegar, jam, sugar, garlic, and cayenne pepper and mix. Add ham steak, seal bag, and attach zipper-lock bag with frozen peach slices. Label bags and freeze.

2. *To thaw and reheat:* Thaw ham steak in refrigerator overnight. Keep peach slices frozen. Prepare and preheat grill. Place ham steak on grill 4 to 6 inches from medium coals; reserve marinade. Place frozen peach slices in grill basket or thread them on metal skewers.

3. Grill ham for 3 to 5 minutes on each side, until glazed and thoroughly heated, brushing once with marinade. Grill peach slices for 4 to 5 minutes, until hot and softened, brushing once with marinade. Discard remaining marinade. Serve with hot cooked rice or couscous.

Estimating Charcoal Grill Temperature

To estimate how hot your charcoal is, hold your hand about six inches above the coals. If you can keep your hand there comfortably for two seconds, the grill temperature is 400°F to 450°F; four seconds, the grill temperature is about 350°F; five seconds, the grill temperature is about 300°F.

Serves 4

½ cup peach nectar
2 tablespoons vinegar
2 tablespoons peach jam
2 tablespoons sugar
2 cloves garlic, minced
Pinch cayenne pepper
1 (1½-pound) center-cut
    ham steak
2 cups frozen peach slices

Serves 12

1½ cups peach nectar
6 tablespoons vinegar
6 tablespoons peach jam
6 tablespoons sugar
6 cloves garlic, minced
⅛ teaspoon cayenne
    pepper
3 (1½-pound) center-cut
    ham steaks
6 cups frozen peach slices

Pesto Chicken Packets

Serves 4

4 boneless, skinless chicken breasts
1 onion, chopped
3 cloves garlic, minced
1 lemon
½ teaspoon salt
⅛ teaspoon white pepper
2 cups frozen asparagus pieces
3 blocks frozen Pesto Sauce (page 296), thawed, or ½ cup purchased pesto
½ cup grated Parmesan cheese

Serves 12

12 boneless, skinless chicken breasts
3 onions, chopped
9 cloves garlic, minced
3 lemons
1½ teaspoons salt
⅜ teaspoon white pepper
6 cups frozen asparagus pieces
9 blocks frozen Pesto Sauce (page 296), thawed, or 1½ cups purchased pesto
1½ cups grated Parmesan cheese

These packets can also be made with pork chops or fish fillets. To cook without freezing, just place the packets on the grill and cook as directed.

1. Tear off four 18" × 12" pieces of heavy-duty aluminum foil. Place 1 chicken breast in the center of each piece. Divide onion and garlic among pieces. Thinly slice lemon, removing seeds. Divide among packets and sprinkle each with salt and pepper. Divide frozen asparagus among packets. Top each packet with 2 tablespoons pesto and sprinkle with cheese.

2. Fold foil over chicken and vegetables, and seal edges with a double fold, leaving some room for expansion. Place packets in zipper-lock bags, seal, label, and freeze.

3. *To thaw and cook:* Thaw packets overnight in refrigerator. Prepare and preheat grill. Cook packets 4 to 6 inches from medium coals for 18 to 25 minutes or until chicken is thoroughly cooked and vegetables are tender, turning once.

Swordfish Kabobs

These kabobs have a wonderful flavor from the lemon and bay leaves. To serve without freezing, marinate kabobs in lemon juice mixture for 8 to 10 hours in refrigerator, then grill as directed.

1. Cut swordfish into 1½-inch cubes. Thread onto 10-inch metal skewers, alternating with bay leaves and onion wedges. In small bowl, combine remaining ingredients and mix to blend. Place kabobs on parchment-lined cookie sheets and pour lemon mixture over kabobs. Flash freeze kabobs until frozen solid. Place kabobs in 1-gallon zipper-lock bag, label, seal bag, and freeze.

2. *To thaw and cook:* Thaw kabobs overnight in refrigerator. Prepare and preheat grill; oil grill rack. Cook kabobs 4 to 6 inches from medium coals for 3 to 4 minutes per side, until swordfish flakes when tested with fork. Discard bay leaves.

Wooden Skewers

If you choose to use wooden skewers when you're grilling, be sure to soak them in cold water for at least 30 minutes before adding the food. Then the skewers won't burn up and fall apart while on the grill.

Serves 6

2 pounds swordfish steaks
20 to 24 bay leaves
2 onions, cut into wedges
⅓ cup lemon juice
¼ cup olive oil
1 teaspoon salt
⅛ teaspoon pepper
1 teaspoon dried thyme
  leaves

Serves 18

6 pounds swordfish steaks
60 to 72 bay leaves
6 onions, cut into wedges
1 cup lemon juice
¾ cup olive oil
1 tablespoon salt
⅜ teaspoon pepper
1 tablespoon dried thyme
  leaves

Flank Steak Fajitas

Serves 4

---

1 pound flank steak
¼ cup lemon juice
2 tablespoons orange juice
3 tablespoons olive oil
⅛ teaspoon crushed red
  pepper flakes
1 jalapeno pepper, minced
3 cups frozen bell peppers
  and onions
1 cup shredded pepper jack
  cheese
6 flour tortillas
Salsa

Serves 12

---

3 pounds flank steak
¾ cup lemon juice
6 tablespoons orange juice
9 tablespoons olive oil
⅜ teaspoon crushed red
  pepper flakes
3 jalapeno peppers, minced
9 cups frozen bell peppers
  and onions
3 cup shredded pepper jack
  cheese
18 flour tortillas
Salsa

To serve without freezing, marinate steak in refrigerator
for at least 2 hours, then prepare as directed.

---

1. Place flank steak in large zipper-lock bag. In small bowl, combine lemon and orange juices, olive oil, red pepper flakes, and jalapeno pepper and mix well. Pour over flank steak, seal bag, and turn several times to coat. Place frozen bell peppers and onions in separate zipper-lock bag, seal, and attach to bag with flank steak.

2. Place cheese in another zipper-lock bag, and tortillas in another. Place all bags into a gallon zipper-lock bag; label, seal, and freeze. Reserve salsa in refrigerator or pantry.

3. *To thaw and cook:* Thaw steak, cheese, and tortillas in refrigerator overnight. Keep peppers and onions frozen. Prepare and preheat grill. Grill flank steak 4 to 6 inches from medium heat for 4 to 5 minutes on each side until desired doneness. While steak is grilling, place frozen bell peppers and onions in a grill basket. Grill for 3 to 5 minutes, until heated. Wrap stacked flour tortillas in foil and place on grill for final 2 to 3 minutes of cooking time. Let flank steak stand, covered, for 4 to 5 minutes; then slice across the grain into thin strips. Serve in warmed tortillas with peppers and onions, cheese, and salsa.

All-American Burgers

To cook these classic burgers without freezing, simply grill as directed. Top them with slices of cheese and serve on toasted buns with your favorite condiments.

1. In large bowl, combine beef, steak sauce, water, seasoning, salt, and pepper and mix gently. Form into 8 patties. Flash freeze burgers in single layer on cookie sheet. When frozen, pack into rigid containers, with waxed paper separating layers.

2. Spread butter in thin layer on cut sides of hamburger buns and place in zipper-lock bag. Attach bag of hamburger buns to meat, seal, label, and freeze. Reserve cheese in refrigerator.

3. *To thaw and cook:* Thaw burgers and buns overnight in refrigerator. Prepare and preheat grill. Cook burgers 6 inches from medium coals for 8 to 10 minutes, turning once, until thoroughly cooked, topping with cheese during last minute of cooking time. Grill buns, cut-side down, until toasted. Serve burgers on toasted buns with condiments.

Serves 8

2 pounds lean ground beef
3 tablespoons steak sauce
2 tablespoons water
1 tablespoon Grill Seasoning (page 308)
1 teaspoon salt
⅛ teaspoon pepper
2 tablespoons butter
8 hamburger buns
8 slices American cheese

Serves 12

6 pounds lean ground beef
9 tablespoons steak sauce
6 tablespoons water
3 tablespoons Grill Seasoning (page 308)
1 tablespoon salt
⅜ teaspoon pepper
6 tablespoons butter
24 hamburger buns
24 slices American cheese

Shrimp Kabobs

Serves 4

1½ pounds frozen large shrimp,
peeled and deveined
3 tablespoons lemon juice
3 tablespoons olive oil
2 teaspoons sugar
2 cloves garlic, minced
½ teaspoon dried tarragon leaves
2 onions, cut into wedges
2 lemons, cut into wedges

Serves 12

4½ pounds frozen large shrimp,
peeled and deveined
9 tablespoons lemon juice
9 tablespoons olive oil
6 teaspoons sugar
6 cloves garlic, minced
1½ teaspoons dried tarragon
leaves
6 onions, cut into wedges
6 lemons, cut into wedges

To cook without freezing, thaw shrimp and marinate in lemon mixture for 10 minutes. Thread onto skewers with onions and lemons and cook as directed.

1. Place frozen shrimp in large zipper-lock bag. Combine lemon juice, olive oil, sugar, garlic, and tarragon; pour into small zipper-lock bag. Attach another bag with onions and lemons. Label bags, seal, and freeze.

2. *To thaw and cook:* Thaw all bags overnight in refrigerator. Prepare and preheat grill. Place shrimp in a medium bowl and pour lemon marinade over. Let stand 10 to 15 minutes, then thread shrimp onto metal skewers with onion and lemon wedges.

3. Grill kabobs 6 inches from medium coals for 4 to 6 minutes, brushing with marinade and turning once, until shrimp are pink and opaque and onions are crisp-tender. Discard any remaining marinade.

Grilled Turkey Cutlets

Serves 4

4 (6-ounce) turkey cutlets
3 cloves garlic, minced
1 teaspoon ground cumin
⅛ teaspoon cayenne pepper
2 tablespoons honey
2 tablespoons mustard
1 tablespoon olive oil
1 teaspoon salt

Serves 12

12 (6-ounce) turkey cutlets
9 cloves garlic, minced
1 tablespoon ground cumin
⅜ teaspoon cayenne pepper
6 tablespoons honey
6 tablespoons mustard
3 tablespoons olive oil
1 tablespoon salt

These cutlets are perfect for a hot summer evening. To grill without freezing, marinate the cutlets for 2 to 24 hours in the refrigerator, then cook as directed.

1. Place turkey cutlets in large zipper-lock bag and add remaining ingredients. Seal bag and knead to mix. Label bag, seal, and freeze.

2. *To thaw and cook:* Thaw overnight in refrigerator. Prepare and preheat grill. Drain cutlets and grill 6 inches from medium coals for 4 minutes on each side until juices run clear and turkey is thoroughly cooked.

Flank Steak Sandwiches

To serve these sandwiches without freezing, marinate steak in refrigerator for 2 to 3 hours, then cook as directed.

1. Cut several slits in flank steak on both sides with sharp knife. Place in zipper-lock bag. In small bowl, combine lemon juice, oil, garlic, honey, ginger, and pepper and whisk to mix. Pour over flank steak, seal bag, and knead to work the marinade into the meat.

2. Spread split buns with butter and place in another zipper-lock bag. Put the cheese in a third zipper-lock bag. Attach all bags together, seal, label, and freeze.

3. *To thaw and cook:* Thaw bags overnight in refrigerator. Prepare and preheat grill. Grill flank steak 6 inches from medium coals for 4 to 5 minutes on each side until meat thermometer registers 145°F to 160°F. Remove steak from grill, cover with foil, and let sit for 5 to 10 minutes.

4. Place buns, cut-side down, on grill and cook for 1 to 2 minutes. Turn buns over and sprinkle with cheese. Close grill and cook until cheese melts, about 1 to 2 minutes. Slice flank steak thinly against the grain and make sandwiches with the cheese-coated buns. Serve with mayonnaise and mustard, if desired.

Serves 6

1½ pounds flank steak
¼ cup lemon juice
3 tablespoons olive oil
3 cloves garlic, minced
1 tablespoon honey
1 teaspoon ground ginger
⅛ teaspoon pepper
6 hoagie buns, split
2 tablespoons butter
3 cups shredded Muenster cheese

Serves 18

3 (1½-pound) flank steaks
¾ cup lemon juice
9 tablespoons olive oil
9 cloves garlic, minced
3 tablespoons honey
1 tablespoon ground ginger
⅜ teaspoon pepper
18 hoagie buns, split
6 tablespoons butter
9 cups shredded Muenster cheese

Grilled Steak and Veggies

Serves 4

---

2 teaspoons Grill Seasoning
  (page 308)
1 pound sirloin tip steak
2 tablespoons apple cider
  vinegar
1 tablespoon olive oil
4 ears frozen corn
2 tablespoons butter
1 teaspoon dried basil leaves
1 (16-ounce) package frozen
  asparagus pieces
2 tablespoons water

Serves 12

---

2 tablespoons Grill
  Seasoning (page 308)
3 pounds sirloin tip steak
6 tablespoons apple cider
  vinegar
3 tablespoons olive oil
12 ears frozen corn
6 tablespoons butter
1 tablespoon dried basil
  leaves
3 (16-ounce) packages
  frozen asparagus pieces
6 tablespoons water

If you can't find frozen ears of corn, use loose-pack frozen corn and reduce the grilling time by about half. To serve without freezing, marinate steak in refrigerator for 2 to 3 hours, then cook as directed.

---

1. Rub seasoning into both sides of steak. Coat steak with vinegar and olive oil and place in zipper-lock bag; seal, label, and freeze.

2. Tear off four 12" × 18" sheets of heavy-duty aluminum foil and place corn in center. Mix together butter and basil and spread on corn. Divide asparagus pieces among foil and sprinkle with water. Bring short edges of foil together and fold twice. Fold long edges over twice and seal. Label packages and freeze.

3. *To thaw and cook:* Thaw steak and corn packages overnight in refrigerator. Prepare and heat grill. Place packets on grill 4 to 6 inches from medium coals. Cover grill and cook for 14 to 19 minutes, turning once, or until vegetables are tender. Cook steak 4 to 5 minutes per side, turning once, until desired doneness. Slice steak thinly across the grain and serve with vegetables.

Marinated Steak with Blue Cheese Butter

You could use any cut of tender steak in this delicious recipe. To cook without freezing, marinate steaks in refrigerator for 1 to 2 hours, then cook as directed below. Refrigerate blue cheese butter until ready to serve.

Serves 4–6

4 (1-inch-thick) boneless
    ribeye steaks
¼ cup apple cider vinegar
¼ cup honey
2 tablespoons soy sauce
1 tablespoon Dijon mustard
1 teaspoon salt
⅛ teaspoon white pepper
¼ cup butter, softened
¼ cup crumbled blue cheese
1 tablespoon heavy cream

1. Place each steak in a zipper-lock bag. In small bowl, combine vinegar, honey, soy sauce, mustard, salt, and pepper and mix to blend. Pour equal amounts in each bag over steaks and seal bags.

2. In small bowl, combine butter, cheese, and cream and blend well. Divide into four portions and place in four small zipper-lock bags. Attach to bags with steaks, seal, label, and freeze.

3. *To thaw and cook:* Thaw overnight in refrigerator. Prepare and preheat grill. Grill thawed steaks 4 to 5 minutes per side, 4 to 6 inches from medium-hot coals, until desired doneness. When steaks are cooked, place on serving plate and top each with blue cheese butter. Cover steaks and let stand 5 to 6 minutes before serving.

Serves 12–18

12 (1-inch-thick) boneless
    ribeye steaks
¾ cup apple cider vinegar
¾ cup honey
6 tablespoons soy sauce
3 tablespoons Dijon mustard
1 tablespoon salt
⅜ teaspoon white pepper
¾ cup butter, softened
¾ cup crumbled blue cheese
3 tablespoons heavy cream

Chop First or Measure First?

The order of words in a recipe's ingredient list gives you a clue to their preparation. The word chopped before the ingredient means you first chop the ingredient, then measure it. The same word after the ingredient means you first measure the ingredient, then chop.

Pepper Jack Burger Packets

Serves 4

1 pound lean ground beef
1 cup shredded pepper jack
cheese
1 tablespoon Worcestershire
sauce
2 teaspoons Grill Seasoning
(page 308)
1 tablespoon water
2 cups baby carrots
2 tablespoons butter
2 cups frozen hash brown
potatoes
½ cup grated Parmesan
cheese
½ teaspoons dried oregano
leaves

Serves 12

3 pounds lean ground beef
3 cups shredded pepper jack
cheese
3 tablespoons
Worcestershire sauce
6 teaspoons Grill Seasoning
(page 308)
3 tablespoons water
6 cups baby carrots
6 tablespoons butter
6 cups frozen hash brown
potatoes
1½ cups grated Parmesan
cheese
1½ teaspoons dried oregano
leaves

These packets are a meal in one! To serve without freezing, just grill the packets until the meat is cooked and vegetables are tender, about 15 to 20 minutes, turning once.

1. Tear off four 12" × 18" sheets of heavy-duty aluminum foil and set aside. In medium bowl, combine beef, pepper jack cheese, Worcestershire sauce, seasoning, and water and mix gently. Form into 4 hamburger patties and place one in center of each foil sheet.

2. Divide baby carrots among foil sheets and dot with butter. In medium bowl, toss together potatoes with Parmesan and oregano, then divide among foil sheets. Bring short edges of foil together and fold twice. Fold long edges over twice and seal. Label packages and freeze.

3. *To thaw and cook:* Thaw packages overnight in refrigerator. When ready to eat, prepare and heat grill. Place packets on grill 4 to 6 inches from medium coals. Cover grill and cook for 15 to 25 minutes, turning once, until vegetables are tender and meat is thoroughly cooked to 160°F.

CHAPTER 15
TV Dinners

Pot Roast Dinner

Serves 6

12 slices Pot Roast (page 67)
3 cups refrigerated mashed potatoes
¼ cup grated Parmesan cheese
2 tablespoons olive oil
2 cloves garlic, minced
1 pound fresh asparagus
2 cups water
½ teaspoon salt
⅛ teaspoon pepper

Serves 18

36 slices Pot Roast (page 67)
9 cups refrigerated mashed potatoes
¾ cup grated Parmesan cheese
6 tablespoons olive oil
6 cloves garlic, minced
3 pounds fresh asparagus
6 cups water
1½ teaspoons salt
⅜ teaspoon pepper

When you make the pot roast for these delicious dinners, serve the rest for supper on cooking day or reserve for other recipes.

1. When the Pot Roast is cooked according to the recipe, cut 12 slices about ¼-inch thick. Set out an oven/microwave-safe plate for each serving. Place two slices of roast on each plate and spoon some juices from the roast over the slices.

2. Divide mashed potatoes among the plates and sprinkle with Parmesan cheese. In heavy skillet, heat olive oil and sauté garlic for 2 to 3 minutes until fragrant. Add asparagus and water and bring to a boil. Cover and cook asparagus for 6 to 8 minutes, or until crisp-tender. Drain and place on plates next to mashed potatoes and sprinkle asparagus with salt and pepper. Cover each plate with heavy duty aluminum foil, seal well, label, and freeze.

3. *To thaw and reheat in oven:* Place frozen, still-wrapped containers into preheated 400°F oven and bake for 20 to 30 minutes or until all food is hot.

   To reheat in microwave (one at a time): Remove foil from plates and cover with microwave-safe plastic wrap, vented at one corner. Microwave on high for 4 minutes, then turn beef slices over and microwave on high for another 4 minutes. Let stand for 2 minutes before eating.

Pesto Chicken Dinner

Make your own pesto or use purchased pesto for this delicious dinner. If you like, you can substitute frozen carrot coins for the baby carrots, and use plain rice instead of the chicken-flavored rice mix.

1. Heat olive oil in heavy skillet. Sprinkle chicken breasts with salt and pepper and cook in olive oil over medium heat for 10 to 12 minutes, or until thoroughly cooked, turning once. Set out an oven/microwave-safe plate for each serving. Place a chicken breast on each plate and place in refrigerator while preparing remainder of meal.

2. Place baby carrots in medium saucepan and cover with water. Bring to a boil, then reduce heat and simmer for 4 to 5 minutes, or until carrots are crisp-tender. Plunge carrots into ice water, drain, divide among plates, and dot with butter.

3. In medium saucepan, combine rice mix and water and bring to a boil. Reduce heat, cover saucepan, and simmer for 15 to 18 minutes or until rice is almost tender. Spoon onto plates. Spread pesto over chicken and sprinkle with Muenster cheese. Cover plates with heavy-duty foil, label, and freeze.

4. *To thaw and reheat in oven:* Place frozen, wrapped dinners in preheated 400°F oven and bake for 20 to 30 minutes or until chicken and carrots are thoroughly heated.

   To reheat in microwave (one at a time): Remove foil from plates and cover with microwave-safe plastic wrap, vented at one corner. Microwave on high for 4 minutes, then rotate plate and microwave on high for another 4 minutes. Let stand for 2 minutes before eating.

Serves 4

2 tablespoons olive oil
4 boneless, skinless chicken breasts
½ teaspoon salt
⅛ teaspoon pepper
2 cups baby carrots
2 tablespoons butter
1 cup Chicken Rice Mix (page 306)
2 cups water
2 blocks frozen Pesto Sauce (page 296), thawed
1 cup grated Muenster cheese

Serves 12

6 tablespoons olive oil
12 boneless, skinless chicken breasts
1½ teaspoons salt
⅜ teaspoon pepper
6 cups baby carrots
6 tablespoons butter
3 cups Chicken Rice Mix (page 306)
6 cups water
6 blocks frozen Pesto Sauce (page 296), thawed
3 cups grated Muenster cheese

Beef Rouladen Dinner

Serves 4

---

4 Beef Rouladen rolls
   (page 76)
2 cups green beans, trimmed
2 cups water
½ teaspoon salt
Pinch pepper
2 tablespoons butter
½ teaspoon dried tarragon
   leaves
2 cups frozen potato wedges

Serves 12

---

12 Beef Rouladen rolls
   (page 76)
6 cups green beans, trimmed
6 cups water
1½ teaspoons salt
⅛ teaspoon pepper
6 tablespoons butter
1½ teaspoons dried tarragon
   leaves
6 cups frozen potato wedges

You can use frozen green beans if you'd like; don't defrost them, just dot with butter and tarragon as directed below. Southern hash browns would be a good substitute for the frozen potato wedges.

---

1. Set out an oven/microwave-safe plate for each serving. Place one Beef Rouladen roll on each plate and place in refrigerator while preparing vegetables.

2. Combine green beans, water, and salt in heavy skillet and bring to a boil. Reduce heat and simmer for 5 to 6 minutes or until beans are crisp-tender. Plunge beans into ice water, then drain beans and divide among plates next to Beef Rouladen. Dot beans with butter and sprinkle with tarragon. Place frozen potato wedges on plates. Wrap dinners in heavy-duty foil, label, and freeze.

3. *To thaw and reheat in oven:* Place frozen, wrapped dinners in preheated 400°F oven and bake for 25 to 35 minutes or until meat and vegetables are thoroughly heated.

   To reheat in microwave (one at a time): Remove foil from dinner and cover with microwave-safe plastic wrap, vented at one corner. Microwave on high for 4 minutes. Rotate container 90° and microwave on high for 3 to 4 minutes or until thoroughly heated. Let stand 2 minutes before eating.

Apple Glazed Pork Roast Dinner

Any frozen vegetable can be substituted for the corn and broccoli.
Asparagus and carrots would be a good combination.
Make sure to refrigerate the pork roast within 1 hour of cooking.

1. Set out an oven/microwave-safe plate for each serving. Place two slices of the cooked roast on each plate and top each with some of the sauce.

2. Place frozen corn next to pork and sprinkle with basil leaves. Place broccoli next to pork; dot with butter and sprinkle with Parmesan cheese. Wrap plates in heavy-duty foil, label, and freeze.

3. *To thaw and reheat in oven:* Place frozen, wrapped dinners in pre-heated 400°F oven and bake for 25 to 35 minutes or until Pork Roast and vegetables are thoroughly heated.

   To reheat in microwave (one at a time): Remove foil from dinner and cover with microwave-safe plastic wrap, vented at one corner. Microwave on high for 4 minutes. Rotate container 90° and microwave on high for 3 to 4 minutes or until thoroughly heated. Let stand 2 minutes before eating.

How Important Are the Measurements?

Measurements in baking are critical; measurements in cooking are less strict. A cake batter, for instance, is a precise chemical formula that must be followed for success. Measurements for a stew or soup, on the other hand, are much less rigid.

Serves 4

8 slices Apple Glazed Pork Roast (page 134)
1 cup sauce from Apple Glazed Pork Roast
2 cups frozen corn
1 teaspoon dried basil leaves
2 cups frozen broccoli spears
2 tablespoons butter
¼ cup grated Parmesan cheese

Serves 12

24 slices Apple Glazed Pork Roast (page 134)
3 cups sauce from Apple Glazed Pork Roast
6 cups frozen corn
1 tablespoon dried basil leaves
6 cups frozen broccoli spears
6 tablespoons butter
¾ cup grated Parmesan cheese

Fish Fillet Dinner

Serves 4

1 tablespoon olive oil
1 onion, chopped
2 cloves garlic, minced
4 (½-inch-thick) fish fillets
2 tablespoons lemon juice
1 cup Fish Broth (page 304)
2 cups cut green beans
2 tablespoons butter
4 frozen, unbaked folded
 Homemade Biscuits
 (page 260)

Serves 12

3 tablespoons olive oil
3 onions, chopped
6 cloves garlic, minced
12 (½-inch-thick) fish fillets
6 tablespoons lemon juice
3 cups Fish Broth (page 304)
6 cups cut green beans
6 tablespoons butter
12 frozen, unbaked folded
 Homemade Biscuits
 (page 260)

Use any type of mild fish fillet for this easy dinner.
Orange roughy, halibut, or cod would all work well. You could also
substitute your favorite frozen vegetables for the green beans.

1. In large skillet, heat olive oil and cook onion and garlic until almost tender. Add fish fillets to skillet and sprinkle with lemon juice. Pour broth over all, cover pan, reduce heat, and simmer for 10 to 12 minutes, until fish flakes easily when tested with fork. Set out an oven/microwave-safe plate for each serving. Lift fish and vegetables out of pan using slotted spoon and divide among plates; place in freezer.

2. Place green beans in medium saucepan and cover with water. Bring to a boil, then reduce heat and simmer for 4 minutes. Drain beans well and divide among plates next to fish. Dot beans with butter. Place one frozen biscuit on each plate. Wrap dinners in heavy-duty foil, seal, label, and freeze.

3. *To thaw and reheat:* Peel foil away from biscuits but leave rest of dinner covered. Bake the frozen dinners in preheated 400°F oven for 18 to 22 minutes, or until fish and vegetables are thoroughly heated and rolls are tender and golden. (Microwaving is not recommended.)

Shrimp Pesto Dinner

Shrimp and pesto is a wonderful combination. If you can't find pearl onions, chop 1 medium onion and sauté it in a bit of olive oil until crisp-tender.

1. Set out an oven/microwave-safe plate for each serving. Divide shrimp among plates and top each portion with pesto. Place in freezer while preparing rest of meal.

2. In heavy saucepan, combine brown rice and broth and bring to a boil. Reduce heat, cover, and simmer for 30 to 35 minutes, until rice is almost tender. Cool in refrigerator.

3. Divide cooled rice and frozen vegetables among the plates. Dot carrots and onions with butter. Wrap plates in heavy-duty foil, label, and freeze.

4. *To thaw and reheat in oven:* Place frozen, wrapped dinners in preheated 400°F oven and bake for 18 to 25 minutes or until shrimp, rice, and vegetables are thoroughly heated.

   To reheat in microwave (one at a time): Remove foil from dinner and cover with microwave-safe plastic wrap, vented at one corner. Microwave on high for 4 minutes. Rotate plate 90° and microwave on high for 3 to 4 minutes, until thoroughly heated. Let stand 2 minutes before eating.

Serves 4

1 pound frozen uncooked medium shrimp
4 blocks frozen Pesto Sauce (page 296), thawed
1 cup brown rice
2 cups Chicken Broth (page 301)
2 cups frozen sliced carrots
1 cup frozen pearl onions
2 tablespoons butter

Serves 12

3 pounds frozen uncooked medium shrimp
12 blocks frozen Pesto Sauce (page 296), thawed
3 cups brown rice
6 cups Chicken Broth (page 301)
6 cups sliced frozen carrots
3 cups frozen pearl onions
6 tablespoons butter

Ham and Polenta Dinner

Serves 4

4 slices hickory-smoked
    ham
2 tablespoons peach jam
2 tablespoons barbecue
    sauce
2 cups frozen broccoli
2 cups water
½ cup yellow cornmeal
¼ teaspoon salt
2 tablespoons melted butter

Serves 12

12 slices hickory-smoked
    ham
6 tablespoons peach jam
6 tablespoons barbecue
    sauce
6 cups frozen broccoli
6 cups water
1½ cups yellow cornmeal
¾ teaspoon salt
6 tablespoons melted butter

Polenta is simply cooked cornmeal. It is similar to mashed potatoes, but with a grainier texture and nutty flavor.

1. Set out an oven/microwave-safe plate for each serving. Divide ham among plates. In small bowl, combine peach jam and barbecue sauce and mix well. Brush over ham slices. Divide frozen broccoli among the four plates.

2. In medium saucepan, bring water to a boil. Add cornmeal and salt all at once and cook over medium heat for 12 to 14 minutes until thickened. Stir in butter until combined. Divide among the four plates. Wrap plates in heavy-duty foil, seal, label, and freeze.

3. *To thaw and reheat in oven:* Place frozen, wrapped dinners in preheated 400°F oven and bake for 20 to 30 minutes or until dinners are thoroughly heated.

To reheat in microwave (one at a time): Remove foil from dinner and cover with microwave-safe plastic wrap, vented at one corner. Microwave on high for 4 minutes. Rotate 90° and microwave on high for 3 to 4 minutes, until thoroughly heated. Let stand 2 minutes before eating.

Beef Stroganoff Dinner

Beef Stroganoff is a delicious dinner choice that is so easy to make. You could substitute baby carrots for the frozen corn.

1. In heavy saucepan, cook egg noodles as directed on package until almost al dente; drain, rinse with cold water, and drain again. Set out an oven/microwave-safe plate for each serving. Divide noodles among plates and top with the cooled Beef Stroganoff. Refrigerate.

2. Divide frozen corn and snow peas among plates. Dot corn with 2 tablespoons butter. In small bowl, combine 2 tablespoons melted butter and honey mustard and mix well. Drizzle over snow peas. Wrap plates in heavy-duty foil, seal, label, and freeze.

3. *To thaw and reheat in oven:* Place frozen, wrapped dinners in preheated 400°F oven and bake for 20 to 30 minutes or until dinners are thoroughly heated.

   To reheat in microwave (one at a time): Remove foil from dinner and cover with microwave-safe plastic wrap, vented at one corner. Microwave on high for 4 minutes. Rotate 90° and microwave on high for 3 to 4 minutes, until thoroughly heated. Let stand 2 minutes before eating.

Substituting Pasta

You can substitute different pastas from those called for in recipes as long as the pasta is approximately the same size and shape. Linguine can be substituted for spaghetti; shells can be substituted for egg noodles.

Serves 4

2 cups egg noodles
4 cups Beef Stroganoff
(page 66)
2 cups frozen corn
2 cups frozen snow peas
2 tablespoons butter
2 tablespoons melted butter
2 tablespoons honey
mustard

Serves 12

6 cups egg noodles
12 cups Beef Stroganoff
(page 66)
6 cups frozen corn
6 cups frozen snow peas
6 tablespoons butter
6 tablespoons melted butter
6 tablespoons honey
mustard

Roast Chicken Dinner

Serves 4

---

4 pieces Sticky Roast
    Chicken (page 106)
2 cups frozen corn
1 tablespoon butter
3 tablespoons butter
½ teaspoon garlic powder
4 (1-inch-thick) slices French
    bread

Serves 12

---

12 pieces Sticky Roast
    Chicken (page 106)
6 cups frozen corn
3 tablespoons butter
9 tablespoons butter
1½ teaspoons garlic powder
12 (1-inch-thick) slices
    French bread

This homey combination is great for busy school nights; each member of your family can bake a warm, hearty dinner when he or she gets home from studying or after-school activities.

---

1. When chicken has cooled, slice chicken, including a piece of skin with each piece; discard bones. Set out an oven/microwave-safe plate for each serving. Divide chicken slices among plates.

2. Divide corn among plates and dot with butter. In small bowl, combine butter and garlic powder and mix well. Spread over French bread slices and place them next to corn on plates. Wrap plates in heavy-duty foil, label, seal, and freeze.

3. *To thaw and reheat:* Place frozen, wrapped dinners in preheated 400° oven and bake for 15 minutes; peel foil back to uncover French bread and return to oven. Bake for 5 to 15 minutes longer or until dinners are thoroughly heated. (Microwaving is not recommended.)

Ham Rolls Dinner

This elegant meal is perfect for company or to treat your family. You could substitute frozen green beans or frozen corn for the asparagus, if you'd like.

---

1. Set out an oven/microwave-safe plate for each serving. Divide Ham Rolls among plates and top each with sauce. Sprinkle with Parmesan cheese. Divide asparagus pieces among plates and dot evenly with butter. Divide carrots among plates and dot evenly with butter. Wrap each plate in heavy-duty foil, label, seal, and freeze.

2. *To thaw and reheat in oven:* Place frozen, wrapped dinners in preheated 400°F oven and bake for 20 to 30 minutes or until dinners are thoroughly heated.

   To reheat in microwave (one at a time): Remove foil from dinner and cover with microwave-safe plastic wrap, vented at one corner. Microwave on high for 4 minutes. Rotate 90° and microwave on high for 3 to 4 minutes, until thoroughly heated. Let stand 2 minutes before eating.

Choose Your Own Entrée

When you're putting together your own TV dinners, almost any entrée recipe can be used as long as it is fully cooked before freezing. Two exceptions are shrimp and scallops; they should be packaged in the dinner uncooked.

Serves 4

---

4 Wild Rice Ham Rolls
  (page 146)
1 cup sauce from Wild Rice
  Ham Rolls
¼ cup grated Parmesan
  cheese
2 cups frozen asparagus
  pieces
2 tablespoons butter
2 cups sliced frozen carrots
2 tablespoons butter

Serves 12

---

12 Wild Rice Ham Rolls
  (page 146)
3 cups sauce from Wild Rice
  Ham Rolls
¾ cup grated Parmesan
  cheese
6 cups frozen asparagus
  pieces
6 tablespoons butter
6 cups sliced frozen carrots
6 tablespoons butter

Spaghetti and Meatballs

Serves 6

1 (8-ounce) package
   spaghetti pasta
1 recipe Italian Meatballs
   (page 52)
1 (26-ounce) jar pasta sauce
½ cup grated Parmesan
   cheese
3 cups frozen broccoli florets
2 tablespoons butter

Serves 18

3 (8-ounce) packages
   spaghetti pasta
3 recipes Italian Meatballs
   (page 52)
3 (26-ounce) jars pasta
   sauce
1½ cups grated Parmesan
   cheese
9 cups frozen broccoli florets
6 tablespoons butter

You could substitute purchased frozen fully cooked meatballs for the homemade meatballs in this easy dinner. Serve with some crusty garlic bread.

1. Cook pasta according to package directions until almost al dente. Drain and rinse with cold water; drain again. Set out an oven/microwave-safe plate for each serving. Divide pasta among plates. In large bowl, combine cooled meatballs with pasta sauce. Divide among plates, covering pasta. Sprinkle with grated cheese. Divide frozen broccoli among plates and dot with butter. Wrap plates in freezer wrap, label, seal, and freeze.

2. *To thaw and reheat in oven:* Unwrap dinners and re-wrap in foil. Place dinners in preheated 400°F oven and bake for 20 to 30 minutes or until dinners are thoroughly heated.

   To reheat in microwave (one at a time): Remove freezer wrap from dinner and cover with microwave-safe plastic wrap, vented at one corner. Microwave on high for 4 minutes. Rotate 90° and microwave on high for 3 to 4 minutes, until thoroughly heated. Let stand 2 minutes before eating.

Beefy Enchilada Dinner

This authentic Mexican dinner is just like takeout,
but you control the ingredients!

1. Set out an oven/microwave-safe plate for each serving. Place two enchiladas on each plate. Top each with enchilada sauce. Divide refried beans among the plates and sprinkle each with Cheddar cheese. Store in refrigerator while preparing rice.

2. In heavy saucepan, sauté onion in olive oil until crisp-tender. Add broth and bring to a boil. Add rice and paprika and bring to a boil. Lower heat, cover pan, and simmer for 15 minutes or until rice is almost tender. Divide among plates next to refried beans. Wrap plates in heavy duty foil, seal, label, and freeze.

3. *To thaw and reheat in oven:* Place frozen, wrapped dinners in preheated 400°F oven and bake for 20 to 30 minutes or until dinners are thoroughly heated.

   To reheat in microwave (one at a time): Remove foil from dinner and cover with microwave-safe plastic wrap, vented at one corner. Microwave on high for 4 minutes. Rotate 90° and microwave on high for 3 to 4 minutes, until thoroughly heated. Let stand 2 minutes before eating.

Serves 4

8 Beefy Enchiladas (page 46)
⅔ cup enchilada sauce
2 cups refried beans
¼ cup shredded Cheddar cheese
½ cup minced onion
1 tablespoon olive oil
2 cups Chicken Broth (page 301)
1 cup white rice
¼ teaspoon smoked paprika

Serves 12

24 Beefy Enchiladas (page 46)
2 cups enchilada sauce
6 cups refried beans
¾ cup shredded Cheddar cheese
1½ cups minced onion
3 tablespoons olive oil
6 cups Chicken Broth (page 301)
3 cups white rice
¾ teaspoon smoked paprika

Chicken Fingers Dinner

Serves 4

1 (16-ounce) package
  frozen breaded chicken
  fingers
1 teaspoon smoked paprika
2 cups refrigerated mashed
  potatoes
1 egg yolk
¼ cup grated Parmesan
  cheese
2 cups frozen baby peas
2 tablespoons butter
½ teaspoon dried basil
  leaves
¼ cup honey mustard salad
  dressing
3 tablespoons mayonnaise

Serves 12

3 (16-ounce) packages
  frozen breaded chicken
  fingers
1 tablespoon smoked
  paprika
6 cups refrigerated mashed
  potatoes
3 egg yolks
¾ cup grated Parmesan
  cheese
6 cups frozen baby peas
6 tablespoons butter
1½ teaspoons dried basil
  leaves
¾ cup honey mustard salad
  dressing
9 tablespoons mayonnaise

This dinner is perfect for kids. If your children are picky,
omit the basil from the peas and the paprika from the chicken
and serve plain old ketchup for a dipping sauce.

1. Set out an oven/microwave-safe plate for each serving. Sprinkle chicken fingers with paprika and divide among plates.

2. In small bowl, combine potatoes, egg yolk, and Parmesan cheese and mix to blend. Divide among plates. Divide peas among plates, dot with butter, and sprinkle with basil. Wrap plates in heavy-duty foil, seal, label, and freeze. Reserve salad dressing and mayonnaise in refrigerator.

3. *To thaw and reheat:* Place frozen, wrapped dinners in preheated 400°F oven and bake for 18 to 25 minutes or until dinners are thoroughly heated.

To reheat in microwave (one at a time): Remove foil from dinner and cover with microwave-safe plastic wrap, vented at one corner. Microwave on high for 4 minutes. Rotate 90° and microwave on high for 3 to 4 minutes until thoroughly heated. Let stand 2 minutes before eating. Combine salad dressing and mayonnaise in small bowl for dipping sauce.

Meatloaf Dinner

Mom's comfort food! You can make your own mashed potatoes for this easy recipe, or substitute hash brown potatoes sprinkled with Parmesan cheese.

1. Set out an oven/microwave-safe plate for each serving. Divide meatloaf slices among plates. In small bowl, combine gravy and water and blend well. Spoon over meatloaf slices.

2. In medium bowl, combine mashed potatoes, egg yolk, and Parmesan cheese and mix until combined. Divide among plates next to meatloaf. Divide green beans among plates; drizzle with olive oil and sprinkle with thyme leaves. Wrap each plate in heavy-duty foil; seal, label, and freeze.

3. *To thaw and reheat in oven:* Place frozen, wrapped dinners in preheated 400°F oven and bake for 20 to 30 minutes or until meatloaf and vegetables are thoroughly heated.

   To reheat in microwave (one at a time): Remove foil from dinner and cover with microwave-safe plastic wrap, vented at one corner. Microwave on high for 4 minutes. Rotate 90° and microwave on high for 3 to 4 minutes, until thoroughly heated. Let stand 2 minutes before eating.

Serves 4

4 (1-inch-thick) slices Mom's Favorite Meatloaf (page 58)
½ cup bottled beef gravy
1 tablespoon water
2 cups refrigerated mashed potatoes
1 egg yolk
¼ cup grated Parmesan cheese
2 cups frozen green beans
1 tablespoon olive oil
¼ teaspoon dried thyme leaves

Serves 12

12 (1-inch-thick) slices Mom's Favorite Meatloaf (page 58)
1½ cups bottled beef gravy
3 tablespoons water
6 cups refrigerated mashed potatoes
3 egg yolks
¾ cup grated Parmesan cheese
6 cups frozen green beans
3 tablespoons olive oil
¾ teaspoon dried thyme leaves

Stuffed Manicotti Dinner

Serves 4

---

8 Stuffed Manicotti shells
(page 47)
1 cup pasta sauce
½ cup grated Parmesan
cheese
2 cups frozen cauliflower
and broccoli mix
2 tablespoons butter
½ teaspoon dried thyme
leaves

Serves 12

---

24 Stuffed Manicotti shells
(page 47)
3 cups pasta sauce
1½ cups grated Parmesan
cheese
6 cups frozen cauliflower
and broccoli mix
6 tablespoons butter
1½ teaspoons dried thyme
leaves

Any frozen vegetable would be a good addition
to this easy Italian TV dinner. Serve with a fresh baby
spinach salad and some crisp breadsticks.

1. Set out an oven/microwave-safe plate for each serving. Place two manicotti shells on each plate. Pour pasta sauce over shells and sprinkle with cheese. Divide frozen vegetables among plates, dot with butter, and sprinkle with thyme. Wrap plates in heavy-duty foil, label, seal, and freeze.

2. *To thaw and reheat in oven:* Place frozen, wrapped dinners in preheated 400°F oven and bake for 20 to 30 minutes or until manicotti and vegetables are thoroughly heated.

To reheat in microwave (one at a time): Remove foil from dinner and cover with microwave-safe plastic wrap, vented at one corner. Microwave on high for 4 minutes. Rotate 90° and microwave on high for 3 to 4 minutes, until thoroughly heated. Let stand 2 minutes before eating.

Pork Chops and Potatoes Dinner

Any recipe for pork chops can be used instead
of the Honey Mustard Pork Chops; just make sure they are
thoroughly cooked before packaging with the dinners.

1. Cook pork chops as directed in recipe; cool in refrigerator. Set out an oven/microwave-safe plate for each serving. Put one pork chop on each plate. Divide asparagus pieces among plates. In medium bowl, combine potatoes, olive oil, and Parmesan cheese and toss to mix. Divide among plates. Wrap plates in heavy-duty foil; seal, label, and freeze.

2. *To thaw and reheat:* Place frozen, wrapped dinners in preheated 400°F oven and bake for 15 minutes. Peel back foil from potatoes, return to oven, and bake for 5 to 15 minutes longer until dinners are thoroughly heated. (Microwaving is not recommended.)

Planning Attractive Meals

When planning a meal, take into consideration the color, temperature, and texture of foods. The more colorful the meal, the healthier it is. Serve cold foods along with hot and warm foods. And vary textures from crunchy to smooth to crisp.

Serves 6

6 Honey Mustard Pork
  Chops (page 133)
2 cups frozen asparagus
  pieces
2 cups frozen shredded hash
  brown potatoes
2 tablespoons olive oil
½ cup grated Parmesan
  cheese

Serves 18

18 Honey Mustard Pork
  Chops (page 133)
6 cups frozen asparagus
  pieces
6 cups frozen shredded hash
  brown potatoes
6 tablespoons olive oil
1½ cups grated Parmesan
  cheese

Seafood Crepes Dinner

These elegant crepes are perfect for a special occasion dinner; imagine serving TV dinners to company! Accompany this dinner with some crusty sourdough bread.

Serves 8

1 recipe Basic Crepes
(page 300)
2 cups Chicken Broth
(page 301)
1 cup basmati rice
2 cups small frozen cooked
shrimp
1 (12-ounce) can crabmeat,
drained
1 (16-ounce) jar Alfredo
sauce
1 cup frozen baby peas
1 cup shredded Gouda
cheese
2 cups frozen asparagus
pieces
2 tablespoons butter
½ cup water

Serves 24

3 recipes Basic Crepes
(page 300)
6 cups Chicken Broth
(page 301)
3 cups basmati rice
6 cups small frozen cooked
shrimp
3 (12-ounce) cans crabmeat,
drained
3 (16-ounce) jars Alfredo
sauce
3 cups frozen baby peas
3 cups shredded Gouda
cheese
6 cups frozen asparagus
pieces
6 tablespoons butter
1½ cups water

1. Prepare crepes and cool. Bring broth to a boil in medium saucepan and stir in rice. Cover pan, reduce heat, and simmer for 10 to 15 minutes or until rice is almost tender.

2. Meanwhile, in large bowl, combine frozen shrimp, drained crabmeat, half of Alfredo sauce, frozen peas, and Gouda and mix gently. Place large spoonful of this mixture on each crepe and roll up. Set out an oven/microwave-safe plate for each serving. Place 2 filled crepes on each plate and top with remaining Alfredo sauce.

3. Divide frozen asparagus among plates and dot with butter. Divide rice among plates and sprinkle each serving with 1 tablespoon water. Wrap dinners in heavy-duty foil, seal, label, and freeze.

4. *To thaw and reheat in oven:* Place frozen, wrapped dinners in preheated 400°F oven and bake for 18 to 25 minutes or until crepes, rice, and asparagus are thoroughly heated.

To reheat in microwave (one at a time): Remove foil from dinner and cover with microwave-safe plastic wrap, vented at one corner. Microwave on high for 4 minutes. Rotate 90° and microwave on high for 3 to 4 minutes, until thoroughly heated. Let stand 2 minutes before eating.

CHAPTER 16
Breakfast and Brunch

Apple Quick Bread

Makes 2 loaves

---

4 medium apples
1 cup butter, softened
2 cups sugar
1 teaspoon cinnamon
4 eggs
3½ cups flour
1 teaspoon baking soda
½ teaspoon baking powder
¼ teaspoon salt
1 cup buttermilk
1 teaspoon vanilla
1 cup chopped pecans

Makes 6 loaves

---

12 medium apples
3 cups butter, softened
6 cups sugar
1 tablespoon cinnamon
12 eggs
10½ cups flour
1 tablespoon baking soda
1½ teaspoons baking
    powder
¾ teaspoon salt
3 cups buttermilk
1 tablespoon vanilla
3 cups chopped pecans

This is great bread for breakfast on the run. You can add a glaze if you like: Combine 1 cup confectioners' sugar, ½ teaspoon vanilla, and 2 to 3 tablespoons milk and mix well, then drizzle over loaves.

1. Preheat oven to 325°F. Generously grease and flour two 9" × 5" loaf pans and set aside. Peel and core apples and chop finely, by hand or in a food processor.

2. In large bowl, combine chopped apples, butter, sugar, cinnamon, and eggs. Stir for 2 to 3 minutes, until blended. Add remaining ingredients and mix well to blend. Pour batter into prepared baking pans. Bake at 325°F for 60 to 75 minutes, until dark golden brown.

3. Cool bread in pans for 5 minutes, then turn out of pans and cool on wire rack. Wrap loaves in freezer-safe plastic wrap, label, and freeze.

4. *To thaw and serve:* Loosen wrapping and thaw loaves 2 to 3 hours at room temperature.

Cool It!

Cool cooked foods as quickly as possible before freezing. Remember, you don't want to raise the internal temperature of your freezer when you add your freshly prepared foods, so don't add hot foods to the freezer.

Breakfast Burritos

These easy and slightly spicy burritos are great to have on hand. You can heat them individually in the microwave, or bake a bunch in the oven. To serve burritos immediately, serve after rolling.

1. In heavy skillet, cook onion and garlic in butter and olive oil, stirring frequently, until crisp-tender. Stir salt and pepper into beaten eggs and add to pan. Cook egg mixture, stirring frequently, until eggs are set. Remove from heat and stir in remaining ingredients except cheeses and tortillas. Stir cheeses together in medium bowl.

2. Place about ⅓ cup scrambled egg mixture on each tortilla and sprinkle with 2 tablespoons mixed cheeses. Roll up tortilla, folding in sides, and secure with a toothpick. Flash freeze in single layer on baking sheet. When frozen solid, wrap each burrito in a microwave-safe paper towel, then pack in zipper-lock bags, label, and freeze.

3. *To thaw and reheat:* Loosen paper towel wrapping and microwave frozen burritos, one at a time, on high power for 2 to 4 minutes, until thoroughly heated. Or remove paper towel wrapping, re-wrap burritos in foil, and bake at 350°F for 20 to 25 minutes, until hot.

24 burritos

1 onion, chopped
3 cloves garlic, chopped
3 tablespoons butter
1 tablespoon olive oil
1 teaspoon salt
⅛ teaspoon pepper
14 eggs, beaten
2 cups chopped ham
1 cup chunky salsa
1 (4-ounce) can chopped green chilies, drained
2 cups shredded pepper jack cheese
2 cups shredded Cheddar cheese
24 (8-inch) whole wheat flour tortillas

72 burritos

3 onions, chopped
9 cloves garlic, chopped
9 tablespoons butter
3 tablespoons olive oil
1 tablespoon salt
⅜ teaspoon pepper
42 eggs, beaten
6 cups chopped ham
3 cups chunky salsa
3 (4-ounce) cans chopped green chilies, drained
6 cups shredded pepper jack cheese
6 cups shredded Cheddar cheese
72 (8-inch) whole wheat flour tortillas

Turkey Apple Sausage

Serves 6–8

1 Granny Smith apple
½ cup finely chopped onion
1 tablespoon olive oil
1 pound ground turkey
¼ pound ground pork
2 tablespoons mustard
½ teaspoon dried sage
   leaves
½ teaspoon dried marjoram
   leaves
1 teaspoon salt
⅛ teaspoon white pepper
2 tablespoons olive oil

Serves 18–24

3 Granny Smith apples
1½ cups finely chopped
   onion
3 tablespoons olive oil
3 pounds ground turkey
¾ pound ground pork
6 tablespoons mustard
1½ teaspoons dried sage
   leaves
1½ teaspoons dried
   marjoram leaves
1 tablespoon salt
⅜ teaspoon white pepper
6 tablespoons olive oil

It's fun to make your own sausage, and this recipe
is so easy. To serve without freezing, simply cook the patties
until no longer pink in center, about 8 to 10 minutes.

1. Peel and finely chop apple. Cook apple and onion in olive oil in heavy skillet until crisp-tender. Cool mixture, then combine with the rest of the ingredients, except remaining olive oil, in large bowl; mix gently.

2. Form sausage mixture into 3-inch patties, each about ½-inch thick. Heat olive oil in heavy nonstick skillet. Cook patties over medium heat for 8 to 10 minutes, turning once, until thoroughly cooked. Cool patties in refrigerator, then individually wrap and place in rigid container. Label container and freeze.

3. *To thaw and reheat:* Remove patties from freezer and microwave for 3 to 4 minutes on medium per sausage patty. Or place frozen patties in baking pan and bake in preheated 400°F oven for 10 to 12 minutes, until thoroughly heated.

Frozen Fruit Medley

You can use any kind of frozen or canned fruit in this easy recipe. To serve without storing, freeze fruit mixture for 2 to 3 hours, then serve.

1. Thaw all frozen ingredients and combine in large bowl. Add remaining ingredients and mix well to blend. Pour into rigid freezer containers, seal, label, and freeze. You can also freeze these in muffin cups for individual servings.

2. *To thaw and serve:* Let mixture stand at room temperature for 30 minutes before serving. Stir and spoon into serving dishes.

Tips for Toasting Nuts

Preheat oven to 350°. Scatter nuts in a single layer on a baking sheet. Bake the nuts until they start to turn golden and you can smell them cooking (not burning). It takes 8 to 10 minutes, depending on the type of nut. Shake the pan once or twice during the process to ensure even toasting.

Serves 8

1 (6-ounce) can frozen lemonade concentrate
1 (6-ounce) can frozen orange juice concentrate
1 (10-ounce) package frozen sliced peaches
1 (9-ounce) package frozen cherries
1 (20-ounce) can crushed pineapple, undrained
½ cup sugar
1½ cups ginger ale
1 teaspoon vanilla
½ teaspoons ground ginger

Serves 24

3 (6-ounce) cans frozen lemonade concentrate
3 (6-ounce) cans frozen orange juice concentrate
3 (10-ounce) packages frozen sliced peaches
3 (9-ounce) packages frozen cherries
3 (20-ounce) cans crushed pineapple, undrained
1½ cups sugar
4½ cups ginger ale
1 tablespoon vanilla
1½ teaspoons ground ginger

Pecan Corn Waffles

Serves 8

1½ cups flour
½ cup yellow cornmeal
⅓ cup sugar
¼ teaspoon salt
½ teaspoon baking powder
3 eggs
½ cup buttermilk
⅓ cup melted butter
1 cup corn
½ cup chopped pecans

Serves 24

4½ cups flour
1½ cups yellow cornmeal
1 cup sugar
¾ teaspoon salt
1½ teaspoons baking
   powder
9 eggs
1½ cups buttermilk
1 cup melted butter
3 cups corn
1½ cups chopped pecans

These crunchy and tender waffles are perfect for a special weekend breakfast or brunch. They can be eaten immediately after cooking in the waffle iron.

1. In large mixing bowl, combine flour, cornmeal, sugar, salt, and baking powder and blend well. In small bowl, combine eggs, buttermilk, and melted butter and beat well. Pour into dry ingredients and stir just until a batter forms. Fold in corn and pecans just until combined.

2. Cook in preheated, oiled waffle iron until golden brown. Cool on wire rack, then place in zipper-lock bags, seal, label, and freeze.

3. *To thaw and reheat:* Bake frozen waffles in toaster oven or regular oven heated to 375°F until hot and crisp, about 4 to 8 minutes. Serve with maple syrup or fruit.

Is the Oil Hot Enough?

The oil should be shimmering with ripples. You can drop in a few bread crumbs and they should start to bubble and fry. If the oil is smoking, the oil is too hot and you should remove the pan from the heat immediately. Never put a hot pan under cold water to cool. It can result in a dangerous situation.

Blueberry Muffins

If you're using frozen blueberries in these delicious muffins, add them to the batter while they are still frozen. You can serve these muffins after baking as soon as they have cooled slightly.

1. Preheat oven to 400°F. Line 24 muffin cups with paper liners and set aside. In large bowl, combine 3 cups flour, oatmeal, ½ cup sugar, baking powder, baking soda, and salt and mix well. In medium bowl, combine buttermilk, oil, melted butter, and eggs and beat until blended. Pour into dry ingredients and mix just until combined.

2. In medium bowl, combine 3 tablespoons flour with blueberries and pecans and toss gently. Fold into batter just until combined. Spoon batter into prepared muffin cups, filling each three-quarters full. In small bowl, combine ¼ cup sugar and cinnamon and mix well. Sprinkle this mixture over muffin batter.

3. Bake in preheated 400°F oven for 18 to 25 minutes or until muffins are golden brown and spring back when lightly touched in center. Remove from pan immediately and cool on wire rack. When muffins are completely cool, flash freeze in single layer on cookie sheets. Place muffins in zipper-lock bags, label, seal, and freeze.

4. *To thaw:* Let muffins stand at room temperature for 1 to 2 hours until thawed. Or microwave each unwrapped frozen muffin for 40 to 50 seconds on high, let stand, and repeat if necessary.

Serves 24

3 cups flour
½ cup ground oatmeal
½ cup sugar
1 tablespoon baking powder
1 teaspoon baking soda
½ teaspoon salt
1½ cups buttermilk
⅓ cup vegetable oil
⅓ cup butter, melted
2 eggs
3 tablespoons flour
3 cups fresh or frozen
    blueberries
2 cups chopped pecans
¼ cup sugar
1 tablespoon cinnamon

Serves 72

9 cups flour
1½ cups ground oatmeal
1½ cups sugar
3 tablespoons baking
    powder
1 tablespoon baking soda
1½ teaspoons salt
4½ cups buttermilk
1 cup vegetable oil
1 cup butter, melted
6 eggs
9 tablespoons flour
9 cups fresh or frozen
    blueberries
6 cups chopped pecans
¾ cup sugar
3 tablespoons cinnamon

Freezer French Toast

Serves 4–6

¼ cup butter
3 eggs
⅓ cup cream
2 tablespoons sour cream
½ cup milk
¼ cup powdered sugar
2 teaspoons vanilla
¼ teaspoon salt
8 slices whole wheat bread

Serves 12–18

¾ cup butter
9 eggs
1 cup cream
6 tablespoons sour cream
1½ cups milk
¾ cup powdered sugar
2 tablespoons vanilla
¾ teaspoon salt
24 slices whole wheat bread

Sour cream adds wonderful flavor and makes the slices of french toast almost cakelike in the center. You can serve without freezing along with maple syrup, powdered sugar, and assorted jams and jellies.

1. Preheat oven to 400°F. Place butter in jelly roll pan and set aside. In shallow bowl, combine eggs, cream, sour cream, milk, sugar, vanilla, and salt and mix well with egg beater until blended.

2. Dip each slice of whole wheat bread into egg mixture and let stand for 1 to 2 minutes until bread absorbs some of the egg mixture. Set bread on platter and place the jelly roll pan in the oven. Heat the pan for 2 to 4 minutes or until butter is melted. Carefully place each piece of coated bread into the hot butter. Bake at 400°F for 4 to 6 minutes until bottom of toast is golden brown. Carefully turn slices with a spatula and bake for 4 to 7 minutes longer, until bottoms are golden brown. Remove from pan and let cool completely on wire rack.

3. Flash freeze slices in single layer on cookie sheets. When frozen solid, pack into zipper-lock freezer bags, label bags, seal, and freeze.

4. *To thaw and reheat:* Place frozen French toast slices in toaster and toast until thoroughly heated and crisp, or bake in preheated 375°F oven for 9 to 12 minutes or until thoroughly heated and crisp.

Freezer Waffles

These waffles are tender and crisp at the same time. You can serve them immediately without freezing. Serve with softened butter, powdered sugar, maple syrup, or various jams and jellies.

1. Sift together flour, sugar, baking powder, and salt and set aside. In large bowl, beat eggs until fluffy. Add milk, cream, vanilla, and oil and mix well. Add dry ingredients all at once and stir just until mixture is blended.

2. Preheat waffle iron and spray with nonstick cooking spray. Pour enough batter onto waffle iron to just fill. Close iron and cook until steaming stops. Remove waffles from iron and cool on wire rack. Flash freeze in single layer on cookie sheet. When frozen solid, pack into zipper-lock bags, label, seal, and freeze.

3. *To thaw and reheat:* Place frozen waffles in toaster or toaster oven and toast until crisp and hot, or microwave each waffle for 1 to 3 minutes on high until hot.

Know Your Oven

All ovens are different, with hot spots and convection air patterns. That is why times for baking or cooking recipes are given in a range. Check the food at the low end of the range to make sure it doesn't overcook; then be sure to write the optimum baking time on the recipe card.

Serves 6

2 cups flour
2 tablespoons sugar
1 tablespoon baking powder
⅛ teaspoon salt
2 eggs
1 cup milk
¾ cup heavy cream
1 teaspoon vanilla
⅓ cup oil

Serves 18

6 cups flour
6 tablespoons sugar
3 tablespoons baking powder
⅜ teaspoon salt
6 eggs
3 cups milk
2¼ cups heavy cream
1 tablespoon vanilla
1 cup oil

Sausage Scones

Serves 8

½ pound bulk pork sausage
1½ cups flour
½ cup whole wheat flour
3 tablespoons sugar
1 tablespoon baking powder
¼ teaspoon salt
¼ cup grated Parmesan
    cheese
⅓ cup heavy cream
1 egg
¼ cup butter, melted

Serves 24

1½ pounds bulk pork
    sausage
4½ cups flour
1½ cups whole wheat flour
9 tablespoons sugar
3 tablespoons baking
    powder
¾ teaspoon salt
¾ cup grated Parmesan
    cheese
1 cup heavy cream
3 eggs
¾ cup butter, melted

These easy scones are perfect for breakfast on the run. To serve immediately without freezing, let cool for a few minutes after baking.

1. Preheat oven to 400°F. In heavy skillet, cook sausage until crumbly and brown. Drain on paper towels. In large bowl, combine dry ingredients and mix to combine. In small bowl, combine cream, egg, and melted butter and beat well; add all at once to dry ingredients along with drained sausage and cheese. Stir until dough forms.

2. Pat out dough into an 8-inch round on ungreased cookie sheet. Cut the circle into 8 wedge-shaped scones. Bake scones at 400° for 11 to 13 minutes, until very lightly browned and set. Cool on wire rack, then flash freeze on cookie sheet. Pack into rigid containers, separating the layers with waxed paper; label, seal, and freeze.

3. *To reheat:* Place frozen scones on baking sheet and bake at 400°F for 10 to 15 minutes, until golden brown and hot. Let cool a few minutes before serving.

Breakfast Pizza

These little pizzas are so fun to make and eat. You can eat them as soon as they are baked. They will taste different every time if you use a mild sausage or one that's spicier and vary the cheese topping.

---

1. Preheat oven to 350°F. Butter split sides of English muffins and toast in toaster oven until light brown and crisp. Set aside. In heavy skillet, cook pork sausage until almost done. Drain off excess fat and add onion. Cook and stir for 3 to 4 minutes, until sausage is cooked and onion is crisp-tender. Remove pork and onion from pan, leaving drippings.

2. In large bowl, beat eggs and milk until combined. Pour into hot skillet and cook over medium heat until just set, about 5 to 8 minutes. Fold sausage and onion mixture into eggs.

3. Divide egg mixture among toasted English muffins and top with cheeses. Place on cookie sheet and bake at 350°F for 10 to 15 minutes or until thoroughly heated and cheese is melted. Cool on wire rack for 30 minutes, then flash freeze in single layer on cookie sheet. When frozen solid, wrap well and place in zipper-lock bags. Seal bag, label, and freeze.

4. *To thaw and reheat:* Microwave frozen pizzas one at a time on high power for 1 to 3 minutes or until thoroughly heated.

Serves 8

---

2 tablespoons butter
4 English muffins, split
½ pound bulk pork sausage
½ cup finely chopped onion
8 eggs, beaten
⅓ cup whole milk
1 cup shredded Colby cheese
½ cup shredded mozzarella cheese

Serves 24

---

6 tablespoons butter
12 English muffins, split
1½ pounds bulk pork sausage
1½ cups finely chopped onion
24 eggs, beaten
1 cup whole milk
3 cups shredded Colby cheese
1½ cups shredded mozzarella cheese

Phyllo Sausage and Egg Roll

Serves 6

½ pound bulk pork sausage
1 tablespoon butter
1 tablespoon olive oil
1 onion, chopped
1 red bell pepper, chopped
6 eggs, beaten
¼ cup heavy cream
¼ teaspoon pepper
10 phyllo pastry sheets,
    thawed
½ cup butter, melted
1 cup shredded Muenster
    cheese

Serves 18

1½ pounds bulk pork
    sausage
3 tablespoons butter
3 tablespoons olive oil
3 onions, chopped
3 red bell peppers, chopped
18 eggs, beaten
¾ cup heavy cream
¾ teaspoon pepper
30 phyllo pastry sheets,
    thawed
1½ cups butter, melted
3 cups shredded Muenster
    cheese

To serve without freezing, bake roll at 350°F for
40 to 50 minutes or until hot, browned, and crisp.

1. In large skillet, cook pork sausage, stirring frequently, until crumbly and well done. Drain on paper towels. Pour off fat from skillet and add butter and olive oil. Heat over medium heat until melted. Cook onion and bell pepper until crisp-tender.

2. Meanwhile, beat eggs with cream and pepper in medium bowl until blended. Pour over vegetable mixture in skillet; cook and stir until eggs are set. Remove from heat and stir in drained pork sausage.

3. Place one phyllo sheet on work surface and brush with melted butter. Place next phyllo sheet on top of the first, and brush with butter. Repeat with remaining 8 sheets. Place egg mixture along center of top sheet and sprinkle with cheese. Roll up phyllo to enclose egg mixture, folding in sides and brushing with butter to seal edges.

4. Wrap roll in freezer paper and freeze until firm. Wrap again in freezer paper, label, seal, and freeze.

5. *To thaw and bake*: Let thaw overnight in refrigerator. Bake in preheated 350°F oven for 50 to 60 minutes or until filling is thoroughly heated and pastry is brown and crisp.

Bran Muffins

These little muffins have a wonderful taste and a very tender texture because of the brown sugar and maple syrup. Serve them while warm with some softened butter for a great healthy breakfast.

1. Preheat oven to 400°F. In large bowl, combine cereal, flours, sugars, baking soda, and salt and mix well to blend. In medium bowl, combine maple syrup, eggs, oil, and buttermilk and beat to blend. Add liquid ingredients to dry ingredients along with raisins and stir just until combined.

2. *To freeze baked muffins:* Line 48 muffin tins with paper liners and fill three-quarters full with batter. Bake at 400°F for 13 to 19 minutes or until muffins are golden brown and tops spring back when touched lightly with fingertip. Cool on wire rack, then pack into rigid containers, seal, label, and freeze.

3. *To freeze batter:* Line 48 muffin tins with paper liners and fill three-quarters full with batter. Flash freeze in single layer on cookie sheet; when frozen solid, pack into rigid containers, separating layers with waxed paper. Seal container, label, and freeze.

4. *To thaw and serve baked muffins:* Let stand at room temperature for 2 to 3 hours until thawed. When thawed, remove paper liners and reheat muffins in microwave on high for 1 minute, if desired.

5. *To thaw and bake batter:* Place frozen unbaked muffins in muffin tins and bake in preheated 400°F oven for 30 to 35 minutes, until muffins are golden brown and tops spring back when touched lightly with fingertip.

Makes 48

1 (15-ounce) box raisin
   bran cereal
4 cups flour
1 cup whole wheat flour
1½ cups sugar
1 cup brown sugar
2 teaspoons baking soda
½ teaspoon salt
½ cup maple syrup
4 eggs, beaten
1 cup safflower oil
4 cups buttermilk
1 cup raisins

Makes 144 muffins

3 (15-ounce) boxes raisin
   bran cereal
12 cups flour
3 cups whole wheat flour
4½ cups sugar
3 cups brown sugar
2 tablespoons baking soda
1½ teaspoons salt
1½ cups maple syrup
12 eggs, beaten
3 cups safflower oil
12 cups buttermilk
3 cups raisins

Cherry Oat Muffins

Serves 24

1 cup oatmeal
1 cup oat bran
⅔ cup brown sugar
1 cup flour
1 teaspoon baking powder
½ teaspoon baking soda
⅛ teaspoon salt
1 cup buttermilk
½ cup safflower oil
2 eggs
1½ cups chopped dried
    cherries

Serves 72

3 cups oatmeal
3 cups oat bran
2 cups brown sugar
3 cups flour
1 tablespoon baking powder
1½ teaspoons baking soda
⅜ teaspoon salt
3 cups buttermilk
1½ cups safflower oil
6 eggs
4½ cups chopped dried
    cherries

Make sure to carefully pick over the dried cherries
to make sure the pits have all been removed. These little muffins
have a wonderful flavor and texture, and they freeze beautifully.

1. Preheat oven to 375°F. Line 24 muffin cups with paper liners and set aside. In large bowl, combine oatmeal, oat bran, brown sugar, flour, baking powder, baking soda, and salt and mix well. In medium bowl, combine buttermilk, oil, and eggs and beat well. Add liquid ingredients to dry ingredients along with chopped cherries and mix just until blended.

2. Fill prepared muffin cups three-quarters full and bake at 375°F for 17 to 21 minutes or until golden brown and tops spring back when lightly touched with finger. Cool on wire rack, then flash freeze in single layer on cookie sheet. When frozen, pack into rigid containers, layers separated by waxed paper.

3. *To thaw:* Let muffins stand at room temperature for 1 to 2 hours until thawed. Or place frozen muffins, one at a time, in microwave and heat on 30 percent power for 2 to 4 minutes, until thawed and warm.

Cranberry Oatmeal Quick Bread

If using frozen cranberries to make this delicious quick bread, chop while frozen, then return to freezer until you're ready to add them to the batter. These little breads taste best if allowed to sit overnight before eating.

1. Preheat oven to 350°F. Grease and flour 8" × 4" loaf pans and set aside. In medium bowl, combine oatmeal and hot water, mix, and let stand for 5 minutes. Meanwhile, cream butter and brown sugar until fluffy. Add sour cream, orange peel, egg, vanilla, and oatmeal mixture and blend. Add flour, baking powder, baking soda, salt, and cinnamon and stir just until combined; then fold in cranberries and walnuts.

2. Spoon batter into prepared pans and bake at 350°F for 55 to 65 minutes or until golden brown and set. Cool 10 minutes; then remove from pans and cool on wire rack. Wrap well in freezer wrap, seal, label, and freeze.

3. *To thaw:* Loosen wrappings and let bread stand at room temperature for 1 to 3 hours, until thawed.

Measuring Liquids

Liquids should be measured in a special measuring cup with a spout. These cups are usually clear plastic or glass. To measure liquids accurately, hold the cup at eye level. The liquid should be exactly on the desired mark on the cup.

Makes 2 loaves

1 cup oatmeal
1¼ cups hot water
¾ cup butter
1½ cups brown sugar
½ cup sour cream
2 tablespoons orange peel
1 egg
1 teaspoon vanilla
2½ cups flour
2 teaspoons baking powder
½ teaspoon baking soda
¼ teaspoon salt
1 teaspoon cinnamon
1 cup chopped cranberries
½ cup finely chopped walnuts

Makes 6 loaves

3 cups oatmeal
3¾ cups hot water
2¼ cups butter
4½ cups brown sugar
1½ cups sour cream
5 tablespoons orange peel
3 eggs
1 tablespoon vanilla
7½ cups flour
2 tablespoons baking powder
1½ teaspoons baking soda
¾ teaspoon salt
1 tablespoon cinnamon
3 cups chopped cranberries
1½ cups finely chopped walnuts

Homemade Biscuits

Serves 24

---

1 package dry yeast
5 tablespoons water
1 teaspoon sugar
4 cups flour
1 cup whole wheat flour
3 tablespoons sugar
1 tablespoon baking powder
1 teaspoon baking soda
¼ teaspoon salt
1 cup butter, softened
1⅓ cups buttermilk
¼ cup melted butter

Serves 72

---

3 packages dry yeast
15 tablespoons water
1 tablespoon sugar
12 cups flour
3 cups whole wheat flour
9 tablespoons sugar
3 tablespoons baking
   powder
1 tablespoon baking soda
¾ teaspoon salt
3 cups butter, softened
4 cups buttermilk
¾ cup melted butter

Bake these biscuits straight from the freezer!
Serve them with butter and maple syrup hot out of the oven.

---

1. In small bowl, combine yeast, water, and 1 teaspoon sugar; let stand for 5 to 8 minutes, until bubbly. In large bowl, combine flours, sugar, baking powder, baking soda, and salt and mix well. Using two knives or a pastry blender, cut in butter until particles are fine. Add yeast mixture and buttermilk and stir just until a dough forms. You may need to add more flour or more buttermilk to reach desired consistency.

2. *For folded biscuits:* Form dough into 2-inch balls and place on work surface. Using hands or rolling pin, press each ball into a small circle. Dip in melted butter, fold over, and flash freeze on cookie sheet.

   For unfolded biscuits: Form dough into 3-inch balls, place on work surface, and flatten to 1-inch thickness with your palm. Dip in melted butter and flash freeze. When frozen solid, place rolls in zipper-lock bag, label, seal, and freeze.

3. *To bake*: Preheat oven to 400°F. Bake folded frozen rolls on parchment-lined cookie sheets for 18 to 22 minutes, until light, fluffy, and golden brown. Bake unfolded 1-inch-thick rolls for 20 to 25 minutes. Remove from cookie sheets and cool briefly on wire rack. Serve warm.

Egg Muffin Sandwiches

You could substitute Homemade Biscuits (page 260) for the English muffins. To serve these little sandwiches without freezing, microwave each on high for about 50 to 60 seconds to melt cheese.

1. Spread butter on split sides of English muffins and toast in toaster oven until light golden brown. Set aside. In heavy skillet, cook bacon until crisp; remove from skillet and drain on paper towels. Pour off all but 1 tablespoon bacon drippings from skillet.

2. In large bowl, beat eggs with milk and seasonings. Pour into hot drippings and cook over medium-low heat, stirring frequently, until just set. Remove from heat, and then crumble bacon and stir into egg mixture.

3. Place one slice American cheese on half of each English muffin. Top with egg mixture, dividing evenly among muffins. Top egg mixture with remaining cheese slices and cover with remaining English muffin halves. Flash freeze sandwiches in single layer on cookie sheet until solid. Wrap in microwave-safe paper towel, then pack into zipper-lock bags. Label bags, seal, and freeze.

4. *To thaw and reheat:* Place frozen, wrapped muffins, one at a time, in microwave and heat on high power for 1 to 3 minutes, until thoroughly heated and cheese has melted.

Serves 8

2 tablespoons butter
8 English muffins, split
6 slices bacon
8 eggs
⅓ cup evaporated milk
¼ teaspoon salt
⅛ teaspoon white pepper
½ teaspoon dried thyme leaves
16 slices American cheese, unwrapped

Serves 24

6 tablespoons butter
24 English muffins, split
18 slices bacon
24 eggs
1 cup evaporated milk
¾ teaspoon salt
⅜ teaspoon white pepper
1½ teaspoons dried thyme leaves
48 slices American cheese, unwrapped

Divinity Salad

Serves 8

1 (10-ounce) can crushed
  pineapple
3 tablespoons reserved
  pineapple juice
1 (8-ounce) package cream
  cheese, softened
1 cup mayonnaise
¼ cup buttermilk
½ cup honey
1 cup finely chopped
  apricots
1 cup heavy cream
3 tablespoons powdered
  sugar
½ cup finely chopped
  toasted pecans

Serves 24

3 (10-ounce) cans crushed
  pineapple
9 tablespoons reserved
  pineapple juice
3 (8-ounce) packages cream
  cheese, softened
3 cups mayonnaise
¾ cup buttermilk
1½ cups honey
3 cups finely chopped
  apricots
3 cups heavy cream
9 tablespoons powdered
  sugar
1½ cups finely chopped
  toasted pecans

This delicious salad makes a refreshing breakfast
on a hot day, or a wonderful addition to
a summer cookout. You can also freeze it in an 8-inch
round pan for 3 to 4 hours; then simply cut into wedges to serve.

1. Thoroughly drain pineapple, reserving juice; set aside. In large bowl, beat cream cheese until light and fluffy. Gradually add mayonnaise and beat until very fluffy. Add buttermilk, pineapple juice, and honey and mix well until blended.

2. Add drained pineapple and chopped apricots to cream cheese mixture. In small bowl, combine cream and powdered sugar and beat until stiff peaks form. Fold into cream cheese mixture along with pecans.

3. Spoon salad into paper-lined muffin cups and flash freeze in single layer until solid. Store in zipper-lock bags; label, seal bags, and freeze.

4. *To serve:* Let salad stand at room temperature for 15 to 20 minutes.

CHAPTER 17
Sandwiches

Meatball Marinara Sandwiches

Serves 4

---

1 pound lean ground beef
¼ cup dry bread crumbs
3 tablespoons milk
1 egg
½ teaspoon salt
⅛ teaspoon pepper
1 (14-ounce) jar tomato
    pasta sauce
4 hoagie buns
1 cup shredded Monterey
    jack cheese

Serves 12

---

3 pounds lean ground beef
¾ cup dry bread crumbs
9 tablespoons milk
3 eggs
1½ teaspoons salt
⅜ teaspoon pepper
3 (14-ounce) jars tomato
    pasta sauce
12 hoagie buns
3 cups shredded Monterey
    jack cheese

To serve these sandwiches immediately, combine hot meatballs and sauce in saucepan and simmer for 4 to 5 minutes. Broil and assemble sandwiches as directed.

---

1. In large bowl, combine beef, bread crumbs, milk, egg, salt, and pepper and mix gently but thoroughly. Form into 24 meatballs and place on baking sheet. Bake at 350°F for 20 to 30 minutes, until meatballs are thoroughly cooked. Cool in refrigerator.

2. Combine cooled meatballs with pasta sauce and place in zipper-lock bag. Slice hoagie buns and place in zipper-lock bag. Place cheese in zipper-lock bag. Combine all bags in one larger bag; label, seal, and freeze.

3. *To thaw and reheat:* Thaw hoagie buns at room temperature overnight. Thaw meatballs and sauce and cheese in refrigerator overnight. Pour meatballs and sauce into saucepan and heat until sauce bubbles and meatballs are thoroughly heated. Toast sliced hoagie buns under broiler. Place meatballs and sauce on one half of each toasted bun and top with cheese. Place filled halves of hoagie buns on broiler pan and broil 4 to 6 inches from heat for 4 to 5 minutes, until cheese melts. Assemble sandwiches and serve.

French Dip Sandwiches

These sandwiches are stuffed with very tender beef cooked in the Slow Cooker or in your oven. To serve immediately, slice and toast buns and make sandwiches with sliced beef and strained broth.

1. Trim excess fat off beef and rub with salt and pepper. Heat olive oil in large skillet and brown beef on all sides, about 8 to 10 minutes. Place beef in 4-quart slow cooker with remaining ingredients except buns and butter. Cover and cook on low for 8 to 9 hours, until beef is very tender. Or, bake in large covered casserole at 350°F for 3 hours or until beef is very tender.

2. Remove beef from broth and strain broth. Cool beef and broth in refrigerator. When meat is cool, slice thinly against the grain. Place slices in zipper-lock bag and cover with strained broth. Slice sandwich buns in half and spread cut sides with butter. Place buns in a zipper-lock bag and attach to meat bag, label, and freeze.

3. *To thaw and reheat:* Thaw everything overnight in refrigerator. Place beef and broth in large skillet and heat over low heat until very hot. Brown the split buns in toaster oven or under broiler. Make sandwiches with beef and buns; serve broth on side for dipping.

Serves 6

2 pounds bottom round beef roast
1 teaspoon seasoned salt
⅛ teaspoon pepper
2 tablespoons oil
3 cups Beef Broth (page 302)
1 bay leaf
2 shallots, chopped
1 teaspoon dried thyme
½ cup apple juice
6 crusty French sandwich buns
2 tablespoons butter

Serves 18

6 pounds bottom round beef roast
1 tablespoon seasoned salt
⅜ teaspoon pepper
6 tablespoons oil
9 cups Beef Broth (page 302)
3 bay leaves
6 shallots, chopped
1 tablespoon dried thyme
1½ cups apple juice
18 crusty French sandwich buns
6 tablespoons butter

Tuna Sandwiches

Serves 4

1 (3-ounce) package cream cheese, softened
2 tablespoons Miracle Whip
1 (6-ounce) can chunk tuna, drained
¼ cup chopped green onions
¼ cup shredded carrot
1 tablespoon lemon juice
2 tablespoons butter, softened
8 slices whole wheat bread

Serves 12

3 (3-ounce) packages cream cheese, softened
6 tablespoons Miracle Whip
3 (6-ounce) cans chunk tuna, drained
¾ cup chopped green onions
¾ cup shredded carrot
3 tablespoons lemon juice
6 tablespoons butter, softened
24 slices whole wheat bread

Cream cheese and Miracle Whip make a delicious sandwich spread that isn't affected by freezing. You can use any cooked chopped meat in this easy recipe. The sandwiches can be served immediately without freezing.

1. In medium bowl, combine cream cheese and Miracle Whip and beat until smooth. Stir in tuna, onions, carrot, and lemon juice. Blend well to combine.

2. Spread softened butter thinly on each slice of bread and spread tuna filling to make sandwiches. Wrap in freezer wrap and place in gallon freezer bag. Label sandwiches and freeze.

3. *To thaw:* Let thaw overnight in refrigerator, or add to brown bag lunches in the morning and let thaw until lunchtime. (Make sure sandwiches are eaten within 2 hours of being completely thawed.)

Substitution Suggestions

Consider using smoked meats in place of regular meats. There are excellent smoked chickens, pork tenderloins, and chops available at specialty stores. Substituting with a smoked meat can add a whole new flavor to the old standby recipes.

Pimiento Cheese Sandwiches

Using whole pimientos and chopping them yourself makes a better-textured spread. You could use white sandwich bread instead of whole wheat if you'd prefer; make sure it's a firm, thinly sliced white bread.

1. Drain pimientos and chop coarsely. In medium bowl, combine cream cheese and Miracle Whip and beat until smooth and fluffy. Add pimientos, Colby cheese, Worcestershire sauce, garlic powder, and pepper and stir gently by hand until blended.

2. Spread a thin layer of butter on one side of each slice of bread. Divide pimiento cheese among bread slices and put together to make sandwiches. Wrap each sandwich in freezer wrap, then place all in large zipper-lock bag. Label sandwiches, seal bag, and freeze.

3. *To thaw:* Let thaw overnight in refrigerator, or add to brown bag lunches in the morning and let thaw until lunchtime. (Make sure sandwiches are eaten within 2 hours of being completely thawed.)

Reheating in the Microwave

If you want to cook frozen dishes in the microwave oven, be very careful to follow temperature guidelines and use your instant-read thermometer. Microwave ovens can be quite variable, with hot spots, uneven heating, and insufficient heating.

Serves 6

1 (7-ounce) jar whole pimientos, drained
1 (3-ounce) package cream cheese, softened
½ cup Miracle Whip
2 cups shredded Colby cheese
1 teaspoon Worcestershire sauce
⅛ teaspoon garlic powder
Pinch white pepper
3 tablespoons butter
12 slices whole wheat bread

Serves 18

3 (7-ounce) jars whole pimientos, drained
3 (3-ounce) packages cream cheese, softened
1½ cups Miracle Whip
6 cups shredded Colby cheese
1 tablespoon Worcestershire sauce
⅜ teaspoon garlic powder
3 pinches white pepper
9 tablespoons butter
36 slices whole wheat bread

Turkey Pesto Sandwiches

Serves 4

1 (3-ounce) package cream
cheese
¼ cup Miracle Whip
3 blocks frozen Pesto Sauce
(page 296), thawed
¼ cup grated Parmesan
cheese
1 cup chopped smoked
turkey
8 slices cracked wheat bread
2 tablespoons butter,
softened

Serves 12

3 (3-ounce) packages cream
cheese
¾ cup Miracle Whip
9 blocks frozen Pesto Sauce
(page 296), thawed
¾ cup grated Parmesan
cheese
3 cups chopped smoked
turkey
24 slices cracked wheat
bread
6 tablespoons butter,
softened

You can substitute plain cooked turkey for the smoked turkey in these easy sandwiches. They can also be served immediately without freezing, or the spread can be stored in the refrigerator, well covered, and used as desired.

1. In medium bowl, combine cream cheese and Miracle Whip and beat until well blended. Add pesto and Parmesan cheese and mix well. Stir in turkey and mix well.

2. Spread one side of each slice of bread with softened butter. Divide turkey mixture among bread slices and put together to make sandwiches. Place sandwiches in zipper-lock bags, seal, label, and freeze.

3. *To thaw:* Thaw in refrigerator overnight. Or place, still frozen, in lunch boxes in the morning and let thaw. Make sure the sandwiches are eaten at lunch when thawed.

Sandwich Spreading Tip

When making sandwiches, use frozen bread slices. They are easier to spread with butter and the sandwich spread, and will make the sandwich freeze faster, preserving the quality of the filling.

Garlic Roast Beef Sandwiches

Roasting garlic makes it nutty and sweet, adding a perfect touch to tender roast beef. The garlic spread can be stored, well covered, in the refrigerator and used as desired.

1. Place unpeeled garlic on a square of heavy-duty foil and drizzle with olive oil. Fold foil over garlic, sealing edges; place on cookie sheet; and roast in 400°F oven for 20 to 25 minutes, until garlic is soft. Let cool until easy to handle. Press garlic out of skins with your fingers and place in small bowl. Add Miracle Whip, whipped cream cheese, and white pepper and mix well until blended.

2. Spread butter on one side of each slice of bread. Spread garlic mixture over butter and lay roast beef on top. Top with another slice of bread, butter-side down. Place each sandwich in zipper-lock bag. Seal bags, label, and freeze.

3. *To thaw:* Thaw in refrigerator overnight. Or place, still frozen, in lunch boxes in the morning and let thaw. Make sure the sandwiches are eaten at lunch when thawed.

Serves 4

6 cloves garlic
2 teaspoons olive oil
3 tablespoons Miracle Whip
2 tablespoons whipped
    cream cheese
Pinch white pepper
2 tablespoons butter,
    softened
8 slices sourdough bread
½ pound cooked roast beef,
    sliced

Serves 12

1 head garlic
2 tablespoons olive oil
9 tablespoons Miracle Whip
6 tablespoons whipped
    cream cheese
3 pinches white pepper
6 tablespoons butter,
    softened
24 slices sourdough bread
1½ pounds cooked roast
    beef, sliced

Hummus Sandwiches

Serves 4

1 (16-ounce) can garbanzo
  beans, drained
2 tablespoons lemon juice
¼ cup sesame paste
1 tablespoon olive oil
1 teaspoon toasted sesame
  oil
¼ cup toasted sesame seeds
¼ cup chopped green
  onions
8 slices whole wheat bread
2 tablespoons butter,
  softened

Serves 12

3 (16-ounce) cans garbanzo
  beans, drained
6 tablespoons lemon juice
¾ cup sesame paste
3 tablespoons olive oil
1 tablespoon toasted
  sesame oil
¾ cup toasted sesame seeds
¾ cup chopped green
  onions
24 slices whole wheat bread
6 tablespoons butter,
  softened

This recipe for hummus also makes a delicious appetizer dip for fresh vegetables or as a sandwich spread for chicken or roast beef sandwiches. Store it, well covered, in the refrigerator for up to 1 week.

1. In food processor or blender, combine drained garbanzo beans, lemon juice, sesame paste, olive oil, and sesame oil and process until almost smooth. Remove from processor to medium bowl and stir in toasted sesame seeds and green onions.

2. Spread one side of each slice of bread with butter and divide hummus among bread slices. Make sandwiches and place in zipper-lock bags. Label bags, seal, and freeze.

3. *To thaw:* Thaw in refrigerator overnight. Or place, still frozen, in lunch boxes in the morning and let thaw. Make sure the sandwiches are eaten at lunch when thawed.

Open Face Pizza Sandwiches

These little sandwiches are like mini pizzas, except with more filling. To serve without freezing, bake the completed sandwiches in preheated 350°F oven for 15 to 20 minutes or until hot and bubbly.

1. In medium bowl, combine all ingredients except cheeses and English muffins. Toast the split English muffins and let cool completely. Place one slice of processed mozzarella cheese onto each muffin half. Divide tomato mixture among muffins and top with diced mozzarella cheese and Parmesan cheese.

2. Flash freeze the sandwiches on cookie sheet until frozen solid. Place into zipper-lock bags, label, seal, and freeze.

3. *To reheat in oven:* Unwrap frozen sandwiches, place on cookie sheet, and bake in preheated 375°F oven for 20 to 30 minutes or until thoroughly heated and cheese is melted and bubbly.

   To reheat in microwave: Wrap sandwiches in microwave-safe paper towels and microwave each frozen sandwich for 1 to 3 minutes on high power or until thoroughly heated.

What's Your Favorite Bread?

When making sandwiches for the freezer, use your imagination when choosing bread. Tortillas, English muffins, Boboli pizza crusts, focaccia bread, and all types of sandwich bread will work well.

Serves 8

1 cup frozen vegetable protein crumbles
1 (8-ounce) can tomato sauce
2 tablespoons tomato paste
½ cup chopped onion
1 tablespoon Spaghetti Sauce Mix (page 304)
8 slices processed mozzarella cheese
1 cup diced mozzarella cheese
¼ cup grated Parmesan cheese
8 English muffins, split

Serves 24

3 cups frozen vegetable protein crumbles
3 (8-ounce) cans tomato sauce
6 tablespoons tomato paste
1½ cups chopped onion
3 tablespoons Spaghetti Sauce Mix (page 304)
24 slices processed mozzarella cheese
3 cups diced mozzarella cheese
¾ cup grated Parmesan cheese
24 English muffins, split

Curried Chicken Salad Wraps

Serves 4

1½ cups cooked, cubed chicken
⅓ cup Miracle Whip
3 tablespoons mango chutney
1 teaspoon curry powder
¼ cup golden raisins
¼ cup chopped green onions
⅓ cup crushed pineapple,
  well drained
4 (8-inch) flour tortillas

Serves 12

4½ cups cooked, cubed chicken
1 cup Miracle Whip
9 tablespoons mango chutney
1 tablespoon curry powder
¾ cup golden raisins
¾ cup chopped green onions
1 cup crushed pineapple, well
  drained
12 (8-inch) flour tortillas

These wraps can be served without freezing; in that case, you can place lettuce leaves on the tortillas before adding the chicken salad.

1. In medium bowl, combine all ingredients except flour tortillas and mix well to blend. Place flour tortillas on work surface and divide chicken mixture among them. Roll up each tortilla, enclosing filling; then cut in half crosswise. Wrap each filled tortilla half in freezer wrap and place in zipper-lock bags. Seal bags, label, and freeze.

2. *To thaw:* Let thaw in refrigerator overnight. Or place, still frozen, in lunch boxes in the morning and let thaw. Make sure the sandwiches are eaten at lunch when thawed.

Updated Peanut Butter Sandwiches

Serves 4

1 cup chunky peanut butter
⅓ cup crushed granola
½ cup chopped salted
  peanuts
1 tablespoon butter, softened
2 tablespoons whipped honey
4 (8-inch) whole wheat flour
  tortillas

Serves 12

3 cups chunky peanut butter
1 cup crushed granola
1½ cups chopped salted peanuts
3 tablespoons butter, softened
6 tablespoons whipped honey
12 (8-inch) whole wheat flour
  tortillas

This sandwich is almost a dessert! The sweet granola and the creamy honey add a depth of flavor to the peanut butter; and the whole wheat flour tortillas don't get soggy when the filling thaws.

1. In medium bowl, combine all ingredients except tortillas and blend well. Divide mixture among the flour tortillas and spread to the edges. Roll up the tortillas, enclosing the filling. Cut sandwiches in half crosswise, then place in zipper-lock bags, label, seal, and freeze.

2. *To thaw*: Let thaw in refrigerator overnight. Or place, still frozen, in lunch boxes in the morning and let thaw. Make sure the sandwiches are eaten at lunch when thawed.

Mexican Pita Sandwiches

Because these sandwiches are assembled after thawing, the lettuce stays nice and crisp.

1½ cups chopped roast beef
¼ cup refried beans
½ cup kidney beans, rinsed
1 jalapeno pepper, seeded and diced
¼ cup salsa
⅓ cup crumbled queso fresco cheese
4 whole wheat pita breads, cut in half
2 cups bagged lettuce

1. In medium bowl, combine beef, refried beans, kidney beans, peppers, salsa, and cheese and blend well. Divide this mixture into quarters and place each quarter into zipper-lock freezer bag. Label bags, seal, attach zipper-lock bag with two halves pita bread to each, and freeze. Reserve lettuce in refrigerator.

Serves 12

4½ cups chopped roast beef
¾ cup refried beans
1½ cups kidney beans, rinsed
3 jalapeno peppers, seeded and diced
¾ cup salsa
1 cup crumbled queso fresco cheese
6 cups bagged lettuce

2. *To thaw:* Place ½ cup lettuce in zipper-lock bag and place in lunch box along with frozen filling and pita breads. Let thaw during the morning, then assemble sandwiches by placing lettuce in pita breads and topping with thawed beef mixture. Make sure sandwiches are eaten at lunch when thawed.

Stuffed Hot Tuna Sandwiches

Serves 6

1 (3-ounce) package cream cheese, softened
¼ cup Miracle Whip
1 (6-ounce) can chunk light tuna, drained
1 cup shredded Colby cheese
¼ cup grated Parmesan cheese
2 tablespoons capers, drained
¼ cup minced yellow bell pepper
2 tablespoons butter, softened
6 (6-inch) crusty sandwich rolls

You can bake these sandwiches without freezing in a preheated 375°F oven for 15 to 20 minutes, until sandwiches are hot and cheese is melted.

1. In medium bowl, beat cream cheese and Miracle Whip until smooth. Add all remaining ingredients except butter and sandwich rolls and mix gently to combine. Slice sandwich rolls in half lengthwise and pull out some of the soft centers (reserve to make bread crumbs for other recipes). Thinly spread butter into rolls. Make sandwiches with tuna filling and wrap each sandwich in foil. Place sandwiches into zipper-lock bags, seal, label, and freeze.

Serves 18

3 (3-ounce) packages cream cheese, softened
¾ cup Miracle Whip
3 (6-ounce) cans chunk light tuna, drained
3 cups shredded Colby cheese
¾ cup grated Parmesan cheese
6 tablespoons capers, drained
¾ cup minced yellow bell pepper
6 tablespoons butter, softened
18 (6-inch) crusty sandwich rolls

2. *To thaw and heat:* Place wrapped frozen sandwiches on baking sheet and bake in preheated 375°F oven for 25 to 35 minutes, until filling is hot and cheese is melted.

Egg Salad Supreme Sandwiches

Serves 4

6 eggs
¼ cup minced red bell
  pepper
¼ cup minced red onion
2 tablespoons drained pickle
  relish
⅛ teaspoon salt
Pinch pepper
¼ cup plain yogurt
¼ cup Miracle Whip
2 tablespoons butter,
  softened
4 (8-inch) crusty hoagie
  buns, sliced

Serves 12

18 eggs
¾ cup minced red bell
  pepper
¾ cup minced red onion
6 tablespoons drained pickle
  relish
⅜ teaspoon salt
3 pinches pepper
¾ cup plain yogurt
¾ cup Miracle Whip
6 tablespoons butter,
  softened
12 (8-inch) crusty hoagie
  buns, sliced

If you don't like pickle relish, omit it and add 1 tablespoon lemon juice to the egg salad filling. These sandwiches can be served immediately or refrigerated up to 6 hours before eating.

1. Place eggs in medium saucepan and cover with cold water. Bring to a boil over high heat; then cover pan, remove from heat, and let stand 15 minutes. Place pan in sink and run cold water into pan until eggs have cooled. Crack eggs slightly against the side of pan and let sit another 5 minutes in the cold water. Peel eggs and coarsely chop.

2. Combine chopped eggs with remaining ingredients except butter and hoagie buns and mix gently. Spread a thin layer of butter on cut sides of hoagie buns and make sandwiches with the egg salad. Wrap sandwiches in freezer paper, place in zipper-lock bags, label, seal, and freeze.

3. *To thaw*: Let thaw in refrigerator overnight. Or place, still frozen, in lunch boxes in the morning and let thaw. Make sure the sandwiches are eaten at lunch when thawed.

Salmon Salad Wraps

You can substitute tiny canned shrimp, drained canned crabmeat, or drained canned tuna for the salmon in these delicious wraps.

1. Drain canned salmon and carefully remove skin and bones. Flake salmon into a medium bowl and set aside. In another medium bowl, combine cream cheese and mayonnaise and beat until smooth. Mix with remaining ingredients except butter and tortillas. Spread butter evenly on tortillas. Spread filling over butter and roll up, enclosing filling. Place in zipper-lock bags, seal, label, and freeze.

2. *To thaw*: Let thaw in refrigerator overnight. Or place, still frozen, in lunch boxes in the morning and let thaw. Make sure the sandwiches are eaten at lunch when thawed.

Serves 6

1 (15-ounce) can red sockeye salmon
1 (3-ounce) package cream cheese, softened
⅓ cup mayonnaise
¼ cup honey mustard salad dressing
½ teaspoon dried thyme leaves
¼ cup minced green onion
2 cups frozen corn
2 tablespoons butter
6 (6-inch) corn tortillas

Serves 6

3 (15-ounce) cans red sockeye salmon
3 (3-ounce) packages cream cheese, softened
1 cup mayonnaise
¾ cup honey mustard salad dressing
1½ teaspoons dried thyme leaves
¾ cup minced green onion
6 cups frozen corn
6 tablespoons butter
18 (6-inch) corn tortillas

Cannellini Bean Spread Wraps

This spread is similar to hummus but is milder; it makes an excellent sandwich spread or an appetizer dip served with vegetables. The sandwiches can be served immediately, or wrapped and stored in the refrigerator up to 6 hours.

1. In blender container or food processor, combine drained beans with remaining ingredients except tortillas. Blend or process until mixture is almost smooth. Spread mixture on tortillas and roll up, enclosing filling. Cut sandwiches in half and place in zipper-lock bags; label, seal, and freeze.

2. *To thaw*: Let thaw in refrigerator overnight. Or place, still frozen, in lunch boxes in the morning and let thaw. Make sure the sandwiches are eaten at lunch when thawed.

Serves 4

1 (16-ounce) can cannellini beans, drained
2 tablespoons lemon juice
1 (3-ounce) package cream cheese, softened
3 tablespoons olive oil
⅓ cup grated Parmesan cheese
⅛ teaspoon cayenne pepper
½ teaspoon dried marjoram leaves
4 (10-inch) jalapeno-flavored flour tortillas

Serves 12

3 (16-ounce) cans cannellini beans, drained
6 tablespoons lemon juice
3 (3-ounce) packages cream cheese, softened
9 tablespoons olive oil
1 cup grated Parmesan cheese
⅜ teaspoon cayenne pepper
1½ teaspoons dried marjoram leaves
12 (10-inch) jalapeno-flavored flour tortillas

Ham and Pineapple Sandwiches

Serves 6

1 (3-ounce) package cream
   cheese, softened
3 tablespoons Miracle Whip
1 (8-ounce) can crushed
   pineapple
1½ cups cubed smoked ham
¼ cup minced green bell
   pepper
⅛ teaspoon pepper
¼ cup minced green onion
2 tablespoons butter,
   softened
1 (12-inch) round loaf
   focaccia bread

Serves 18

3 (3-ounce) packages cream
   cheese, softened
9 tablespoons Miracle Whip
3 (8-ounce) cans crushed
   pineapple
4½ cups cubed smoked ham
¾ cup minced green bell
   pepper
⅜ teaspoon pepper
¾ cup minced green onion
6 tablespoons butter,
   softened
3 (12-inch) round loaf
   focaccia breads

Ordinary canned ham can be substituted for the
smoked ham in this delicious recipe. If you can't find focaccia bread,
use a Boboli pizza crust carefully cut in half.

1. In medium bowl, combine cream cheese and Miracle Whip and beat until smooth. Drain pineapple, reserving 2 tablespoons juice (from each can). Add this reserved juice to bowl and mix well. Stir in drained pineapple and remaining ingredients except butter and focaccia bread, and mix well.

2. Split focaccia bread in half and spread a thin layer of butter on both cut sides. Place ham salad filling on bottom half of bread and top with second half. Using serrated knife, cut filled bread into 6 wedges. Wrap each wedge in freezer paper, then place in zipper-lock bags, seal, label, and freeze.

3. *To thaw:* Let thaw in refrigerator overnight. Or place, still frozen, in lunch boxes in the morning and let thaw. Make sure the sandwiches are eaten at lunch when thawed.

CHAPTER 18
Sweet Endings

German Chocolate Pound Cake

Serves 8–10

1 cup butter, softened
2 teaspoons vanilla
2 cups sugar
4 eggs
3 cups flour
½ teaspoon baking soda
½ teaspoon salt
1 (4-ounce) package
    German sweet chocolate
1 cup buttermilk

Serves 24–30

3 cups butter, softened
6 teaspoons vanilla
6 cups sugar
12 eggs
9 cups flour
1½ teaspoons baking soda
1½ teaspoons salt
3 (4-ounce) packages
    German sweet chocolate
3 cups buttermilk

This delicious light chocolate cake can be served as soon as it is cooled.

1. Preheat oven to 300°F. Grease and flour 10-inch tube pan and set aside. In large bowl, combine butter, vanilla, and sugar and beat until light and fluffy. Add eggs, one at a time, beating well after each addition. Combine flour with baking soda and salt; sift into a medium bowl.

2. Melt chocolate in microwave oven or in small, heavy pan over low heat. Let cool for 10 to 15 minutes. Add flour mixture alternately with buttermilk to butter mixture, beginning and ending with dry ingredients. Beat well after each addition before adding next ingredient. Add melted chocolate and blend well.

3. Pour batter into prepared pan. Bake at 300°F for 80 to 90 minutes or until toothpick inserted in center comes out clean. Cool cake on wire rack for 15 minutes, then remove from pan and cool completely. Cut cake into quarters. Wrap each piece of cake well in freezer wrap; seal, label, and freeze.

4. *To thaw:* Loosen wrapping slightly and let cake stand at room temperature for 3 to 4 hours, until thawed. If desired, drizzle with a simple chocolate frosting made by combining 1 cup powdered sugar, 1 teaspoon vanilla, 2 tablespoons cocoa, and 2 to 3 tablespoons cream.

Apple Peach Pie

3 Granny Smith apples
2 tablespoons lemon juice
½ cup sugar
2 teaspoons cinnamon
3 tablespoons flour
2 cups frozen peach slices
2 tablespoons butter
2 9-inch Pie Crusts (page 299)

To bake without freezing, combine frozen peach slices, apples, and remaining ingredients except pie crust. Fill crust and bake as directed.

1. Peel, core, and slice apples and toss with lemon juice. In medium bowl, combine sugar, cinnamon, and flour and mix well to blend. Add apple slices and toss to coat. Add frozen peaches and bits of butter and mix gently to coat.

2. Pour fruit mixture into disposable 9-inch pie pan; wrap, seal, label, and freeze. Wrap pie crusts for freezing and attach to fruit mixture.

Serves 24

9 Granny Smith apples
6 tablespoons lemon juice
1½ cups sugar
2 tablespoons cinnamon
9 tablespoons flour
6 cups frozen peach slices
6 tablespoons butter
6 9-inch Pie Crusts (page 299)

3. *To thaw and bake:* Let frozen pie crusts stand at room temperature for 30 to 45 minutes, until thawed. Keep filling frozen. Place one crust in bottom of 9-inch pie pan. Remove frozen fruit mixture from disposable pan and place in pie crust. Top with remaining crust, seal and flute edges, and cut decorative holes in top for venting. Bake in preheated 400°F oven for 15 minutes, then lower heat to 350°F and bake for 40 to 55 minutes longer or until crust is deep golden brown and juices are bubbling in center of pie. Let cool before slicing.

Caramel Cashew Bars

Makes 24 bars

For crust:

2 cups flour
1 cup brown sugar
½ cup butter, melted
2 cups halved cashews

For topping:

1 cup butter
¾ cup brown sugar
2 cups milk chocolate
   chunks

Makes 72 bars

For crust:

6 cups flour
3 cups brown sugar
1½ cups butter, melted
6 cups halved cashews

For topping:

3 cups butter
2¼ cups brown sugar
6 cups milk chocolate
   chunks

These simple bars are very decadent. To serve without freezing, cool bars completely and then cut into 24 squares.

---

1. Preheat oven to 350°F. Combine flour, first quantity of brown sugar, and the melted butter in medium bowl and mix until crumbly. Press into 13" × 9" pan. Sprinkle cashews over crust and set aside.

2. In medium saucepan, combine remaining butter and brown sugar. Cook over medium heat, stirring constantly, until melted together. Boil this mixture for 1 minute. Immediately drizzle over cashews. Bake at 350°F for 17 to 21 minutes or until the entire surface is bubbly. Remove from oven.

3. Sprinkle hot bars with chocolate chunks, then cover with foil. Let stand for 3 to 4 minutes until chocolate melts, then swirl knife through chunks to marble with the caramel topping. Let cool completely. Cut into bars. Flash freeze bars until frozen solid. Wrap individually in freezer wrap and place in zipper-lock bag. Label bag and freeze.

4. *To thaw:* Let bars stand at room temperature for 2 to 3 hours.

Frozen Peanut Squares

Serves 10–12

Serve these easy and delicious bars after freezing for 3 to 4 hours. Top them with a dollop of whipped cream and some chopped salted peanuts.

2 cups chocolate sandwich
  cookie crumbs
¼ cup melted butter
½ cup finely chopped salted
  peanuts
1½ cups powdered sugar
¾ cup crunchy peanut
  butter
1 quart vanilla ice cream
1 cup heavy cream, whipped
¼ cup grated milk chocolate

1. In large bowl, combine cookie crumbs, butter, and peanuts and mix well. Press into bottom of 13" × 9" pan and set aside. In small bowl, combine powdered sugar and peanut butter until mixed and crumbly and set aside.

2. In large bowl, beat vanilla ice cream until softened (about 40 seconds) and fold in whipped cream. Spread half of ice cream mixture over cookie crust. Sprinkle with half of peanut butter mixture. Repeat layers, ending with peanut butter mixture, and sprinkle with grated chocolate. Freeze until solid; then wrap, seal, label, and freeze.

3. *To serve*: Let dessert stand at room temperature for 20 minutes before slicing.

Serves 30–36

6 cups chocolate sandwich
  cookie crumbs
¾ cup melted butter
1½ cups finely chopped
  salted peanuts
4½ cups powdered sugar
2¼ cups crunchy peanut
  butter
3 quarts vanilla ice cream
3 cups heavy cream,
  whipped
¾ cup grated milk chocolate

Is Your Oven Accurate?

Use an oven thermometer to ensure accuracy of temperature. Many oven temperature gauges are off by 25°F or more. Adjust the temperature setting so the thermometer registers the correct temperature, then make a note of the change in setting.

Granola Cookies

Makes about 36

½ cup butter, softened
¼ cup honey
¼ cup brown sugar
1 egg
½ cup sour cream
2 teaspoons vanilla
2 bananas, mashed
1½ cups flour
1 teaspoon baking powder
¼ teaspoon salt
2 cups granola cereal
1 cup chocolate chips

Makes about 108

1½ cups butter, softened
¾ cup honey
¾ cup brown sugar
3 eggs
1½ cups sour cream
2 tablespoons vanilla
6 bananas, mashed
4½ cups flour
1 tablespoon baking powder
¾ teaspoon salt
6 cups granola cereal
3 cups chocolate chips

These hearty cookies are full of honey and granola. You could substitute golden raisins for the chocolate chips if you like. The cookies are ready to eat as soon as they have cooled.

1. In large bowl, combine butter, honey, brown sugar, and egg and beat well. Add sour cream, vanilla, and mashed bananas to butter mixture and mix until blended. Add flour, baking powder, and salt, and stir until a dough forms. Add granola and chocolate chips.

2. Drop teaspoons of dough onto parchment paper–lined cookie sheets. Bake at 375°F for 10 to 14 minutes or until lightly browned. Remove to wire rack to cool. Cool cookies completely, then layer in rigid container, with waxed paper separating the layers. Label, seal, and freeze.

3. *To thaw:* Loosen container wrappings and let stand at room temperature for 1 to 2 hours, until cookies are soft.

Measuring Flour

To measure flour accurately, spoon flour into a measuring cup; do not use the cup to scoop flour out of the container. Using the back of a knife, level off the flour even with the measuring cup's top.

Gold Rush Bars

These delicious bars could be made with dried peaches or dried apples instead of the dried apricots. Store unfrozen bars, tightly covered, at room temperature for up to 4 days.

1. Preheat oven to 325°F. Grease 13" × 9" pan and set aside. In heavy saucepan, combine dried apricots, nectar, water, orange juice, and sugar. Bring to a boil, then reduce heat and simmer mixture, stirring frequently, until apricots are soft, about 10 to 15 minutes. Puree half of this mixture in a food processor or blender; return to pan with unpureed mixture, stir in first quantity butter, and let cool.

2. In large bowl, combine brown sugar, softened butter, and shortening and mix until fluffy. Add eggs and vanilla and beat well. Stir in flour, baking soda, and baking powder.

3. Place half of batter in prepared pan. Spread with cooled apricot filling and sprinkle with nuts. Spoon remaining batter over filling and spread as evenly as possible. Bake at 325°F for 55 to 65 minutes or until bars are light golden brown and set. Cut into 25 bars and flash freeze in single layer on baking sheet. Wrap bars individually; then pack into rigid containers. Label package and freeze bars.

4. *To thaw:* Loosen wrapping and let bars stand at room temperature for 3 to 5 hours, until softened.

Makes about 25

1½ cups chopped dried apricots
½ cup apricot nectar
½ cup water
1 tablespoon orange juice
¾ cup sugar
2 tablespoons butter
2 cups brown sugar
1½ cups butter, softened
½ cup solid shortening
2 eggs
2 teaspoons vanilla
2½ cups flour
½ teaspoon baking soda
½ teaspoon baking powder
1 cup chopped walnuts

Makes about 75

4½ cups chopped dried apricots
1½ cups apricot nectar
1½ cups water
3 tablespoons orange juice
2¼ cups sugar
6 tablespoons butter
6 cups brown sugar
4½ cups butter, softened
1½ cups solid shortening
6 eggs
6 teaspoons vanilla
7½ cups flour
1½ teaspoons baking soda
1½ teaspoons baking powder
3 cups chopped walnuts

Pineapple-Orange Pound Cake

Serves 8–10

2½ cups flour
1½ cups sugar
1 tablespoon baking powder
¼ teaspoon salt
¾ cup pineapple-orange
   juice
¾ cup safflower oil
2 teaspoons vanilla
4 eggs
¾ cup ground almonds

Glaze:
1¾ cups powdered sugar
½ cup pineapple-orange
   juice

Serves 24–30

7½ cups flour
4½ cups sugar
3 tablespoons baking
   powder
¾ teaspoon salt
2¼ cups pineapple-orange
   juice
2¼ cups safflower oil
2 tablespoons vanilla
12 eggs
2¼ cups ground almonds

Glaze:
5¼ cups powdered sugar
1½ cups pineapple-orange
   juice

This delicious cake stays very moist because of the glaze added while the cake is hot. You can serve the cake immediately after it cools; top it with a dollop of whipped cream or a scoop of orange sherbet.

1. Preheat oven to 325°F. Generously grease and flour a 12-cup Bundt pan and set aside.

2. Combine all ingredients except for glaze ingredients in large mixing bowl and mix on low speed until blended. Beat at high speed for 2 minutes. Pour into prepared pan. Bake at 325°F for 40 to 50 minutes or until golden and firm.

3. In small bowl, mix powdered sugar and remaining pineapple-orange juice until smooth. Spoon half of this glaze over the hot cake while it's still in the pan. Let cake sit in pan on wire rack for 10 minutes, then invert onto serving plate. Drizzle rest of glaze over cake; then cool completely. Cut cake into quarters. Wrap each piece of cake well in freezer wrap; seal, label, and freeze.

4. *To thaw:* Loosen wrapping slightly and let cake stand at room temperature for 2 to 3 hours, until thawed.

The Best Chocolate Chip Cookies

Using salted nuts instead of adding salt to the batter gives these cookies great flavor. Chilling the dough before baking ensures the cookies will be soft and chewy.

1. In large bowl, combine shortening, butter, brown sugar, and sugar until smooth and fluffy. Add vanilla, eggs, and egg yolk and mix well until combined.

2. In blender or food processor, combine oatmeal and vanilla milk chips. Grind until particles are very fine. Add to butter mixture along with flour and baking soda. Stir in chocolate chips and cashews until blended. Chill dough for at least 2 hours before baking.

3. *To freeze cookie dough:* Roll chilled dough into 1-inch balls and flash freeze. Place in zipper-lock bag and store in refrigerator.

4. *To freeze baked cookies:* Preheat oven to 325°F. Drop dough by rounded tablespoons onto parchment paper–lined cookie sheets. Bake at 325°F for 12 to 16 minutes or until cookies are browned around edges and are set. Remove immediately from cookie sheet and cool on wire rack. Place cooled cookies in rigid container, dividing layers with waxed paper or freezer wrap. Seal package, label, and freeze.

5. *To bake frozen dough:* Place frozen balls of dough on parchment paper–lined cookie sheets and bake in preheated 325°F oven for 14 to 17 minutes or until cookies are light golden brown. Remove immediately from cookie sheet and cool on wire rack.

To thaw frozen cookies: Let wrapped cookies stand at room temperature for 1 to 2 hours.

Makes about 48

½ cup butter-flavored shortening
½ cup butter, softened
1½ cups brown sugar
½ cup sugar
1 tablespoon vanilla
2 eggs
1 egg yolk
½ cup oatmeal
½ cup vanilla milk chips
2¼ cups flour
1 teaspoon baking soda
2 cups semisweet chocolate chips
1 cup milk chocolate chips
1 cup chopped salted cashews

Makes about 144

1½ cups butter-flavored shortening
1½ cups butter, softened
4½ cups brown sugar
1½ cups sugar
3 tablespoons vanilla
6 eggs
3 egg yolks
1½ cups oatmeal
1½ cups vanilla milk chips
6¾ cups flour
1 tablespoon baking soda
6 cups semisweet chocolate chips
3 cups milk chocolate chips
3 cups chopped salted cashews

Fudgy Bars

Makes 24

2 cups chocolate chips
3 tablespoons butter
1 (14-ounce) can chocolate-
  flavored sweetened
  condensed milk
2 cups flour
2 cups quick-cooking rolled
  oats
1½ cups brown sugar
1 teaspoon baking soda
¼ teaspoon salt
1 cup butter, melted
1 cup chopped walnuts

Makes 72

6 cups chocolate chips
9 tablespoons butter
3 (14-ounce) cans chocolate-
  flavored sweetened
  condensed milk
6 cups flour
6 cups quick-cooking rolled
  oats
4½ cups brown sugar
1 tablespoon baking soda
¾ teaspoon salt
3 cups butter, melted
3 cups chopped walnuts

To serve without freezing, let pan cool on a wire rack,
then cut into bars using a sharp knife.

1. Preheat oven to 350°F. In microwave-safe bowl, combine chocolate chips, 3 tablespoons butter, and sweetened condensed milk. Heat on medium power for 2 to 3 minutes, until chips and butter are melted. Stir until smooth and set aside.

2. In large bowl, combine flour, oats, brown sugar, baking soda, and salt. Pour melted butter over and mix until crumbs form. Stir in walnuts. Press one-half of the crumb mixture into a 13" × 9" pan. Stir chocolate mixture again, then pour over crust. Sprinkle remaining crumb mixture over chocolate.

3. Bake at 350°F for 25 to 30 minutes or until light golden brown. Let cool completely, then cut into bars and wrap individually in freezer wrap. Place wrapped bars in rigid container, label, and freeze.

4. *To thaw and serve:* Loosen wrapping around bars and let stand at room temperature for 1 to 2 hours.

Peanut Butter Cookies

Powdered sugar in the dough keeps these cookies tender even through freezing.

1. Preheat oven to 350°F. In large bowl, combine shortening, butter, peanut butter, brown sugar, powdered sugar, and sugar and beat until combined. Add vanilla and eggs and beat well. Add flour, baking soda, and salt and mix until a dough forms. Chill dough for 1 to 2 hours in refrigerator.

2. *To freeze cookie dough:* Form dough into 1-inch balls and press on balls with fork to flatten. Flash freeze dough balls until firm, then package in zipper-lock bag.

3. *To freeze baked cookies:* Form dough into 1-inch balls and place on ungreased cookie sheets. Flatten cookies with fork; then bake at 350°F for 12 to 14 minutes or until light golden brown and set. Remove to wire rack to cool. When completely cooled, pack in rigid containers, with layers separated by waxed paper; seal, label, and freeze.

4. *To bake frozen dough:* Preheat oven to 350°F. Place frozen dough balls on ungreased cookie sheets and bake at 350°F for 14 to 16 minutes or until light golden brown. Cool on wire rack.

   To thaw frozen cookies: Let cookies stand at room temperature for 1 to 2 hours, until softened.

Makes about 36

½ cup butter-flavored shortening
½ cup butter, softened
1 cup peanut butter
¾ cup brown sugar
½ cup powdered sugar
¼ cup sugar
1 teaspoon vanilla
2 eggs
2¼ cups flour
1 teaspoon baking soda
½ teaspoon salt

Makes about 108

1½ cups butter-flavored shortening
1½ cups butter, softened
3 cups peanut butter
2¼ cups brown sugar
1½ cups powdered sugar
¾ cup sugar
1 tablespoon vanilla
6 eggs
6¾ cups flour
1 tablespoon baking soda
1½ teaspoons salt

Frozen Citrus Loaf

Serves 8

---

1 (3-ounce) package
   ladyfingers, split
3 tablespoons orange juice
1 pint orange sherbet
1 pint vanilla ice cream
1 pint lemon sherbet
1 pint raspberry sherbet

Serves 24

---

3 (3-ounce) packages
   ladyfingers, split
9 tablespoons orange juice
3 pints orange sherbet
3 pints vanilla ice cream
3 pints lemon sherbet
3 pints raspberry sherbet

This beautiful loaf must be frozen for 3 to 4 hours before serving. Follow the instructions below for removing from pan and serving.

---

1. If ladyfingers aren't cut in half lengthwise, split them. Dip each lady-finger briefly, cut-side down, in orange juice and place in bottom and up sides of 9" × 5" loaf pan, cut sides toward center.

2. Soften all the ice cream and sherbet by letting stand at room tempera-ture for 20 to 30 minutes. Spoon and spread orange sherbet over lady-fingers. Place in freezer for 10 to 15 minutes to firm. Top with layer of vanilla ice cream and place in freezer for 10 to 15 minutes to firm. Top with a layer of lemon sherbet and freeze for 10 to 15 minutes. Finally, top with a layer of raspberry sherbet, cover well, and freeze until firm. Wrap, label, and store in freezer.

3. *To serve:* Dip loaf pan into a bowl of hot water for 3 to 4 seconds, then invert onto serving plate. Let stand for 10 minutes, then slice and serve with whipped cream.

Avoid Soggy Breads!

Make sure to thoroughly cool breads, cakes, and cookies before wrapping them in freezer paper. If these products are not cool before wrapping, moisture will condense on the surface, making the food soggy.

Coconut Snowballs with Fudge Sauce

These delicious little ice cream balls can be served after freezing for 1 to 2 hours. The fudge sauce is wonderful over any ice cream or cake, and it keeps its soft texture even when frozen.

1. In heavy saucepan, combine powdered sugar, half-and-half, chocolate chips, and butter. Cook over medium heat, stirring constantly, until mixture comes to a boil. Reduce heat and simmer sauce for 8 to 10 minutes, stirring frequently, until thickened. Add vanilla and stir well. Cool sauce in ice-water bath or refrigerator.

2. Slightly soften ice cream. Using ice cream scoop, form balls and place on parchment paper–lined baking sheets. Return to freezer. On shallow plate, combine toasted coconut and amaretti cookie crumbs. Remove ice cream balls from freezer and roll in coconut mixture to coat. Flash freeze in single layer until hard. Then package ice cream balls in rigid container, with waxed paper separating layers. Place fudge sauce in rigid container and attach to snowballs. Label package and freeze.

3. *To thaw and serve:* Let fudge sauce stand at room temperature for 30 to 50 minutes, until softened. Fudge sauce can also be heated in saucepan or microwave. Serve frozen snowballs with fudge sauce drizzled on top.

Serves 8

2 cups powdered sugar
1½ cups half-and-half
2 cups chocolate chips
½ cup butter
1 teaspoon vanilla
1 quart vanilla ice cream
1 cup coconut, toasted
1 cup crushed amaretti cookies

Serves 24

6 cups powdered sugar
4½ cups half-and-half
6 cups chocolate chips
1½ cups butter
1 tablespoon vanilla
3 quarts vanilla ice cream
3 cups coconut, toasted
3 cups crushed amaretti cookies

Banana Snack Cake

Serves 10–12

¾ cup butter, softened
1 cup sugar
¼ cup brown sugar
2 eggs
1 cup mashed banana
    (2 large)
2 teaspoons vanilla
1 teaspoon baking powder
1 teaspoon baking soda
¼ teaspoon salt
2½ cups flour
1 cup milk chocolate chips
1 cup chopped pecans
½ cup brown sugar
3 tablespoons butter

Serves 30–36

2¼ cups butter, softened
3 cups sugar
¾ cup brown sugar
6 eggs
3 cups mashed banana
    (6 large)
2 tablespoons vanilla
1 tablespoon baking powder
1 tablespoon baking soda
¾ teaspoon salt
7½ cups flour
3 cups milk chocolate chips
3 cups chopped pecans
1½ cups brown sugar
9 tablespoons butter

Snack cake is the perfect treat to have on hand for after-school snacks or unexpected company. To serve without freezing, let cake cool for 30 to 40 minutes before slicing.

1. Preheat oven to 350°F. Grease and flour 13" × 9" baking pan. In large mixing bowl, beat first quantity of butter with sugar and first quantity of brown sugar until light and fluffy. Add eggs, mashed banana, and vanilla, beating until smooth. Sift together baking powder, baking soda, salt, and flour and add to banana mixture; mix until blended. Stir in chocolate chips and pour into prepared pan.

2. In small bowl, combine pecans with remaining brown sugar and butter; mix until crumbly. Sprinkle over batter in pan. Bake at 350°F for 25 to 35 minutes or until toothpick inserted in center comes out clean. Cool completely and cut into bars. Wrap each bar individually in freezer wrap and place in large rigid container. Label, seal, and freeze bars.

3. *To thaw and serve:* Loosen wrapping from bars and let stand at room temperature for 1 to 2 hours, until thawed.

Measuring Brown Sugar

Brown sugar must be pressed firmly into the measuring cup or spoon to get an accurate amount. The sugar should hold its shape when turned out of the cup or spoon.

Decadent Brownies

These brownies can be cut and served as soon as they are cool. If you like, frost them with a mixture of ½ cup peanut butter and 1½ cups chocolate chips, melted together until smooth.

1. Preheat oven to 350°F. Grease a 13" × 9" pan and set aside. Combine sugar, butter, and water in large saucepan and cook over medium heat until mixture comes to a boil. Remove from heat and add chocolate chips; stir until melted. Add vanilla and eggs and beat well. Stir in flour, cocoa, baking powder, and salt and mix. Stir in pecans.

2. Spread batter in prepared pan and bake at 350°F for 25 to 35 minutes or until toothpick inserted near center of pan comes out clean. Do not overbake. Cool brownies on rack, then cut into bars and wrap each bar in freezer wrap. Pack into rigid container, seal, label, and freeze.

3. *To thaw and serve:* Thaw brownies for 1 to 2 hours at room temperature until soft.

Assembly-Line Cooking

Plan your assembly lines, preparation order, and cooking order after you have chosen your recipes and made your shopping and on-hand lists. Set up stations where different tasks are performed. Once the ingredients are prepped, combine as the various recipes instruct.

Makes 12

1½ cups sugar
⅔ cup butter
5 tablespoons water
1 cup semisweet chocolate chips
2 teaspoons vanilla
4 eggs
1½ cups flour
¼ cup cocoa
½ teaspoon baking powder
¼ teaspoon salt
1 cup chopped pecans

Makes 36

4½ cups sugar
2 cups butter
15 tablespoons water
3 cups semisweet chocolate chips
2 tablespoons vanilla
12 eggs
4½ cups flour
¾ cup cocoa
1½ teaspoons baking powder
¾ teaspoon salt
3 cups chopped pecans

White Chocolate Shortbread

Serves 12

---

1 cup unsalted butter, softened
½ cup powdered sugar
1 teaspoon vanilla
¼ teaspoon salt
1½ cups flour
½ cup rice flour
½ cup white chocolate chips, ground
1 cup chopped cashews
1 cup white chocolate chips

Serves 36

---

3 cups unsalted butter, softened
1½ cups powdered sugar
1 tablespoon vanilla
¾ teaspoon salt
4½ cups flour
1½ cups rice flour
1½ cups white chocolate chips, ground
3 cups chopped cashews
3 cups white chocolate chips

Rice flour makes this shortbread very crisp. Ground white chocolate makes it very tender. Put together, they make a fantastic cookie. To serve without freezing, let cool for 45 minutes and break into pieces.

1. Preheat oven to 375°F. In large bowl, combine butter, sugar, and vanilla and beat until fluffy. Combine salt, flour, and rice flour in small bowl and add to butter mixture along with ground white chocolate chips. Mix until a dough forms. Stir in cashews and whole white chocolate chips.

2. Press into ungreased 13" × 9" pan and bake at 375°F for 15 to 25 minutes or until light golden brown around edges. Cool completely on wire rack; then break shortbread into pieces. Place in rigid freezer container, separating layers with freezer paper. Seal package, label, and freeze.

3. *To thaw and serve:* Let package stand at room temperature for 1 to 2 hours, until shortbread is thawed.

Raspberry Daiquiri Pie

This pie is good to have on hand for summer entertaining.
To serve immediately, freeze pie for 2 to 3 hours, until firm,
then cut into slices.

1. In small bowl, combine pretzels, melted butter, and sugar and blend well. Press into bottom and up sides of 9-inch pie pan and set aside.

2. In large bowl, combine condensed milk and cream cheese and beat until smooth and well blended. Add raspberries with syrup and lime juice and mix well. Fold in thawed whipped topping until blended. Pour into prepared pie shell. Cover and freeze until firm. Wrap pie in freezer paper, seal, label, and freeze.

3. *To serve:* Let pie stand at room temperature for 20 minutes before slicing. Top with raspberry syrup and whipped topping, if desired.

Freezing Whipped Cream

Whipped cream can be frozen. Beat the cream with some powdered sugar until stiff peaks form, then dollop or pipe the cream onto a cookie sheet. Freeze until firm, then place in single layer in rigid containers and freeze.

Serves 8

1½ cups crushed pretzels
½ cup butter, melted
⅓ cup sugar
1 (14-ounce) can sweetened
 condensed milk
1 (8-ounce) package cream
 cheese, softened
2 cups frozen raspberries in
 syrup, thawed
2 tablespoons lime juice
2 cups frozen whipped
 topping, thawed

Serves 24

4½ cups crushed pretzels
1½ cups butter, melted
1 cup sugar
3 (14-ounce) cans sweetened
 condensed milk
3 (8-ounce) packages cream
 cheese, softened
6 cups frozen raspberries in
 syrup, thawed
6 tablespoons lime juice
6 cups frozen whipped
 topping, thawed

Ginger Cookies

½ cup butter
¼ cup solid shortening
1 cup sugar
1 egg
¼ cup honey
2 cups flour
2 teaspoons baking soda
¼ teaspoon salt
1 teaspoon ground ginger
¼ teaspoon ground nutmeg
¼ cup finely chopped
*   crystallized ginger*

Makes about 108

1½ cups butter
¾ cup solid shortening
3 cups sugar
3 eggs
¾ cup honey
6 cups flour
2 tablespoons baking soda
¾ teaspoon salt
1 tablespoon ground ginger
¾ teaspoon ground nutmeg
¾ cup finely chopped
*   crystallized ginger*

These old-fashioned cookies have an extra snap of crystallized ginger along with ground ginger. They are delicious with a glass of cold milk, or served with midmorning coffee or tea.

1. Preheat oven to 375°F. In large bowl, combine butter, shortening, and sugar and mix until fluffy. Stir in egg and honey and beat well to combine. Add remaining ingredients and mix to combine.

2. *To freeze unbaked dough:* Form dough into 1-inch balls and flash freeze dough balls until firm; then package in zipper-lock bag.

3. *To freeze baked cookies:* Form dough into 1-inch balls and place on parchment paper–lined cookie sheets. Bake at 375°F for 9 to 13 minutes or until cookies are golden around edges. Let stand on cookie sheet for 2 minutes, then remove to wire rack to cool. When completely cooled, pack in rigid containers, with layers separated by waxed paper; seal, label, and freeze.

4. *To bake frozen dough:* Preheat oven to 375°F. Place frozen dough balls on ungreased cookie sheets and bake at 375°F for 14 to 16 minutes or until light golden brown. Cool on wire rack.

To thaw frozen cookies: Let cookies stand at room temperature for 1 to 2 hours until softened.

Chapter 19
Mixes and Basic Recipes

Pesto Sauce

**Makes about
1½ cups**

1½ cups fresh basil leaves
1½ cups baby spinach leaves
4 cloves garlic, peeled
1 tablespoon lemon juice
½ cup grated Parmesan
    cheese
¼ cup pine nuts, toasted
¼ cup chopped salted
    cashews, toasted
¼ teaspoon white pepper
⅓ cup extra-virgin olive oil
2–3 tablespoons water

Makes about 4 ½ cups

4½ cups fresh basil leaves
4½ cups baby spinach leaves
12 cloves garlic, peeled
3 tablespoons lemon juice
1½ cups grated Parmesan
    cheese
¾ cup pine nuts, toasted
¾ cup chopped salted
    cashews, toasted
¾ teaspoon white pepper
1 cup extra-virgin olive oil
6–8 tablespoons water

Spinach helps keep the pesto nice and green, and adds to the nutrition of this easy sauce. Using salted cashews instead of adding salt seems to increase the depth of flavor.

---

1. Combine basil, spinach, garlic, lemon juice, and cheese in food processor or blender and pulse several times until mixture is fine. Then add pine nuts, cashews, and white pepper; pulse several times until mixture is fine and evenly blended. While machine is running, slowly add olive oil until a thick paste forms.

2. If necessary, add water to mixture until desired consistency. Pour pesto into ice cube trays and freeze until firm. Package frozen cubes in zipper-lock bags, label, seal, and freeze.

3. *To thaw and use:* Remove from freezer and let stand at room temperature for 30 to 40 minutes before using to coat cooked pasta or in other recipes.

Taco Seasoning Mix

Add this mix to browned ground beef and tomato sauce to make a filling for tacos or enchiladas. Two tablespoons of the mix equal an envelope of purchased seasoning mix blend.

1. Combine all ingredients in small bowl and mix well with fork to blend. Pour into small zipper-lock bag or rigid container; label, and store in cool, dry place or freeze.

2. Use 2 tablespoons to substitute for a 1.25-ounce package of commercial taco seasoning mix. To make taco sauce from this mix, in medium saucepan, combine 2 tablespoons of the mix, an 8-ounce can tomato sauce, and ¼ cup water; bring to a simmer over medium heat. Simmer for 5 to 10 minutes to blend flavors, and use as a substitute for 1 cup taco sauce in any recipe.

Need It Twice, Chop It Once

You'll find that you probably use the same ingredients in many recipes. So gather all of the same items together and process them all at once. Peel, rinse, and chop all the onions and place in a zipper-lock bag. Wash, core, seed, and chop all the green or red peppers you'll need; some may be cut into strips or even left whole.

Makes 6 batches

⅓ cup dried minced onion
2 tablespoons dried minced garlic
¼ cup chili powder
1 tablespoon ground cumin
1 tablespoon ground coriander
1 tablespoon smoked paprika
4 teaspoons sugar
4 teaspoons salt
¼ teaspoon black pepper
¼ teaspoon white pepper
½ teaspoon red pepper
2 tablespoons cornstarch

Makes 18 batches

1 cup dried minced onion
6 tablespoons dried minced garlic
¾ cup chili powder
3 tablespoons ground cumin
3 tablespoons ground coriander
3 tablespoons smoked paprika
4 tablespoons sugar
4 tablespoons salt
¾ teaspoon black pepper
¾ teaspoon white pepper
1½ teaspoons red pepper
6 tablespoons cornstarch

Pizza Crust

Makes 6 crusts

6 cups white flour
3 cups cornmeal
3 envelopes dry yeast
1 tablespoon sugar
1 tablespoon salt
¼ teaspoon cayenne pepper
9 tablespoons olive oil
4 cups warm water
3 cups whole wheat flour

Makes 18 crusts

18 cups white flour
9 cups cornmeal
9 envelopes dry yeast
3 tablespoons sugar
3 tablespoons salt
¾ teaspoon cayenne pepper
1⅔ cups olive oil
12 cups warm water
9 cups whole wheat flour

Make a bunch of these crusts and keep them in your freezer; then when you want pizza, pull out a crust, bake it as directed, top it with fun toppings, bake again, and eat!

1. In large bowl, combine 1 cup white flour, cornmeal, dry yeast, sugar, salt, pepper, and olive oil; mix well. Add warm water and beat until a batter forms. Cover and let stand for 30 minutes. Add whole wheat flour and enough remaining white flour to form a firm dough.

2. Knead dough for 8 minutes on floured board. Place dough in greased mixing bowl, turning to grease top. Cover and let rise in warm place for 1 hour. Punch down dough and divide into 6 balls. Sprinkle work surface with flour and roll out each ball into 12-inch circle. Place dough on cookie sheets and flash freeze.

3. When dough is frozen solid, wrap well, label, and seal. To use, bake frozen rounds at 400°F for 10 to 15 minutes, until just beginning to brown. Top with pizza ingredients and bake according to pizza recipe.

Food Processor Tips

To mince garlic in a full-size food processor, peel the garlic cloves and trim the root end. If garlic is older, split the clove lengthwise and remove the center shoot, which can be somewhat bitter when cooked. Fit the metal blade in the work bowl. With the motor running, drop the garlic down the feed tube, 1 to 2 cloves at a time, until minced. Do not put all the garlic in at once, as it won't mince evenly.

Pie Crust

When you have several rounds of pastry stored in your freezer, a main dish pie or dessert is only minutes away. Fit the thawed rounds into a 9-inch pie pan and flute edges. Use as directed in recipe.

1. Place flour, salt, and sugar in a large bowl. Cut in cold butter, shortening, and cold cream cheese until small, even crumbs form. Sprinkle 6 tablespoons buttermilk into bowl, tossing crumbs with fork until a dough forms. You may need to add more buttermilk or more flour to achieve the correct consistency.

2. Gather dough into a ball, wrap in plastic wrap, and chill in refrigerator for at least 2 hours. Then, divide dough into 6 balls. On lightly floured surface, roll out each ball into an 11-inch round. Flash freeze rounds on cookie sheets. When frozen solid, wrap in freezer wrap, label, seal, and freeze.

3. *To thaw and use:* Let frozen pastry stand at room temperature for 30 to 45 minutes, until thawed. Use as directed in recipes.

Makes 6 crusts

4 cups flour
½ teaspoon salt
2 teaspoons sugar
½ cup butter
½ cup shortening
2 (3-ounce) packages cream
   cheese
6–8 tablespoons buttermilk

Makes 18 crusts

12 cups flour
1½ teaspoons salt
2 tablespoons sugar
1½ cups butter
1½ cups shortening
6 (3-ounce) packages cream
   cheese
1 cup plus 2–6 tablespoons
   buttermilk

Basic Crepes

2 eggs
1 cup whole milk
2 tablespoons canola oil
1 cup flour
1 teaspoon sugar
¼ teaspoon salt
3 tablespoons butter

Makes about 24–36 crepes

6 eggs
3 cups whole milk
6 tablespoons canola oil
3 cups flour
1 tablespoon sugar
¾ teaspoon salt
9 tablespoons butter

The tiny amount of sugar in these crepes ensures that they brown beautifully. These thin, delicate crepes may be filled as soon as they cool.

1. In medium bowl, beat eggs until foamy. Add milk and oil and beat until combined. Combine flour, sugar, and salt; add all at once to egg mixture and mix with wire whisk until smooth. Cover and refrigerate for at least 1 hour before making crepes.

2. When ready to make crepes, preheat a 6-inch skillet over medium-high heat. Add a small pat of butter and swirl pan so butter coats bottom as it melts. Spoon ¼ cup of batter into pan and immediately swirl batter around pan to make a solid circle. (Don't worry if there are small holes in the batter.) Cook over medium-high heat for 2 to 3 minutes, until bottom of crepe is lightly browned.

3. Using fork, gently pull edge of crepe up and flip crepe over. Cook on second side for 1 to 2 minutes, until set. Place crepe on kitchen towel and let cool. Repeat with remaining batter, adding a tiny amount of butter to pan before pouring batter.

4. When crepes are cool, they can be stacked, separated by waxed paper. Place cooled crepes in large zipper-lock bags, about 8 per bag, separated by waxed paper or freezer paper. Label bag, seal, and freeze.

5. *To thaw and use:* Let crepes stand at room temperature for 1 to 2 hours. Fill with desired filling as recipe directs.

Chicken Broth

When you make your own broth, you control the fat and sodium content. If you omit the salt from this recipe, add a few cloves of garlic for richer flavor.

1. Place all ingredients in large stockpot. Bring to a boil over high heat; then reduce heat, partially cover pot, and simmer for 2 hours.

2. Remove the chicken from the broth and set aside (pull the meat from the bones and use in recipes or freeze to use later). Strain broth through a sieve and refrigerate overnight. The next day, remove fat from top of broth and strain again through cheesecloth. Freeze broth in 1-cup portions in 1-pint zipper-lock bags.

3. *To thaw and reheat:* Thaw overnight in refrigerator or place frozen broth in saucepan and heat over low heat until liquid. Use in recipes as desired.

Preparing Meat

Processing and cooking meats in bulk is one of the biggest time-savers in once-a-month cooking. Use your Slow Cooker to cook a beef roast overnight. Then in the morning, you'll just cool and cube the beef and use it in your recipes. Place cut-up chicken pieces on a foil-lined baking sheet and bake until done; then let them cool, and chop and slice the amounts you need for your recipes.

Makes 2 quarts

1 (6-pound) stewing
  chicken
2 onions, thickly sliced
2 carrots, chunked
2 stalks celery, chunked
2 teaspoons salt
1 bay leaf
1 teaspoon dried basil leaves
¼ teaspoon white pepper
2½ quarts water

Makes 6 quarts

3 (6-pound) stewing
  chickens
6 onions, thickly sliced
6 carrots, chunked
6 stalks celery, chunked
5 teaspoons salt
3 bay leaves
1 tablespoon dried basil
  leaves
¾ teaspoon white pepper
7½ quarts water

Beef Broth

Makes 1 gallon

---

 4 pounds beef shanks
3 pounds beef bones
3 onions, thickly sliced
4 carrots, chunked
 ⅓ cup water
4½ quarts water
6 cloves garlic
3 stalks celery, chunked
5 tablespoons tomato paste
½ teaspoon pepper
2 teaspoons salt
1 bay leaf
1 teaspoon dried thyme
    leaves

Makes 3 gallons

---

12 pounds beef shanks
9 pounds beef bones
9 onions, thickly sliced
12 carrots, chunked
1 cup water
13½ quarts water
18 cloves garlic
9 stalks celery, chunked
1 cup tomato paste
1½ teaspoons pepper
5 teaspoons salt
3 bay leaves
1 tablespoon dried thyme
    leaves

Homemade beef broth makes the best soups and stews
in the world. If you are watching your fat and sodium intake,
this broth can be made without salt.

---

1. Preheat oven to 450°F. When purchasing beef, have butcher cut shanks into 3-inch pieces and crack the bones. In large roasting pan, place shanks, bones, onion, and carrot; pour ⅓ cup water over. Roast, uncovered, in 450°F oven for 50 to 60 minutes, until meat and vegetables are well browned.

2. Remove beef and vegetables from pan and place in large stockpot. Pour off fat from roasting pan and add 2 cups water. Set pan over high heat and bring liquid to a boil, scraping pan bottom and sides with spoon to loosen drippings. Pour into stockpot along with remaining water.

3. Add remaining ingredients to stockpot and bring to a boil. Reduce heat, partially cover the pan, and simmer for 4 hours (broth will be rich brown color). Strain broth through a sieve into a large saucepan. Cool broth in ice-water bath; then let stand, covered, in refrigerator overnight.

4. Remove fat from surface of broth. Strain broth through cheesecloth. Freeze broth in 1-cup portions in 1-pint zipper-lock bags.

5. *To thaw and reheat:* Thaw overnight in refrigerator or place frozen broth in saucepan and heat over low heat until liquid. Use in recipes as desired.

Vegetable Broth

2 tablespoons olive oil
2 onions, chopped
2 carrots, chopped
1 leek, sliced
3 stalks celery, chopped
5 cloves garlic, minced
1 teaspoon dried thyme
  leaves
1 teaspoon dried marjoram
  leaves
1 bay leaf
2 teaspoons salt
2½ quarts water

This broth can be substituted for beef, chicken, or fish broth in any soup or casserole recipe. If you like a thicker broth, puree some of the vegetables and add back to the broth.

1. Heat olive oil in large stockpot over medium heat. Add onions and carrots; cook and stir until browned. Add leek, celery, and garlic; cook and stir 5 to 10 minutes or until garlic is light golden brown. Add seasonings and water; bring to a boil. Partially cover pan, reduce heat, and simmer for about 2 hours, until flavor is pronounced.

2. If necessary, skim broth, then strain it through a fine mesh strainer. Cool in ice-water bath or refrigerator. Freeze broth in 1-cup portions in 1-pint zipper-lock bags.

3. *To thaw and reheat:* Thaw overnight in refrigerator or place frozen broth in saucepan and heat over low heat until liquid. Use in recipes as desired.

Makes 6 quarts

6 tablespoons olive oil
6 onions, chopped
6 carrots, chopped
3 leeks, sliced
9 stalks celery, chopped
15 cloves garlic, minced
1 tablespoon dried thyme
  leaves
1 tablespoon dried
  marjoram leaves
3 bay leaves
2 tablespoons salt
7½ quarts water

What Is the Difference Between a Simmer and a Boil?

A simmer starts at 190°F and a gentle boil starts at 200°F. A boil starts at 212°F. A cooking thermometer will determine the actual temperature. Simmering is a gentler cooking method and won't cause the ingredients to break up. A hard boil is good for pasta but not for vegetables. Soups and stews are best when cooked at a simmer or gentle boil.

Fish Broth

Makes 1 quart

1 pound white fish trimmings
¼ pound shrimp shells
2 carrots, chopped
2 leeks, chopped
1 onion, chopped
½ teaspoon salt
10 peppercorns
1 bay leaf
¼ cup celery leaves
1 quart water
1 cup white wine

Makes 3 quarts

3 pounds white fish trimmings
¾ pound shrimp shells
6 carrots, chopped
6 leeks, chopped
3 onions, chopped
1½ teaspoons salt
20 peppercorns
3 bay leaves
¾ cup celery leaves
3 quarts water
3 cups white wine

Makes 5 batches

⅓ cup instant minced onion
1 teaspoon garlic powder
⅓ cup cornstarch
1 tablespoon dried basil leaves
1 tablespoon dried oregano leaves
2 tablespoons sugar
1 tablespoon salt
1 teaspoon pepper
2 teaspoons celery seed
¼ cup dried parsley leaves

Makes 15 batches

1 cup instant minced onion
1 tablespoon garlic powder
1 cup cornstarch
3 tablespoons dried basil leaves
3 tablespoons dried oregano leaves
6 tablespoons sugar
3 tablespoons salt
1 tablespoon pepper
2 tablespoons celery seed
¾ cup dried parsley leaves

Do not use fatty fish, such as salmon or tuna, in this broth. It is delicious used in casseroles or sauces that include any type of seafood. Be sure to strain the broth well so no small fish bones slip through.

1. In heavy stockpot, combine all ingredients and bring to a boil. Reduce heat, partially cover pot, and simmer for 20 to 30 minutes. Strain broth through a fine sieve and cool broth in ice-water bath or refrigerator. Portion broth into 1-pint zipper-lock bags (1 cup of broth in each); label, seal, and freeze.

2. *To thaw and reheat:* Thaw overnight in refrigerator or place frozen broth in saucepan and heat over low heat until liquid. Use in recipes as desired.

Spaghetti Sauce Mix

If you are watching your sodium intake, just omit the salt from this easy seasoning mix. You can vary the proportions of spices and herbs to your family's taste.

1. Combine all ingredients in a small bowl and mix well to blend. Pour into tightly closed container and store in a cool, dry place or place in freezer and freeze up to 4 months.

2. *To use:* Combine ⅓ cup of mix with 16 ounces tomato sauce, 6 ounces tomato paste, and 2¾ cups water; simmer for 20 to 25 minutes, until thickened. Or use as directed in recipe.

Condensed Cream Soup Mix

You can substitute just about any spices or herbs
for the thyme and basil. To make flavored soups, add sautéed
mushrooms, cooked chicken or beef, tomato sauce, et cetera.

1. Combine all ingredients in medium bowl and mix well with wire whisk to blend. Store in tightly closed container in a dry, cool place or freeze up to 4 months.

2. *To use as a substitute for a can of condensed soup:* Combine ½ cup mix with 1¼ cups water in a small saucepan and bring to a boil, stirring constantly, until thickened.

Makes 9 batches

2 cups dried milk powder
⅔ cup cornstarch
½ cup instant chicken or beef
   bouillon granules
2 tablespoons dried onion flakes
¼ teaspoon white pepper
1 teaspoon dried thyme leaves
½ teaspoon dried basil leaves

Makes 27 batches

6 cups dried milk powder
2 cups cornstarch
1½ cups instant chicken or
   beef bouillon granules
6 tablespoons dried onion flakes
¾ teaspoon white pepper
1 tablespoon dried thyme leaves
1½ teaspoons dried basil
   leaves

Onion Soup Mix

If you're watching sodium content, use low-sodium beef bouillon
granules, and substitute celery seed for the celery salt.

1. Combine all ingredients and mix well; store in rigid container in cool place. Mix can be stored in freezer for up to 6 months.

2. *To use as an appetizer dip:* Combine ¼ cup mix with 2 cups sour cream, cover, and let stand in refrigerator for 2 to 3 hours.

To use as soup: Combine 2 tablespoons mix in 1½ cups of boiling water per serving. Substitute for purchased onion soup mix in dips and recipes.

Makes 10 batches

1 cup dried minced onions
2 teaspoons onion powder
1 teaspoon garlic powder
¼ cup instant beef bouillon
   granules
¼ cup grated Parmesan cheese
1 teaspoon celery salt
½ teaspoon white pepper
1 teaspoon sugar

Makes 30 batches

3 cups dried minced onions
2 tablespoons onion powder
1 tablespoon garlic powder
¾ cups instant beef bouillon
   granules
¾ cups grated Parmesan cheese
1 tablespoon celery salt
1½ teaspoons white pepper
1 tablespoon sugar

Chicken Rice Mix

Makes 6 batches

---

6 cups uncooked basmati rice
½ cup dry chicken bouillon granules
⅓ cup dried minced onions
2 teaspoons garlic powder
2 teaspoons sugar
1 teaspoon salt
1 teaspoon white pepper
3 tablespoons dried parsley flakes
1 tablespoon dried marjoram leaves
1 tablespoon dried oregano leaves

Makes 18 batches

---

18 cups uncooked basmati rice
1½ cups dry chicken bouillon granules
1 cup dried minced onions
2 tablespoons garlic powder
2 tablespoons sugar
1 tablespoon salt
1 tablespoon white pepper
9 tablespoons dried parsley flakes
3 tablespoons dried marjoram leaves
3 tablespoons dried oregano leaves

Makes 4 cups mix

---

4 cups uncooked basmati rice
¼ cup beef bouillon granules
2 tablespoons dried celery flakes
¼ cup dried onion flakes
1 teaspoon smoked paprika
1 teaspoon dried oregano leaves
1 teaspoon white pepper
1 teaspoon salt

Makes 12 cups mix

---

12 cups uncooked basmati rice
¾ cup beef bouillon granules
6 tablespoons dried celery flakes
¾ cup dried onion flakes
1 tablespoon smoked paprika
1 tablespoon dried oregano leaves
1 tablespoon white pepper
1 tablespoon salt

The basmati rice cooks in less time than long-grain rice and has a wonderful popcornaroma while it cooks.

---

1. Combine all ingredients and mix well; store in cool place in rigid container. Mix may be stored in the freezer for up to 6 months.

2. *To use:* Combine $1^{1/3}$ cups of the rice mix with 2 cups water and 2 tablespoons butter in a heavy saucepan and bring to a boil over medium heat. Cover pan, reduce heat to low, and cook for 15 to 25 minutes, until rice is tender and liquid is absorbed.

Beef Rice Mix

This is such a simple mix to have on hand to dress up any meal. The basmati rice adds a wonderful nutty flavor to the herbs and spices and always cooks up fluffy and tender.

---

1. Combine all ingredients in large bowl and mix until well blended. Store in tightly covered container in cool, dry place. Mix can be stored in tightly closed container in freezer for up to 6 months.

2. *To use:* Bring 2 cups water and 1 tablespoon butter to a boil in a medium saucepan. Add 1 cup of the rice mix, bring back to a boil, then cover pan, reduce heat, and simmer for 15 to 20 minutes, until rice is tender. Remove from heat and let stand, covered, for 5 minutes, then fluff with fork and serve.

Pancake Mix

This mix can be used to make waffles, too.

1. In large bowl, combine all ingredients and mix well with wire whisk. Pour into rigid container and store covered in cool place, or store mix in freezer for up to 6 months.

2. *To use:* Place 1½ cups thawed pancake mix in medium bowl. In small bowl, beat together 1 egg, 2 tablespoons canola oil, and ¾ to 1 cup cold water. Pour into pancake mix and stir just until dry ingredients are blended. In a nonstick skillet, melt butter over medium heat and pour ¼ cup batter for each pancake. Cook until bubbles form on surface and edges begin to brown. Flip pancakes and cook 3 to 4 minutes longer, until pancakes are fluffy and golden brown. Repeat with remaining batter. Makes 6 to 8 pancakes per batch.

Biscuit Mix

You could substitute up to half of the all-purpose flour with whole wheat flour or rye flour. Use this mix in place of purchased all-purpose baking mixes.

1. In large mixing bowl, combine all dry ingredients and mix well until blended. Using two knives or a pastry blender, cut in chilled shortening until particles are fine. Pour into rigid container and store in the refrigerator or freezer for up to 6 months. Use in place of biscuit or baking mixes.

2. *To make biscuits:* Combine ½ cup cold water with about 1 cup thawed mix until dough forms. Divide into six balls and flatten with rolling pin to ½-inch thick. Brush with cream and bake in preheated 425°F oven for 8 to 10 minutes, until golden brown.

Makes 12 batches

9 cups flour
4 cups whole wheat flour
½ cup finely ground oatmeal
1 cup buttermilk powder
1 cup dry milk powder
5 tablespoons baking powder
2 tablespoons baking soda
1⅓ cups sugar
1 tablespoon salt
2 tablespoons vanilla powder

Makes 36 batches

27 cups flour
12 cups whole wheat flour
1½ cups finely ground oatmeal
3 cups buttermilk powder
3 cups dry milk powder
15 tablespoons baking powder
6 tablespoons baking soda
4 cups sugar
3 tablespoons salt
6 tablespoons vanilla powder

Makes 36 biscuits

5 cups flour
1 cup whole wheat flour
3 tablespoons baking powder
2 teaspoons salt
⅓ cup nonfat dry milk powder
2 tablespoons sugar
1½ cups solid shortening, chilled

Makes 108 biscuits

15 cups flour
3 cups whole wheat flour
9 tablespoons baking powder
2 tablespoons salt
1 cup nonfat dry milk powder
6 tablespoons sugar
4½ cups solid shortening, chilled

No Salt Seasoning Mix

Makes ¹/₂ cup

2 tablespoons garlic powder
2 tablespoons onion powder
2 teaspoons dried marjoram leaves
2 teaspoons celery seed
1 tablespoon dry mustard
2 teaspoons white pepper
1 tablespoon black pepper
1 teaspoon cayenne pepper
2 teaspoons smoked paprika

Makes 1¹/₂ cups

6 tablespoons garlic powder
6 tablespoons onion powder
2 tablespoons dried marjoram leaves
2 tablespoons celery seed
3 tablespoons dry mustard
2 tablespoons white pepper
3 tablespoons black pepper
1 tablespoon cayenne pepper
2 tablespoons smoked paprika

This is an excellent mix to keep in a salt shaker and place on the table.

1. Combine all ingredients and mix well. Store in cool place in tightly sealed container, or mixture can be stored in the freezer for up to 6 months.

2. *To use:* This can be sprinkled on meats before cooking, or used at the table in place of salt and pepper.

Makes ¹/₂ cup

2 tablespoons smoked paprika
2 tablespoons onion powder
2 teaspoons cumin
1 tablespoon sugar
2 teaspoons salt
2 teaspoons dried oregano leaves
1 tablespoon granulated garlic
1 teaspoon black pepper
½ teaspoon cayenne pepper

Makes 1¹/₂ cups

6 tablespoons smoked paprika
6 tablespoons onion powder
2 tablespoons cumin
3 tablespoons sugar
2 tablespoons salt
2 tablespoons dried oregano leaves
3 tablespoons granulated garlic
1 tablespoon black pepper
1½ teaspoons cayenne pepper

Grill Seasoning

This seasoning adds great flavor to any meat or vegetable you are going to cook on the grill. Use about 2 teaspoons Grill Seasoning per pound of meat.

1. Combine all ingredients and mix well. Store in cool place in tightly sealed container. Mixture can be stored in the freezer for up to 6 months.

2. This can be sprinkled on meats or vegetables before cooking.

Appendices

Appendix A

Equivalents Chart / 310

Appendix B

Food Preparation Glossary / 312

Commonly Used Cooking Equivalents

Ingredient	Equivalent
1 pound lean ground beef	2½ cups cooked, drained
1 pound ham	3 cups cubed
8 slices bacon	½ cup cooked, drained, crumbled
1 whole chicken	3–4 cups cooked, cubed meat
1½ pounds boneless, skinless chicken breast	3 cups cooked, diced
1½ pounds beef roast	3 cups cooked, cubed
1 pound lamb chops	2 chops
1 pound onions	3 cups chopped
1 bell pepper, chopped	1 cup
3 ounces button mushrooms	1 cup sliced
1 medium cabbage	5 cups shredded
2 ribs celery	1 cup sliced
1 medium apple	1 cup chopped
1 pound apples	3 medium
3 medium bananas	1 cup mashed
1 medium tomato	1 cup chopped
1 orange	5–6 tablespoons juice
1 lemon	2–4 tablespoons juice
1 lime	1½–2 tablespoons juice
1 pound potatoes	4–5 cups chopped
1 pound broccoli	2 cups florets
1 pound carrots	2½ cups sliced
1 pound cauliflower	3 cups chopped
1 pound cranberries	4 cups
1 pound fennel bulb	3 cups sliced
1 pound grapes	2½ cups seedless
1 pound melon	1 cup diced
1 medium head lettuce	4–6 cups torn
1 pound fresh spinach	¾ cup cooked, drained

Commonly Used Cooking Equivalents

Ingredient	Equivalent
1 pint strawberries	2 cups sliced
1 pound sweet potatoes (2 large)	2 cups cubed
8 ounces (2 cups) uncooked noodles	4 cups cooked, drained
1 pound rice (2¼ cups uncooked)	6¾ cups cooked
2 slices bread	1 cup soft bread crumbs
4 slices bread, oven dried	1 cup dry bread crumbs
1 pound flour	4 cups
1 pound (2 cups) dried beans	6 cups cooked
10-ounce can condensed broth	2½ cups broth
3 cups cornflakes	1 cup crushed
1 cup uncooked couscous	2½–3 cups cooked
1 pound lasagna noodles	16–24 noodles
18 ounces peanut butter	2 cups
6 ounces pecan pieces	1½ cups
1 pound sugar	2 cups
1 pound brown sugar	2¼ cups packed
1 pound powdered sugar	3¾ cups
1 egg	¼ cup egg substitute
1 pound firm cheese (Cheddar)	4 cups shredded
1 pound hard cheese (Parmesan)	3 cups grated
4 whole large eggs	1 cup
7–8 egg whites	1 cup
1 pound frozen corn	1⅔ cups kernels
10 ounces frozen green peas	1½ cups
10 ounces frozen peppers and onions	2¼ cups
10-ounce package frozen vegetables	1½ cups
16 ounces frozen tortellini	3 cups cooked
1 pound frozen potato wedges	3 cups cooked
1 pound hash brown potatoes	2½ cups cooked

GLOSSARY

additives:
Strictly regulated ingredients and chemicals added to food to help improve texture and flavor and to extend the shelf life of products.

al dente:
Italian term that translates as "to the tooth." It refers to the most desired texture of cooked pasta, with a slight resistance in the center when chewed.

ascorbic acid:
An organic acid also known as vitamin C. It is used to help prevent enzymatic browning in fruits and vegetables.

baking powder:
A leavening agent used in baked goods that combines an acid and a base to produce carbon dioxide when mixed with water. The carbon dioxide fills small bubbles in the batter or dough and expands when baked to form the characteristic crumb.

baking soda:
Bicarbonate of soda is used as a leavening agent in baked goods. It combines with an acidic ingredient in the dough or batter to produce carbon dioxide so the product expands while baking.

baste:
To spoon or pour a liquid over foods during cooking to help glaze food and prevent drying.

batter:
A combination of flour and liquid mixed together by stirring or beating to form a pourable mass.

beat:
To rapidly stir a batter with force to incorporate dry and wet ingredients. Beating also incorporates air into the batter or dough.

blanch:
To dip foods, especially fruits and vegetables, into boiling water for a brief period. The blanched food is then plunged into ice water to stop the cooking process. Foods are blanched before freezing to set the color, so the skin will slip off, and to stop enzymatic reactions.

blend:
To stir or gently mix several ingredients together until the separate ingredients are no longer visible.

blind bake:
To bake a pie shell without a filling. Pie crusts that are blind baked are usually lined with foil and filled with pie weights or dried beans to stop the dough from puffing.

boil:
To raise the temperature of a liquid to 212°F or 100°C so that bubbles rise from the bottom of the liquid to the top and break on the surface.

bone:
To remove the bone from meat or fish. A piece of meat that has major bones removed is called partially boned.

braise:
To cook meat in a liquid environment for long periods of time to melt connective tissue and tenderize the product. This wet-heat method of cooking is used on less tender cuts of meat.

broil:
To cook food a few inches away from a burner or flame turned to its highest point. This dry-heat method of cooking can be done in an oven or over a grill.

brown:
To cook over high heat so the exterior turns color to a deep brown while the interior remains uncooked or undercooked.

chop:
To cut in roughly uniform bite-size pieces with a sharp knife. Chopped food is in larger pieces than minced or diced food.

chunk:
To cut food into large, thick pieces. Chunked carrots, for example, are cut into 3 to 4 pieces per carrot.

couscous:
A small-grain semolina, or granular wheat, common in Middle Eastern cooking. Couscous is actually a tiny pasta, not a whole grain.

cream:
To combine a fat and a dry ingredient together until a smooth mass forms. Creaming helps develop the crumb of a baked good, since sugar crystals make tiny holes in the fat.

crepe:
A very thin, delicate pancake of French origin that is used in both dessert and savory dishes.

crumb:
The texture of a baked good. A fine crumb means the air holes in the product are very small. A coarse crumb means the air holes in the product are large.

cut in:
To combine shortening or fat with dry ingredients using two knives or a pastry blender until particles of fat coated with dry ingredients are small and blended.

deglaze:
To pour liquid into a hot pan in which meat has been browned, loosening from the bottom the drippings and brown particles that form during browning.

dice:
To cut with a sharp knife into small, even square pieces, about ⅛ inch to 1/4 inch in diameter.

dock:
To pierce tiny holes in the bottom and sides of unbaked pie crust to help prevent puffing while the crust blind bakes.

dot:
To place small bits of one ingredient on top of another. Usually butter is dotted over pie fillings or pastries.

drain:
To remove the liquid from a food, usually by pouring into a strainer or colander. Some foods, such as frozen spinach, must be thoroughly drained by pressing on them with the back of a spoon to remove as much liquid as possible.

dredge:
To coat food with a light layer of flour, cornstarch, or very fine crumbs.

drippings:
The melted fat, juices, and browned particles left in the bottom of a pan after meat or vegetables have been browned.

drizzle:
To pour a thin liquid mixture in a very fine stream over baked goods or other foods.

dry ingredients:
Flour, salt, baking powder, flavorings, herbs, and other ingredients that are low in water content.

dry rub:
A combination of herbs, salt, pepper, and spices that is rubbed into meats to help flavor and tenderize before cooking.

enzymes:
Molecules, usually proteins, found in cells that help encourage and speed up reactions between chemicals.

fillet:
To remove the bones, skin, and sometimes cartilage from a piece of meat, poultry, or seafood. Also a piece of meat with no bones or skin.

flake:
To gently tease apart cooked meat, especially seafood, along the natural lines of separation or layers between muscles.

flash freeze:
To freeze unwrapped food quickly, usually in a single layer on a cookie sheet or baking pan. Food that is flash frozen is generally small, such as balls of cookie dough or small appetizers.

flute:
To make a decorative border on a pie crust by using the fingers or a utensil to push a pattern into the dough.

fold:
To combine two mixtures by an action of gently cutting a spoon or spatula down through the mixtures, scraping the bottom of the bowl, and turning the mixtures over until combined.

freezer burn:
Food that is improperly wrapped and frozen may have dry hard patches, or freezer burn, caused by moisture evaporating in the cold climate of the freezer. Freezer burn is not dangerous, but it makes the food unpalatable.

fry:
A dry-heat cooking method where the food is surrounded by hot cooking oil until it reaches a safe internal temperature.

glaze:
To pour a thin coating over foods to evenly coat. A glaze is also a thin liquid that flavors foods and dries to a high gloss.

grease:
To coat the surface of a baking pan or sheet with shortening, butter, or oil before adding the batter, preventing the food from sticking after it is cooked.

half-and-half:
A dairy product with fat content halfway between whole milk and heavy cream. Half-and-half is also called coffee cream.

head space:
An air pocket deliberately left in a rigid container that allows for expansion of liquids when frozen.

jelly roll pan:
A large pan with 1-inch sides used to bake cakes used in jelly rolls, or for baking large sheet cakes or bars.

knead:
To physically manipulate dough by pushing and pulling it with your hands until it becomes smooth and resilient.

marinade:
A combination of liquids, acids, and flavorings poured over foods, especially meats, to tenderize and flavor them before cooking.

marinate:
To pour marinade over a food and let it stand for minutes or hours before cooking, to tenderize and flavor the food.

mince:
To cut into very small pieces with a sharp knife or food processor. Minced food is smaller than chopped or diced food.

olive oil:
The oil from pressed olives. Extra-virgin olive oil is from the first "cold" pressing, which uses no chemicals, and has the lowest acid content. Virgin olive oil is also a first pressing, but it has a slightly higher acid content. Olive oil is a combination of different pressings and is usually used for sautéing foods.

oxidation:

Oxidation in food is the combination of air with chemicals in food cells. This process can change the color and texture of food and lead to rancid by-products.

parboil:

To briefly cook foods in boiling water until partially cooked. Vegetables are usually parboiled before being frozen or stir-fried.

pare:

To remove the thin skin or outer covering of fruits and vegetables with a knife or a swivel-bladed vegetable peeler.

partially cover:

To place a cover on a pan or skillet, leaving a small opening for steam to pass through, helping reduce or thicken the sauce.

peel:

To remove the skin or outer covering of fruits and vegetables with a knife or a swivel-bladed vegetable peeler.

pie weight:

Small pebblelike object, usually made of stainless steel or ceramic materials, that is used in blind baking a pie crust to prevent shrinking and puffing.

pinch:

The amount of an ingredient that can be held between the thumb and forefinger. Technically, it is about 1/16 teaspoon.

poach:

To cook meats, fruits, or vegetables in a liquid that is heated to just below a simmer. The poaching liquid, whether water, broth, or wine, will shimmer on the surface when the temperature is correct.

preheat:

To turn on an appliance, whether an oven, grill, or stovetop burner, to heat to baking or cooking temperature before adding foods.

prick:

To poke a food with the tines of a fork or the tip of a sharp knife. Most often, pie crusts are pricked to prevent buckling, shrinking, or puffing.

puree:

To mash food or force it through a sieve, or to process it in a blender or food processor to make a smooth paste.

reduce:

To cook a liquid at a rapid boil, removing much of the water by evaporation, until a thick sauce forms. A reduction is a sauce made by reducing liquid.

roast:

A dry-heat cooking method where foods are cooked at high temperatures in an oven. Usually meats and vegetables are roasted.

roll out:

To manipulate dough or pastry with a rolling pin or other round implement, flattening the dough into a thin and even round or square.

sauté:

To cook food in a small amount of oil or fat over fairly high heat in a short amount of time.

scald:

Also known as blanch; to place a food in boiling water for a short amount of time. Scalded fruits and vegetables are usually cooked just long enough to set color or to remove peel or skin.

score:

To make shallow cuts on a piece of meat or fish that allow marinade, tenderizers, and spices to penetrate the meat and add flavor.

sear:

To heat foods at a very high heat in order to seal in juices and give color to the food. Searing is done with direct heat, as in a broiler, sauté pan, or grill.

seed:
To remove the seeds from a fruit.

shred:
To cut food into thin strips with a grater or attachment on a food processor. Some foods can also be shredded with a knife or with two forks.

sift:
To shake dry ingredients through a fine sifter or sieve to remove lumps, to combine them, and to make them lighter.

simmer:
To cook food in liquid at a temperature just below a boil. Small bubbles rise to the surface and barely break when the liquid is at the proper temperature.

skewer:
A long, thin piece of metal or wood used to hold food in a single row while cooking.

slice:
To cut a food using a knife or food processor to make very thin strips or sections.

soften:
To make a food softer, either by soaking it in water, letting it stand at room temperature, or heating it briefly. Gelatin is softened in water; butter is softened by microwaving.

steam:
To cook food suspended over boiling water so the steam penetrates the food. Since the water doesn't come in contact with the food, steamed foods retain more nutrients and flavor than poached or simmered foods do.

stir-fry:
To cook piece of food over very high heat in a skillet or wok while moving the food constantly around the pan. Foods for stir-frying are cut into similar shapes and sizes so they cook evenly.

strain:
To remove large pieces of foods from a liquid or a puree using a fine mesh strainer or colander lined with cheesecloth.

tart:
A pie, usually baked in a tart pan, which has very shallow, straight sides and a removable bottom. Tarts can be large or bite-size, filled with savory or sweet fillings.

tear:
To rip or break foods, usually greens or herbs, into irregular pieces.

toast:
To brown foods over or under direct heat, whether in a dry saucepan, a broiler, or a toaster.

toss:
To turn food pieces over and under each other to combine. Usually salads and other vegetable mixtures are tossed.

water bath:
A large container filled either with ice water or very hot water that smaller containers of food can be placed into. This method is used to cool food quickly (using an ice-water bath) or warm it gently (using a hot-water bath).

wrap:
To fold something over another ingredient. A wrap is also a sandwich that uses a flat bread such as a tortilla to hold the filling ingredients.

yeast:
A single-celled organism that is preserved, usually by drying, and that multiplies when mixed with water and a food source. Yeast is used to give raised bread its characteristic crumb and flavor.

Index

Dec. 2006